D1541713

The
American
Presidents

The American Presidents
The Office and the Men

I

Washington
to
Buchanan

Edited by
FRANK N. MAGILL

Associate Editor
JOHN L. LOOS

SALEM PRESS
Pasadena, California   Englewood Cliffs, New Jersey

Library of Congress Cataloging-in-Publication Data
Main entry under title:

The American presidents.

   Bibliography: p.
   Includes index.
   1. Presidents—United States—History. 2.
Presidents—United States—Biography. 3.
United States—Politics and government. I.
Magill, Frank Northen, 1907-   . II. Loos, John
L.
E176.1.A657 1986   973'.09'92   85-30338
ISBN 0-89356-525-3 (set)
ISBN 0-89356-526-1 (volume I)

PRINTED IN THE UNITED STATES OF AMERICA

PREFACE

"When in the Course of human events, it becomes necessary for one people to dissolve the political bands which have connected them with another. . ." are the twenty-four words that heralded the formal rupture of ties with the Mother Country, a condition which the American Colonists deemed necessary in order for the citizens of the Colonies to develop into a whole society based on elective principles that applied directly to those being governed.

The idea of a social body considering that ". . . all men are created equal . . . with certain unalienable Rights . . ." was another noble concept new to much of the world at the time (and indeed down through history), and it was not easy for England's power structure to take this pronouncement from the Colonies as a serious threat to the status quo.

Most of those who voluntarily left the security and relative comfort of Great Britain for the wilderness across the sea did so hoping to get a new start in life in a land not locked in a class structure where tradition and bloodline were all-important and unalterable. Thus, the arbitrary restrictions of Great Britain's "Colonial overseers" became more and more intolerable as new generations grew in the Colonies, and at last the breaking point was reached in 1773, when 342 chests of British tea were dumped into Boston Harbor from the decks of British merchant ships by some three score Bostonians garbed as "Mohawks," an action schoolchildren have since known as the Boston Tea Party. Not only were these hardy people who had braved the New World—and all that implies—ready to resist further encroachment on their freedom at the hands of autocratic oppressors, but also they were ready to take up arms in order to end such treatment. In little more than a year after the tea-dumping affair the Colonies and Great Britain were indeed locked in a shooting war. Destiny had waited long enough.

Warfare in the American wilderness was not an activity to which the conventional British military forces were fully attuned. Furthermore, they were forced to bring much of what they required—men, guns, supplies— across three thousand miles of ocean; worst of all, the stubborn rebels never seemed to understand that they were poorly trained, badly equipped, undersupplied, and outgunned. All they had to offer was dedication to a cause and, eventually—for leadership—president-to-be George Washington.

The war surged back and forth inconclusively for several years. At last, with substantial and timely help from the French military establishment, as well as some inept strategy on the part of the British high command, Major General Lord Charles Cornwallis, the ranking British general in the Southern battle area, was trapped with his entire army at Yorktown, Virginia, in

v

1781, and forced to surrender in October of that year—to president-to-be George Washington.

This act of surrender signaled the end of George III's attempts to subdue the rebellious American Colonists by military force. Withdrawal of the English, however, left no political vacuum. Representatives of twelve of the thirteen colonies that had dared to challenge Great Britain had already met in 1774 and 1775 and codified their thinking, which eventually resulted in a Constitution through which, as amended, the emerging nation could be governed, uniformly and without favor to any special class. To administer the letter and spirit of this Constitution, an Office was carefully designed: It should be freely elective, subject to the will of the people; it should be temporary, subject to reiteration or change by the electorate every four years; it should be occupied by one who inspired the confidence of the electorate and commanded the respect of world leaders. The man the framers seemed to be describing was—George Washington.

Washington was duly elected as the first president of the United States and became known thenceforth to innumerable schoolchildren as The Father of Our Country. He promptly set the tone of the office, and the new nation could not have been more fortunate in the choice. His physical appearance and formal demeanor were ideal for the image required of the new leader, and the model has served well many future aspirants.

Washington did not disappoint his constituents. He already had some political experience, having served as a Virginia delegate to the first and second Continental Congresses in 1774 and 1775. His integrity and sense of honor were beyond reproach, and he had earlier demonstrated his lack of ambition to acquire power, through his widely praised act of resigning his commission as supreme commander after the war rather than hang on to it and form a military dictatorship. Indeed, Washington's reputation for favoring civilian power over the military helped the states decide to form a fairly strong federal government and surrender some of their powers to it because Washington was to head up that new power base. It was known that Washington believed that the threat of anarchy by the masses was a greater danger to democracy than a dictatorship would be; thus, the Federal government should have sufficient power and resources to protect itself from all threats.

The importance of George Washington's eight years as America's first president is of such significance that the reader is referred without further discussion here to Professor Charles Royster's 35-page article at the beginning of Volume I describing Washington's two terms in office.

John Adams, the second president, lacked the charisma of his predecessor, though his handling of the XYZ affair, and the peaceful accommodation with France that followed, prevented his term of office from being a complete failure.

The third president, Thomas Jefferson, was perhaps the brightest star of his time, and his two administrations served to upgrade the office of president to the level of esteem it had held under Washington. One of the major reasons for his popular success was the fact that, like Washington, Jefferson had become a national leader prior to achieving the presidency, through his brilliant writing, his ambassadorial service in France, and his vision for the development of the new nation, as exemplified in his contributions to the drafting of the Declaration of Independence. As president, his stature continued to grow through such accomplishments as the Louisiana Purchase, the expansion of public works, the founding of schools, and the signing of the act that closed the international slave trade (a premature hope). On balance, Jefferson must be rated high as a president, surely among our five or six greatest.

Thomas Jefferson's much admired friend, James Madison, followed him as the fourth president of the United States. Like Jefferson, Madison also was a brilliant man with much prior service to the new nation, including membership in the first four Congresses, where he was the author of the first ten amendments to the new Constitution—known as the Bill of Rights. Madison inherited a major problem which eventually resulted in the War of 1812 with Great Britain, primarily over the general issue of free trade on the open seas. England persisted in refusing to honor such a policy, seizing American ships and impressing American sailors at will. As a new member of the family of nations, the United States could not tolerate such abuse, and prepared for war. Although the British captured the city of Washington, burned the "White House," and almost captured the fleeing president, a dramatic victory by General Andrew Jackson over the British at New Orleans in January, 1815, assured that the Treaty of Ghent, signed two weeks earlier and ending the War of 1812, would be fully honored by Great Britain. Madison's long and fruitful career in government ended with James Monroe's election as president in 1817. Without question, President Madison had given his best to his country, and he lived with these memories for nineteen more years.

The last member of the Virginia Dynasty and the last of the generation of those revolutionary leaders who helped form the new nation, James Monroe became the fifth president on March 4, 1817, He was a true republican in thought and his belief in the ability of free men to govern themselves through voluntary mutual agreement was innate.

While still in his late teens, Monroe had fought with distinction in Washington's Continental army, being severely wounded in battle. He ended his military career as a major and with the expressed admiration of General Washington himself. Monroe's political career began at the age of twenty-four with his election to the Virginia House of Delegates. He was a delegate to the Continental Congress in 1783 and was elected to the United States

Senate in 1790. Monroe's two terms as president were characterized by fiscal responsibility in government but deep economic problems for the people, marked by The Panic of 1819 which caused a depression in land prices and agricultural products, as well as severe unemployment. By 1821, however, the economy had recovered, some economics lessons had been learned, and the nation was headed for a decade of prosperity. Meanwhile, territorial expansion had been going on. In The Territorial Treaty of 1819, Spain ceded Florida and the Oregon Country to the United States, adding greatly to the territorial extent and the unification process of the nation. Monroe had now concluded that the Western Hemisphere should be free from foreign intervention, especially by adventurous European rulers, and in 1823 he proclaimed what was to become known as the Monroe Doctrine. This edict stated that the American continents were "henceforth not to be considered as subjects for future colonization by any European powers," probably at the time the most grandiose uncalled political bluff in history—and a fitting climax to the genius of four Virginians and one New Englander who is less than fifty years had turned a disparate group of immigrant descendants into a cohesive, powerful nation that had earned the attention and respect of the world's powers.

The seventh president, Andrew Jackson, was first of all a superb military leader, without whom some of the political successes of his predecessors might have been more difficult. As a president, Jackson was lacking in some of the fine points of diplomacy and all that implies, but he was a fast learner and, in time, mastered the minimal intricacies of protocol required of him in his office. A born warrior, Jackson's national reputation was made in the Battle of New Orleans at the end of the War of 1812. His plan for the defense of the city was phenomenal, with casualties running 20 to 1 in his favor against seasoned British troops. Lacking an established political base, Jackson more or less stumbled into a vacuum and quickly caught on with noncommitted voters. As an outsider on the political scene even after his election, Jackson, always dedicated to democracy, was from the beginning on the side of the little man. Even such things as paper money seemed to him a ploy of bankers to cheat the average citizen. For such reasons, Jackson was the first president of the United States with whom "the man in the street" (or the frontiersman) could relate. Thus Jackson demonstrated to *all* Americans that even they could have a voice in their country's actions.

The six presidents mentioned above were acting often without precedents to guide them, and their administrations have been reviewed at some length here. The remaining thirty-three presidential figures included in this work are also important to the full researcher, and for specifics, the reader henceforth is referred directly to the individual scholarly article that covers the target president, and to Professor Loos's Introduction, which begins on page xi.

PREFACE

It is true that not all the presidents provoked the same degree of interest or exhibited the charisma that mesmerized audiences, but all of them projected something special or they would not have gained the high office. This work is meant to bring forward the distinctive qualities of each man in the office so that the user may find the level of interest that most appeals individually.

The presidential articles here presented are not offered as a type of "media overview" but as scholar-oriented historical essays written by professors with more or less a scholarly lifetime of interest in and study of the presidential figure about whom they have been asked to write. The objective has been to interpret the impact of the man on the office, to stress his contributions to the safety and welfare of the nation, and to show whether the tenor of the office was changed by his administration and if so, how it was changed.

While all the presidents of the United States have been important in one way or another, after Andrew Jackson the next most serious threat to the nation came in the administration of Abraham Lincoln, a crisis that had been long in the making and came to a head with the firing on Fort Sumter by Confederates on April 12, 1861. Professor Robert Johannsen's 43-page article beginning on page 286 of Volume II delineates in master fashionly the background and presidential career of Abraham Lincoln, who presided at the death and resurrection of the United States of America as he knew it, and whose deep travail over these events was ended only with his own assassination on April 14, 1865.

Others leaving indelible marks on the Office of the President include Woodrow Wilson, who, among other things, persuaded the American public in 1917 that it was our duty to help "make the world safe for democracy," rather than stand by and see our traditional allies enslaved by power-mad dictators. Without help from the United States, the Western European Allies would very likely have been defeated.

The only man to break George Washington's nonbinding precedent of only two four-year terms as president is Franklin D. Roosevelt. When he was voted into office in 1933, the country was deep in the grip of one of the nation's worst depressions. Through imagination, innovation, and dramatic "fireside chats" he began the slow process of getting the economy back to normal. His first term was full of economic trial and error, with some successes, some failures, but never a lack of effort. Such concern for the problems of the unfortunate earned for Roosevelt the deep gratitude of those he helped and the goodwill of most of the nation, impressed as it was by the fact that he was "doing something" for those needing relief. His popularity level with the electorate during his first term was extremely high and the margin of his victory for a second term was by far the greatest in American history.

Professor Robert McElvain's 49-page survey of Roosevelt's presidential years begins on page 576 of Volume III, and is highly recommended.

Upon Franklin D. Roosevelt's death on April 12, 1945, Vice President Harry S Truman became the thirty-third president of the United States. His date with destiny at Hiroshima shook the world to its core, and instantly changed forever the way military men even dare give passing thoughts to all-out war.

Following Truman, the nation underwent eight more or less tranquil years under Dwight D. Eisenhower; a sudden soul-searching shock in the brutal assassination of the thirty-fifth president, John F. Kennedy; several years of unprecedented civil upheaval under Lyndon B. Johnson—which finally drove him from office—and the brazen Watergate scandal that eventually caused Richard M. Nixon to resign from the presidential office to which he had been reelected in 1972.

The next president, Gerald R. Ford, attained the office without ever having been elected either to the vice presidency or the presidency, a unique circumstance that required not a single vote from any constituent anywhere. Ford's presidency was ended with the election of Jimmy Carter, of Georgia, as the nation's thirty-ninth president, a sincere, hardworking, inexperienced political figure who succumbed to the glitter of Ronald Reagan after one term.

George Washington's "tone of the office" has ebbed and flowed with the tide of passing events, but in the minds of the serious electorate the legacy of the first president's example remains a beacon on which Americans still focus as a reminder of who they are and from whence they have come.

The complete list of contributing professors, along with their academic affiliation and the identity of the presidential career they chose to discuss, begins on page xxiii in Volume I. I wish to thank each professor individually for the valued contribution to this work. I also wish to express my appreciation to the staff of researchers and proofreaders for their untiring efforts in the processing of the manuscripts.

We wish to thank the White House Historical Association for making available for reproduction the official presidential portraits. As a portrait of President Reagan has yet to be commissioned, his official presidential photograph has been reproduced at the beginning of the chapter on his presidency.

We also wish to thank Imagefinders, Inc., for locating and obtaining copies of the illustrations in this book. Below each illustration, we acknowledge the source from which it was obtained.

Frank N. Magill

INTRODUCTION

The president of the United States is the most powerful and influential popularly elected public official in the world. The only person who represents and speaks for all Americans, he serves as the nation's head of state, chief executive, principal administrator, and legislative leader, as well as commander in chief of its armed forces, director of its foreign affairs, and head of his political party. The Constitution of the United States entrusts some of these manifold duties and responsibilities to the president, but they have been expanded upon and others have been added through the efforts of the men who have held the office or because changes in the nature of the federal government or of America's role in the world necessitated them. Since World War II, the president has come to be not only the leader of the United States, but also of the Western alliance if not the entire non-Communist world.

Americans of the Colonial era would be surprised, and probably aghast, at such expansive presidential power. Their experience under British rule left them extremely suspicious of executive authority. The royal governors, as representatives of the British Crown, had been very unpopular with the colonists, who had looked to their elected assemblies to represent and protect their rights and interests. Thus, when during the Revolution the newly independent states established governments, they generally gave preeminent power to the legislature and strictly limited the role of the governor. They made his term of office very short—usually only one year—carefully restricted his eligibility for reelection, and in a few instances even gave the legislature the right to elect him. In addition, the governor's few powers were essentially determined by the legislature, and, with one minor exception, he had no authority to veto its acts. The one noteworthy exception to this general condition of executive impotence was New York, where the governor was given "the supreme executive power and authority of the state." He was elected directly by the people, his term of office was three years, he was indefinitely eligible for reelection, he had broad veto and pardoning powers, and he was the commander in chief of the state militia.

In actual practice, the legislatively dominated state governments left much to be desired from the point of view of the conservative classes. They proved to be lacking in stability and energy and prone to adopting unwise and unfair laws designed to satisfy the demands of one faction or special interest group or another. They were considered by the propertied classes to be far too democratic.

The Articles of Confederation, the frame of national government under which the states operated after 1781, near the end of the Revolution, also reflected the Americans' suspicion of executive power. The Articles provided for only one governing body, a Congress in which each of the states was represented by between two and seven delegates but in which each had only one vote. Administrative and executive functions were performed by committees of Congress and a few administrative departments: foreign affairs, treasury, war, navy, and post office. Congress under the Articles could not govern the country effectively. Lacking the power to levy taxes (it had to rely for funds on requisitions on the states, which were largely ignored, and on borrowing, especially from abroad), it had difficulty paying the war debt and its operating expenses. Without the power to impose tariffs, it was unable to protect American merchants and manufacturers from ruthless foreign competition. Faced with the growing discontent and occasional uprisings of poor, debt-ridden farmers and workers, the Articles of Confederation could not maintain law and order and protect the interests of the conservative, propertied classes.

The perceived failings of both the legislatively dominated state governments and the Articles of Confederation led to a movement for a stronger, more effective central government which in 1787 culminated in the calling of the Constitutional Convention. Although summoned to correct the failings of the Articles of Confederation, soon after assembling the members of the convention decided instead of amending the Articles to draft an entirely new constitution which would embody the principle of separation of powers, with an independent executive, legislature, and judiciary. They were influenced in their decision and guided in their planning for such a government by the writings of great political philosophers, such as John Locke, William Blackstone, and Montesquieu, and by their knowledge of and experience with the colonial and recently established state governments as well as the Articles of Confederation.

Convinced of the need for a strong executive, in spite of the considerable opposition of those who represented the widespread fear of monarchy in the country, the Constitutional Convention voted to follow the example of New York and create a strong executive in the form of a single individual with enough power to instill the office with vigor that would reach throughout the land. To assure the executive's independence of the legislature, he was to be elected by special electors in each state who would be chosen as the state legislature should direct. The framers rejected the idea of popular election of the executive because they considered the people to be too ignorant or too easily subject to being misled by designing persons to make a proper choice. The president so chosen was to serve for a fixed term of office—four years—and was to be eligible for reelection for an indefinite number of terms. (With the adoption of the Twenty-second Amendment in 1951, he could be reelected only once.) Neither the president nor any other member of the executive branch could be a member of Congress, thus preventing the possibility of the development of a cabinet system of government like that in England. The new Constitution gave the president certain stipulated powers as well as those he might be authorized by Congress to exercise.

Despite the constitutional framers' concern not to create an elective monarch, the powers conferred on the chief executive were great. They were in part influenced in bestowing such a generous grant of authority by the assumption that George Washington, the chairman of the convention, would be the first president. "When men spoke of the great national representative, of the guardian of the people, they were thinking in terms of the Father of His Country," declares the constitutional scholar Charles C. Thach, Jr. Article II of the Constitution, which deals with the executive, states broadly that "the executive Power shall be vested in a President of the United States." It specifically makes the president commander in chief of the armed forces and, with the consent of two-thirds of the senators, empowers that individual to make treaties and appoint the principal military, judicial, and administrative officers of the government. The president can also independently appoint other inferior officers of the government, grant pardons for offenses against the United States, call Congress into special session and recommend "measures" to it, and invoke a suspensive veto of all its enactments. The president is responsible for the execution of all the laws of the United States and can be removed only upon impeachment for and conviction by Congress of treason, bribery, or other high crimes and misdemeanors.

The executive provided for in the Constitution, declared James Wilson, the member of the convention who was the chief advocate of a strong executive, is "the man of the people"—representative of and responsible to them. Wilson also considered the American presidency to be "unique," a judgment in which Thach concurred nearly two centuries later when he concluded that it "has proved a governmental creation, differing from its predecessors and its derivatives in a most decisive fashion." For a brief review of the events leading to the presidential office, readers may wish to examine Professor Magill's preface, begining on page v.

As the framers of the Constitution assumed, Washington was unanimously elected the first president and was inaugurated on April 30, 1789. "The office," as the great authority on the presidency Edward S. Corwin has stated, "got off to a good start under a very great man." As president, Washington did not seek to be a popular leader; rather he was "an Olympian figure, above the fray—a symbol of American nationhood." He avoided personal involvement in political controversies and the deliberations of Congress, but his secretary of the Treasury, Alexander Hamilton, did steer through that body a major economic program. Washington's Administration also conducted important relations with the powers of Western Europe—Britain, France, and Spain—to settle problems growing out of the American and French revolutions. At home, the president acted decisively to assert the power of the federal government by suppressing the insurrectionary threat of frontier farmers who refused to pay the excise tax on the whiskey they sold. Through wise and judicious conduct, Washington by the end of his second term had established the presidency on very secure ground.

Washington's immediate successors, like him, came from the leaders of the Revolution and the struggle to create the new government. They were very able men, but in large part their historical reputations owe more to their accomplishments before they became president than to their performance as chief executives.

John Adams, the second president, although a great statesman and political philosopher, was an unsuccessful chief executive because, strong-minded and convinced of his moral superiority, he proved a poor political and popular leader. Relations with revolutionary France dominated his administration, and he considered the avoidance of all-out war with that country the principal achievement of his presidency.

When he took office in 1801, Thomas Jefferson brought to the presidency a new philosophy and style of government. Under him and his successors and friends from Virginia—the "Virginia Dynasty"—the president gave up most of his autonomy and, in deference to the republican principle of legislative supremacy, acquiesced in congressional domination of the national government. Jefferson was, however, an exceptionally shrewd and practical politician who, as the chief founder and leader of the first national political party, the Democratic Republicans, skillfully managed Congress by personal influence. Although having little success in protecting American rights on the high seas by economic means during the Napoleonic Wars, Jefferson was particularly proud of his purchase of Louisiana from France, which almost doubled the territory of the United States.

Lacking the political skill and will of his predecessor, James Madison, despite his well-established greatness as a political thinker and statesman, was a weak and ineffectual president. Unable, even unwilling, to lead Congress, he bungled into a war against England in 1812 for which the country was completely unprepared. Exercising the war power reluctantly and uncertainly, he proved to be a poor commander in chief. Nevertheless, the war, although not a military success, did inspire in the American people a feeling of nationalism such that it has been called the Second War for American Independence.

James Monroe, best known for his famous doctrine claiming American hegemony in the Western Hemisphere, was personally popular but, like his predecessor Madison, had no clearly articulated policy or program. A passive president, in most matters he deferred to Congress and took no legislative initiative.

Although a brilliant diplomat and the nation's greatest secretary of state,

John Quincy Adams was an ineffective president. Self-righteous and opinionated, the second Adams to hold the office was, like his father, a poor popular, as well as legislative and political, leader. Despite his superb credentials, he even failed in his diplomatic endeavors. His power and authority were undermined by the supporters of Andrew Jackson, who, throughout Adams' term of office, waged a vindictive and relentless campaign to assure his defeat in 1828.

The new president, Jackson, was the nation's first truly popular leader. The "Jacksonian democracy" which he ushered in was marked by the extension of political power from the propertied aristocracy to virtually all citizens, which at that time meant only all adult, white males. Jackson spoke and acted as the representative of all the people and as the one person with the special duty of protecting their rights and liberties. He reasserted the independence of his office from Congress by reviving and expanding the removal and veto powers, and from the courts by claiming to have as much authority to interpret the Constitution as the judges. On at least one occasion he allegedly even refused to enforce a decision of the Supreme Court with which he disagreed. He threatened to use military force to compel South Carolina to obey the federal tariff laws when her legislature presumed to nullify them. Neither at that time nor at any other, however, did Jackson challenge in any fundamental way the federal principle which recognized the broad rights and powers of the states.

Following Jackson, until Lincoln assumed the office in 1861, the nation had a succession of relatively weak and passive presidents—Martin Van Buren, William Henry Harrison, John Tyler, James K. Polk, Zachary Taylor, Millard Fillmore, Franklin Pierce, and James Buchanan—each of whom served for only one term or less. As the sectional crisis over slavery worsened, the people seemed to believe that a strong, assertive chief executive might threaten the delicate compromises and accommodations that were worked out in Congress in an effort to prevent a rupture of the Union. Moreover, they appeared to feel safer with leaders who had no pronounced views or strong national policies or programs. In some respects, the one exception among these eight undistinguished presidents was Polk, who led the country in a successful, though rather unpopular, war to obtain a large territory in the Southwest from Mexico and who was an effective administrator and commander in chief.

Abraham Lincoln, judged by many historians to be America's greatest president, raised the power and importance of the presidential office to heights far above those claimed for it by any of his predecessors and became in some respects a virtual dictator. With the secession of the Southern states and the threatened dissolution of the Union, Lincoln faced a situation which was not only unique in American history but the greatest crisis ever faced by the nation. To deal with it, he had, in his words, "to think anew and act anew," and he relied mainly upon the president's war power as commander in chief, an insurrection being deemed to be a war. At first he acted—calling out the militia, enlarging the regular army and navy beyond their legal limits, ordering a blockade of the southern coast, suspending the writ of habeas corpus—only until Congress could ratify and reinforce what he had done. Later, however, he acted without seeking congressional authorization and even in violation of the Constitution itself, as when he issued the Emancipation Proclamation or declared martial law in certain areas in the North. Lincoln justified all that he did on the ground that the people demanded it and the preservation of the Union required it. His actions, according to historian Clinton Rossiter, "raised the Presidency to a position of constitutional and moral ascendancy that left no doubt where the burden of crisis government in this country would thereafter rest."

During the tenure of the eight presidents who followed Lincoln in the last third of the nineteenth century—Andrew Johnson, Ulysses S. Grant, Rutherford B. Hayes, James A. Garfield, Chester A. Arthur, Grover Cleveland, Benjamin Harrison, and William McKinley—Congress again became the dominant branch of the national government. The strongest of these generally passive chief executives was Cleveland, the only president in the nation's history to serve two nonconsecutive terms of office. A "defensive" president, Cleveland, like the other presidents of his generation, believed in a laissez-faire role for the national government but tried, especially through the use of his veto power, to keep the government honest, fair, and impartial in its treatment of all elements of population.

In 1898, pressured by Congress and the public, Cleveland's successor, William McKinley, led the country into war with Spain. From this conflict the United States emerged as a world power with territorial possessions extending from the Caribbean to the western Pacific. This new status led to the substantial enhancement of the role of the president as the nation's acknowledged leader in the field of foreign affairs.

Theodore Roosevelt became the first of the "new" twentieth-century presidents. A very popular chief executive, he brought color and excitement to the office. "He was," as Rossiter states, "a brilliant molder and interpreter of public opinion and an active leader of Congress." Roosevelt claimed to have the right and duty to do anything necessary for the public welfare unless such action was forbidden by the Constitution or laws. He conducted the nation's foreign affairs with vigor and took the lead in securing from Congress legislation to regulate big business. He was also the first president to act as a mediator in an industrial dispute, but he did not envision or advocate for the national government such a positive role in economic and social matters as that inaugurated by his distant cousin a generation later. Roosevelt's hand-picked successor, Robert Taft, had a much more modest view of the proper role of the president. He believed that the chief magistrate could do only those things which he was expressly empowered to do by the Constitution or the laws, and he was quite content to leave the legislative initiative to Congress.

The balance of power shifted again with the accession to the presidency of Woodrow Wilson, who was through most of his two terms a very strong chief executive. A popular leader, he was both a good administrator and an exceptionally shrewd head of his party. Wilson dealt most effectively with the legislative branch and achieved a high level of vigorous and responsible government. During World War I he obtained from Congress extensive emergency powers, especially over the economy. In the end, however, because of the excessively partisan spirit in which he conducted his office, serious health problems, and a stubborn and uncompromising stand on the Treaty of Versailles, he lost support with the people and Congress and failed as a leader in foreign relations.

Wilson, like other strong presidents in times of crisis, was followed by a succession of largely passive chief executives—Warren G. Harding, Calvin Coolidge, and Herbert Hoover—all of whom held a relatively modest view of the position and powers of the president and of the proper functions of the national government. Despite his belief in "rugged individualism," however, Hoover did propose to Congress some rather novel economic measures to deal with the economic crisis which began with the stock market crash in 1929.

The failure of Hoover's efforts to revive the economy helped ensure the victory in 1932 of Franklin D. Roosevelt, the only person to be elected to the presidency four times. During his long tenure of slightly more than twelve years, the nation experienced the greatest depression in its history and its greatest war. In dealing with these crises, Roosevelt significantly enlarged the powers of the president and of the national government. In attacking the Great Depression, Roosevelt claimed for the federal government a positive role of unprecedented proportions in the economic and social affairs of the nation, introducing the welfare, or social service, state, which rested upon the "idea that the government should be active and reformist rather than simply protective of the established order of things." In legislating this new order, Congress intruded as never before into areas that had been traditionally reserved to the states. At the same time, the president assumed a far larger role than ever before in the initiation and passage of legislation, and Congress endowed the president with extraordinary legislative powers. During World War II the president, as commander in chief, assumed still greater powers over the economy and the people, even to the extent of seriously violating, in the name of national security, the constitutional rights of the Japanese Americans who were living on the West Coast. The war and the accompanying emergence of the United States as the greatest power in the world also resulted in greatly increased presidential power in international affairs.

Inasmuch as the United States has remained the greatest economic and military power in the world since World War II, all the presidents since Roosevelt have had an unusually important role in conducting the nation's foreign affairs and in serving as spokesmen for the Western alliance and other non-Communist nations. Furthermore, since the dropping of two atomic bombs on Japan in 1945, the world has lived in a state of greater or less crisis which has served to magnify the role of the president as commander in chief as well as chief diplomat. Similarly, since the inception of the social service state under Roosevelt, the role of the national government and of the president in the social and economic life of the nation has remained large.

Harry S Truman, who succeeded Roosevelt near the end of the war, was a strong party leader and an active president. Foreign affairs dominated his administration and focused on three important decisions which he made: (1) to drop atom bombs on Hiroshima and Nagasaki, (2) to pursue a "cold war" policy of containment toward the Soviet Union, and (3) to fight the North Koreans when they invaded South Korea. Although these decisions were generally popular, Truman's inability to bring the Korean War to a successful conclusion finally contributed decisively to the president's growing unpopularity and the defeat of his party in the 1952 presidential election.

Following Truman, Dwight D. Eisenhower, a wartime hero and great popular leader with a winning personality, was more than anything else a symbol of national unity. Not a party leader, Eisenhower sought in both legislative and foreign affairs essentially to maintain the status quo by drawing on the support of moderate and conservative elements in both major parties. In contrast to what some considered the staid style of Eisenhower, John F. Kennedy, a charismatic popular leader, projected an image of youth, vigor, and great confidence. Although he painted appealing visions of greatness for America, he was not an effective legislative leader, and his short administration was noteworthy more for its style than its substance. Even in the field of foreign affairs the record was mixed. The Soviets' construction of the Berlin Wall and the Bay of Pigs invasion fiasco diminished American prestige and influence, but the Cuban Missile Crisis was a defensive success.

Lyndon Johnson, Kennedy's successor, brought to the presidency great skill and experience as a legislative leader, and in the emotional aftermath of Kennedy's assassination he secured the passage of an impressive body of social and economic legislation which significantly enlarged the social welfare role of the national government with the avowed—though unrealized—goal of abolishing poverty in the United States. Although a great leader of Congress, Johnson failed in the all-important role of commander in chief. His inability to bring an end to the increasingly costly and discouraging war

INTRODUCTION

in Vietnam ultimately cost the president his popular support and forced his decision not to seek reelection.

As president, Richard M. Nixon was a vigorous aggrandizer of power. His presidency has been described as "imperial" in part, at least, because of his somewhat successful efforts to wrest power, especially in budgetary matters, from Congress and to concentrate the power of the executive branch more directly under his control. An active and shrewd diplomatic leader with a reputation as an ardent anti-Communist, he achieved a significant relaxation of tensions, or détente, between the United States and the Soviet Union, as well as initiating the establishment of diplomatic relations with the People's Republic of China. Reelected in a landslide, less than two years later he became the only president to resign his office. He did so under the threat of impeachment growing out of charges of criminal misconduct in connection with an attempted burglary of the Democratic National Committee headquarters in the Watergate apartment complex in Washington by persons associated with his reelection campaign.

With Nixon's resignation, Gerald Ford, who had been appointed vice president following Spiro Agnew's resignation from that office, became the nation's only president who had been elected to neither office. The presidency which Ford assumed, already weakened by the events of Nixon's second term that brought him to office, was further enfeebled by Ford's unpopular pardon of Nixon. Ford sought, for the most part, only to continue the Nixon policies and programs, but even though he had been a popular veteran congressman, he was not an effective legislative leader and played a largely negative role by vetoing many congressional measures which he deemed to be fiscally irresponsible.

Capitalizing on the Watergate scandal and a general public disaffection with the government in Washington, Jimmy Carter won election to the presidency as an outsider. Taking office with no clearly defined policies, having no strong power base in his party, and apparently unable to establish good relations with Congress, he proved an ineffective legislative leader. Even his limited successes in Middle Eastern diplomacy failed to produce a larger settlement of international problems in the region.

Under Ronald Reagan the presidency has recovered its strong leadership position. A remarkably talented and persuasive communicator, Reagan is the most popular president since Franklin D. Roosevelt. The first truly conservative president since Hoover, he has espoused a clearly articulated policy of reducing the role of the national government in the nation's social and economic affairs while strengthening its military posture. A pragmatist, he has succeeded in securing the enactment of substantial parts of his program by exhibiting a willingness to compromise in his dealings with Congress. Similarly, in relations with the Soviet Union, he began, in his second term, to move from a confrontational stance to one of negotiation with the goal of achieving lowered tensions and armaments reduction.

Today, nearly two hundred years after its creation, the office of president is perhaps stronger and more popular than it has ever been. Since the days of Washington, the presidential office has grown enormously in power and importance. This expansion has not been regular of steady, but has occurred primarily in times of crisis or emergency, such as depressions and wars. Regardless of the situation, the power and influence of the office has depended upon the personality of its occupant. Presidents who have enhanced the power of the office have been dynamic, popular leaders who have actively and energetically sought power with the purpose of making a lasting impact on the country, or even the world—of changing things in so fundamental a way that history would take note of them and what they had done. To accomplish their purposes they have actively courted and depended upon the support of the people. They have communicated their views and their goals to the citizenry, and they have claimed to act for them and their posterity. In the hands of lesser men with smaller ambitions and aims, the presidency has at times shrunk in importance and power, but in the long run the nation's thirty-nine presidents have succeeded in making this uniquely American political office the greatest instrument of democratic government in the world.

John L. Loos

LIST OF CONTRIBUTORS

	PRESIDENT	ACADEMIC AFFILIATION
Wayne R. Austerman	*Zachary Taylor* *Millard Fillmore*	Staff Historian USAF Space Command Peterson AFB
Robert A. Becker	*John Adams*	Louisiana State University
Michael Les Benedict	*Ulysses S. Grant*	The Ohio State University
Mark T. Carleton	*Gerald R. Ford*	Louisiana State University
Daniel Feller	*Andrew Jackson*	Assistant Editor The Papers of Andrew Jackson University of Tennessee
James E. Fickle	*William Henry Harrison* *John Tyler* *Benjamin Harrison*	Memphis State University
Gaines M. Foster	*Lyndon B. Johnson*	Louisiana State University
William E. Gienapp	*Franklin Pierce* *James Buchanan*	University of Wyoming
Louis L. Gould	*William McKinley*	University of Texas at Austin
Hugh D. Graham	*John F. Kennedy*	University of Maryland Baltimore County
Ellis W. Hawley	*Herbert Hoover*	University of Iowa
Joan Hoff-Wilson	*Richard M. Nixon*	Indiana University
Robert W. Johannsen	*James K. Polk* *Abraham Lincoln*	University of Illinois
Burton I. Kaufman	*Dwight D. Eisenhower*	Kansas State University
Ralph Ketcham	*John Quincy Adams*	Syracuse University
Richard S. Kirkendall	*Harry S Truman*	Iowa State University
Richard N. Kottman	*Calvin Coolidge*	Iowa State University
Richard B. Latner	*James Monroe*	Newcomb College Tulane University

xxi

Anne C. Loveland	*Jimmy Carter*	Louisiana State University
Richard Lowitt	*William H. Taft*	Iowa State University
Robert M. McColley	*Thomas Jefferson*	University of Illinois
Donald R. McCoy	*Warren G. Harding*	University of Kansas
Robert S. McElvaine	*Franklin D. Roosevelt*	Millsaps College
Burl Noggle	*Woodrow Wilson*	Louisiana State University
James S. Olson	*Ronald Reagan*	Sam Houston State University
Allan Peskin	*James A. Garfield* *Chester A. Arthur*	Cleveland State University
George C. Rable	*Andrew Johnson*	Anderson College
Randy Roberts	*Grover Cleveland*	Sam Houston State University
Charles W. Royster	*George Washington*	Louisiana State University
Robert A. Rutland	*James Madison*	Editor in Chief Papers of James Madison University of Virginia
Terry L. Seip	*Rutherford B. Hayes*	University of Southern California
William C. Widenor	*Theodore Roosevelt*	University of Illinois
Major L. Wilson	*Martin Van Buren*	Memphis State University

CONTENTS
VOLUME I

page

LIST OF ILLUSTRATIONS
VOLUME I

page

The American Presidents

GEORGE WASHINGTON

1789–1797

George Washington stands unique among presidents of the United States in the near unanimity with which politically influential Americans agreed that he should be elected. No other president has enjoyed a comparable degree of public confidence upon entering the office, and few if any other presidents have had equal scope for defining the chief executive's place in the federal government and the nation's life. The symbolic prestige attached to the presidency in the last two hundred years comes not only from its constitutionally defined powers but also from the implicit expectation that each new incumbent may achieve some of the unifying popular respect commanded by Washington.

The Character of a Leader: Ambition and Self-Control

Rather than deriving this respect from his position as president, Washington brought to the office the esteem he had won personally by virtue of his character and career. Little in Washington's youth gave promise of the exceptional stature he later attained; yet, beginning in those early years, he developed the circumspection and reliability that became integral to his public career. Washington was born February 22, 1732 (New Style), in Westmoreland County on the northern neck of Virginia, near the Potomac River. His mother, Mary Ball Washington, was the second wife of Augustine Washington. Augustine's grandfather John had emigrated from England to Virginia in 1657–1658. George was eleven years old when his father died. Augustine's adult son by an earlier marriage, Lawrence Washington, filled some of the role of a father for George until Lawrence died in 1752. First by lease and then by ownership, Lawrence's estate, Mount Vernon, became George's property and his preferred home for the rest of his life.

Washington grew to adulthood in an agricultural, slaveholding society that combined the stability of a self-perpetuating gentry leadership with the volatility of expanding settlement, immigration, and natural population increase. Through Lawrence's marriage to the daughter of Colonel William Fairfax, George came into contact with the comparatively cosmopolitan proprietary family, including Thomas Lord Fairfax, whose holdings included much of northernmost Virginia as far west as the Shenandoah Valley. The prospective value of this land lay in peopling it with tenants or buyers. Washington worked with a Fairfax surveying team in the Shenandoah Valley in 1748 and was appointed Culpeper County surveyor in 1749. Like other surveyors, the eighteen-year-old acquired land on his own account, in addition to inheriting Ferry Farm, which had belonged to his father. Washington was a home-taught and self-taught youth; he did not attend college. His reading tended toward history, biography, novels, and practical works on agriculture and the military. The ambition that Thomas Jefferson, James Madison, and John Adams manifested through intellectual self-development George Washington sought to realize in the world of plantation and military affairs.

In 1753 and 1754, as a major and then a lieutenant colonel in the Virginia militia, Washington became conspicuous in his activities as Governor Robert Dinwiddie's emissary to the chiefs of the Six Nations and to the French who were constructing a chain of forts from Lake Erie to the Ohio River. Washington's first skirmish with the French late in May, 1754, is often described as the beginning of the Seven Years' War. His military career during the war, although it attracted attention and won respect, was linked to several reverses: In July, 1754, he surrendered his command to a much larger French force from Fort Duquesne; in the summer of 1755 he served as an aide-de-camp with General Edward Braddock's expedition against Fort Duquesne, which ended in ambush and rout; as colonel and commander in chief of Virginia militia, he spent two frustrating years trying to protect the Shenandoah Valley and western Virginia with about three hundred men and inadequate supplies. Moreover, in 1755 and 1757 Washington stood for election to the Virginia House of Burgesses and was twice defeated. At the same time, he unsuccessfully sought a regular commission in the Royal Army.

After cooperating with the last expedition against Fort Duquesne in 1758, which ended in French withdrawal and the establishment of Fort Pitt at the forks of the Ohio, Washington returned to civil life. He won election to the House of Burgesses in 1758. In January, 1759, he married Martha Dandridge Custis, a wealthy widow, and settled with her and her children at Mount Vernon. For fifteen years he enjoyed the life of a family man, planter, colonial legislator, and justice of the peace; and yet, to decorate his home, Washington ordered portrait busts of Alexander the Great, Julius Caesar, Charles XII of Sweden, Frederick II of Prussia, Prince Eugene, and the Duke of Marlborough—all famous commanders. When his London agent could not get them, Washington declined to accept busts of poets and philosophers as substitutes. His own appearance was imposing: he was six feet, three inches tall and weighed 209 pounds. His shoulders were narrow, but his arms, hands, legs, and feet were large. He had great strength yet was graceful in posture and movement. He was an excellent dancer and an expert horseman. His large head had a prominent nose and a firm mouth.

His eyes were gray-blue, and in his forties he began to use spectacles to read.

By the time that Washington attained national stature as commander in chief of the Continental Army in 1775, the character that buttressed his popular standing was well formed. As a young man, he was emotional, effusive, audacious, and ambitious. These traits remained with him throughout his life, but he schooled himself to keep these manifestations of his passionate nature under rigorous control. He had purposefully chosen a life of outward stability and inward disappointment. He gained the rewards of equanimity at the cost of curbing his strongest inclinations. The cost was high. Washington often said that he would not relive his life if given the chance.

As revolutionary war commander and as president, George Washington won an unequaled public respect for integrity and reliability. He maintained this public, ideal character while remaining privately aware of the gap between his studied moderation of demeanor and his emotional preference for bold risks, high honors, impulsive attachments, and strong aversions. Without ever losing the enthusiastic temperament of his youth, he subjected it to the control of his will, so that his public expression of his deepest anxieties or strongest joys remained temperate. Only rarely—as in his occasional angry rages or in his effusive friendship with the marquis de Lafayette—did the young Washington and the inner Washington appear to others without being moderated by the mature, public Washington. After he became a general, he was asked whether he really had written the often-quoted lines from his report of his first skirmish with the French in 1754— "I heard the bullets whistle, and, believe me, there is something charming in the sound." Washington replied, "If I said so, it was when I was young."

Having worked so hard to build it, Washington set a very high value on his reputation. He distinguished his personal honor from the popular opinion of him: Praise did not make him overweening, nor did censure paralyze him, but he tended to believe that anyone who attacked his conduct or reputation thereby impugned his honor. Knowing that his public character was his own creation, maintained at the cost of great effort, he resented suggestions that it had flaws. At the same time, possessing a private distance from his public posture, he could see mistakes he had made and correct them, even when he did not want to admit them. Two of the most intimate views of Washington may provide the best brief summary of his character. Gilbert Stuart, who painted portraits of the public Washington, saw the private Washington clearly: "All his features were indicative of the most ungovernable passions, and had he been born in the forests . . . he would have been the fiercest man among the savage tribes." Lafayette, who knew the private Washington better than most, described the reliability of the public Washington: "Had he been a common soldier, he would have been the bravest in the ranks; had he been an obscure citizen, all his neighbors would have respected him."

The American Revolution: Commander in Chief

By the time that Americans' resistance to the British government's measures to levy colonial taxes and to tighten imperial administration had become armed conflict, George Washington was one of the most important Virginia politicians. On May 27, 1774, he joined the extralegal meeting of burgesses in the Raleigh Tavern in Williamsburg, after the royal governor had dissolved the House; and he was one of Virginia's delegates to the first and second Continental Congresses in 1774 and 1775. He was not a theorist or propagandist of the political thought by which Americans explained their effort to win independence and to establish a republican form of government. Nevertheless, he understood the intellectual bases, as well as the moral vision, on which the American Revolution was undertaken. His wartime addresses to his soldiers went beyond the appeals to discipline and professional pride characteristic of the British commanders' orders to include brief summaries of the significance of civil liberties, self-government, and the prospect for America's greatness. He concluded in 1789 that the "sacred fire of liberty and the destiny of the republican model of government" depended "on the experiment intrusted to the hands of the American people." There were, of course, more learned, more philosophically profound, more articulate explicators of the Revolution than Washington. His standing owed most to the personal reliability that had impressed Virginians before the war and that became integral to American victory.

The Continental Congress appointed Washington to command the American forces on June 15, 1775. The importance of unity among sections while most of the fighting was being done by New Englanders made a military veteran from the most populous colony especially appropriate. He remained commander in chief throughout the war, resigning his commission on December 23, 1783, in a ceremony before Congress. His conduct during these eight years established his unique national fame, which led to his election as the first president of the United States. Three elements of Washington's wartime service underlay his success and the public esteem that he won: his unselfishness, his persevering constancy, and his restraint with power. The tableaux that Americans repeatedly celebrated were Washington's declining to accept a salary as commander in chief, Washington's holding the army together at Trenton or Valley Forge or other crucial times, and—above all—Washington's resigning his commission. These seemed to exemplify the civic-mindedness that should characterize the citizens of a republic, guaranteeing the new nation's survival.

As commander in chief, Washington aspired to be a victorious general who commanded a veteran regular army. He resorted to short-term soldiers,

(Courtesy of the Library of Congress, Washington, D.C.)

Washington Crossing the Delaware
Engraved by F.O. Freeman from the Painting by E. Leutze

militia auxiliaries, and cautious Fabian strategy from necessity rather than preference. Although he achieved some critical victories—especially the Battle of Trenton (December 26, 1776) and the capture of Lord Cornwallis' army at Yorktown (October 18, 1781)—his main accomplishment was the painstaking diligence with which he labored on what he called "minutious details" in the interest of supply, discipline, recruitment, and popular support of the war effort—all of which were in jeopardy during the war. The army's wartime difficulties, symbolized by the hardship of the winter at Valley Forge, Pennsylvania (1777–1778), but prevalent at many other times as well, Washington attributed to the deficiencies of the decentralized, state-oriented government under the Continental Congress and the Articles of Confederation ratified in 1781.

Although Washington grew convinced that the United States needed a stronger central government, he remained scrupulously deferential to civil authorities while he was a general. When a few officers, early in 1783, suggested that the army should defy Congress and refuse to disband until provision had been made for back pay and officers' pensions, Washington called a meeting of officers in camp at Newburgh, New York, to quell any attempt to use the army to influence Congress. Perhaps the most widely praised single act of Washington's life was his resignation. Most of the soldiers had already disbanded; Washington, far from contemplating a dictatorship, felt eager to return to private life. Nevertheless, his voluntary surrender of command—in contrast with generals since antiquity who had seized supreme power—stood for his contemporaries as proof that independence had been won without subversion of the political principles of the Revolution. Here was confirmation that public-spirited citizens could wield power without being corrupted, that self-government could survive. The celebration of Washington's trustworthiness during and after the Revolution did not glorify only one personality but also made a public character a basis for national unity.

The Drafting of the Constitution

The almost universal respect that Washington enjoyed after the war made him a pivotal figure in the establishment of the government created by the Constitution of 1787. Among Americans critical of the weakness of the Confederation government, the prospect of Washington as chief executive of a new government promised more effective central authority. Americans who were suspicious of the powers granted to the new federal government by the Constitution could not convincingly portray him as a potential dictator. The new institutions, like republicanism itself, were experimental, and Washington brought a proven record to a tentative undertaking.

Washington's reluctance was sincere as he wrote in April, 1789: "My movements to the chair of Government will be accompanied by feelings not unlike those of a culprit who is going to the place of his execution." He correctly anticipated that he stood a better chance of partly losing the "good name" he already possessed than of adding luster to it. He preferred private life to public power; yet he had taken an active part in the interstate political mobilization on behalf of a stronger federal government and had presided over the Philadelphia Convention of 1787 in which the Constitution was drafted. He supported ratification of the Constitution by the states and accepted the presidency because he believed that the weakness of the Confederation endangered American liberty and independence. The Continental Congress lacked the power to tax or to coerce. States' neglect denied Congress revenue. The opposition or absence of delegates from a few states could prevent major legislation, and the opposition of any one state could prevent Congress from expanding its powers. Hence, the central government could not pay its foreign or domestic debts; nor could it amass sufficient power to protect the expanding Western settlements from British forts or Indian resistance. It lacked the power to retaliate against discriminatory foreign-trade regulations by European nations and to compel trade reciprocity. A state government confronted with unrest—such as Massachusetts when farmers in 1786 closed courts to protest heavy taxation—could not rely on a national government to maintain order. As Washington and

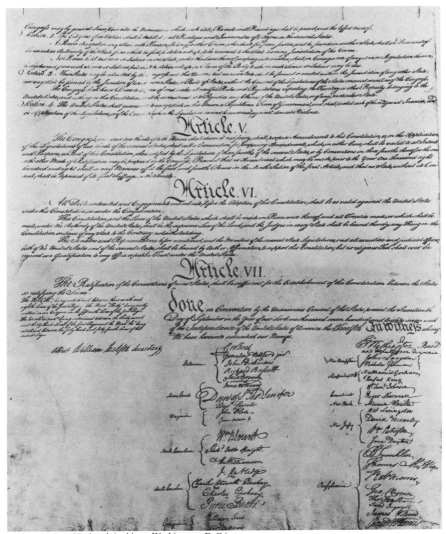

(Courtesy of the National Archives, Washington, D.C.)

Signatures on the United States Constitution

other supporters of strong central government understood history, the prospect of anarchy was an even greater threat to republics than the danger of dictatorship. In fact, weak government would give way to mob rule, ending in tyranny. Washington entered the presidency keenly aware of the fragility of American unity and of the suspicion with which the conduct of the new government would be watched. Yet these centrifugal forces were the very influences that helped convince him to lend his influence to greater political centralization.

Establishing the Presidency

When Washington took the oath of office as president in New York City on April 30, 1789, two states—North Carolina and Rhode Island—had not yet ratified the Constitution. Furthermore, large numbers of Americans in such important states as Virginia, New York, and Pennsylvania had opposed adoption of the new form of government, thinking its powers too great. Political alignments within the states were highly complex and diverse. Some states, such as New York, Rhode Island, and New Jersey, had two-party divisions of long standing; in Pennsylvania the state constitution of 1776 divided political allegiances between its supporters and its critics; in most states, even those as different as Georgia and New Hampshire, political coalitions shifted according to personal, familial, and patronage loyalties. Small wonder that Washington, preparing to appoint federal officials, feared that a "single disgust excited in a particular State, on this account, might perhaps raise a flame of opposition that could not easily, if ever, be extinguished."

One of the first measures of the new government, designed to allay some of the concern provoked by its powers, was Congress' adoption, on September 25, 1789, of twelve amendments to the Constitution, of which ten were eventually ratified by three-fourths of the state legislatures. These amendments were an explicit recognition of rights reserved by the people, not to be violated by the United States government. They included prohibition of a national religious establishment and of federal abridgment of free speech, freedom of the press, peaceable petition and assembly, or the right to bear arms in the common defense. Other amendments prohibited arbitrary quartering of soldiers in private homes and regulated the procedures for the arrest and trial of persons accused of crime. The ninth amendment provided that other rights, not specified in this list, remained intact; and the tenth amendment read: "The powers not delegated to the United States by the Constitution, nor prohibited by it to the States, are reserved to the States respectively, or to the people." The ratification of these amendments—the Bill of Rights—was completed on December 15, 1791. Meanwhile, North Carolina had ratified the Constitution and joined the federal government on November 29, 1789. Rhode Island, under pressure from internal threats of secession, did so on May 29, 1790.

Despite the fact that Americans considered their country to be "the rational empire of human liberty and equality, founded upon the natural rights of mankind and sovereignty of the people," the first federal officeholders, including President Washington, devoted much attention to rituals of official behavior and to the mystique of precedent. The Federalists, as supporters of the Constitution called themselves, commanded a large majority in both houses of Congress. There were only three or four Anti-Federalist senators and no more than thirteen Anti-Federalist representatives. Some Federalists, especially in the Senate and above all Vice President John Adams, believed that the government needed not only the rational consent of its citizens but also the emotional attachment inspired by awe at its magnificence. Thus, senators proposed to exalt Washington with a quasi-monarchical title, such as "His Excellency"—the form of address often used while he was commander of the army—or "His Elective Highness." Washington himself addressed Congress in person and received congressional delegations with replies, as did the British monarch. He rode in state in a carriage with uniformed outriders; he did not accept invitations or return visits. All of these proposals and practices excited comment, especially criticism from the more egalitarian minded. The House of Representatives refused to adopt a special title for the president, and all holders of the office have since been addressed simply as "Mister President." The controversy was comparatively minor; yet, it first raised one of the fundamental issues of Washington's presidency and of early national period politics: a conflict between the attempt to establish a government that could command obedience and the fear that the Revolution would be subverted by monarchical institutions.

George Washington probably overestimated the potential long-term significance of the precedents that he set, ceremonial or substantive. Thomas Jefferson, as president, abandoned Washington's social rules; Andrew Jackson abandoned Washington's practice of vetoing bills only when he deemed them unconstitutional. Washington's fundamental accomplishment was to inaugurate an executive office with strong—and potentially much stronger—authority among a people whose political life in part had long consisted of resistance to centralized executive power. Subject to the Senate's role in ratifying treaties and confirming nominees to office, the president conducted foreign relations, appointed diplomats, federal judges, and other federal officials, and commanded the nation's military forces, including state militias called into federal service. He held office for four years at a time when most state gubernatorial terms were one year or two, and there was no restriction on reelection of the president. He could prevent by veto the enactment of legislation that did not command a two-thirds majority in the House and the Senate.

Early in the first administration Representative James Madison complained to Secretary of State Thomas Jefferson that Washington's followers "had wound up the ceremonials of the government to a pitch of stateliness which nothing but his personal character could have supported, and which no character after him could ever maintain." At the same time that Madison identified a drawback to Washington's distinctive position, he acknowledged its impact. The difficulties in fighting, recruiting, supplying, and financing the American revolutionary war effort had dramatized the deficiencies of state and continental governments with weak executives. No person embodied the impulse to constitutional change so emphatically as Washington.

The "pitch of stateliness" supported by his "personal character" combined augmentation of power with the expectation that it would not be abused.

One of the clearest examples of Washington's personal importance as a nationalizing influence was his travel throughout the United States during his first years in office. In April, 1789, he traveled from Mount Vernon to New York to assume the presidency. In the autumn and winter of 1789–1790 he toured New England, crisscrossing Massachusetts and Connecticut and going as far north as Portsmouth, New Hampshire. In the spring of 1791 he completed an ambitious circuit of the Southern states that covered both the tidewater and the piedmont regions of Virginia, North Carolina, South Carolina, and Georgia. These progressions were an almost unending series of ceremonial addresses, parades, formal greetings, fetes, and honors. Officials welcomed him; choirs serenaded him; girls strewed flowers in his path; tavern keepers played host to his entourage; volunteer companies of horsemen escorted him. After having passed through some of the areas where opposition to the Constitution had been strongest, Washington summarized the main lesson of his tour: "Tranquility reigns among the people, with that disposition towards the general government which is likely to preserve it. They begin to feel the good effects of equal laws and equal protection."

In establishing his administration, Washington neither foresaw nor desired the development of national political parties. Parties, or factions, because they were self-serving and self-perpetuating, were thought to be inimical to the public-spiritedness on which republican institutions were based. The balanced powers of the branches of government were designed to impede any attempt to unite control of the federal authority under one group. The electoral college, in theory, confided the selection of the president and vice president to a few of the best-informed and most judicious citizens. A nonparty ideal of government seemed to prevail at the opening of the Washington Administration.

With James Madison, a central figure in the Constitutional Convention, as an especially prominent leader, the Congress in 1789 enacted legislation to establish the federal judiciary and the executive departments—not yet customarily called a "cabinet"—of State, Treasury, and War. The attorney general was legal counsel to the executive and not the administrator of a department. The Judiciary Act of 1789 established a Supreme Court, two circuit courts, and thirteen district courts, but left the state courts with original jurisdiction over most cases arising under the federal Constitution, laws, or treaties. The Supreme Court was given appellate jurisdiction over cases in which state courts decided against a claim of federal right. This established the principle of federal judicial review of state legislation. Cases not falling under federal jurisdiction, however, could not be appealed beyond the state court systems. Washington appointed firm Federalists to the Supreme Court, with an eye to even geographical distribution and with John Jay of New York as chief justice. As secretary of state, Washington chose Thomas Jefferson, who had been minister to France since 1784. Edmund Randolph became attorney general. The secretary of war, Henry Knox, and the secretary of the treasury, Alexander Hamilton, were men whom Washington had measured during their service in the Continental Army.

Economic Policies: Hamilton's Guiding Vision

Secretary Hamilton took the initiative in defining a domestic legislative program for the administration. An intelligent, ambitious, hardworking man, Hamilton had a vision of governmental policy that encompassed a design for the future of the United States as a populous, industrially productive, powerful, centralized nation. In September, 1780, at a low point of the American effort in the War of Independence, Hamilton—then an aide-de-camp to Washington—had outlined the kinds of measures that he brought to fruition ten years later: executive authority in the hands of departmental administrators, more rigorous federal taxation, and a federally chartered bank that could loan money to the government and attract through the prospect of profits the support of rich men for the government. As secretary of the treasury, Hamilton submitted to Congress in 1790 three reports on provision for the support of the public credit. These contained his plan for funding the national debt, which consisted of approximately $11.7 million owed to Dutch bankers and to the governments of France and Spain, plus $40 million in securities held by foreign investors and by Americans. The Confederation government had been paying interest on the Dutch debt only by contracting additional loans and had allowed interest payments on the rest of the debt to fall into arrears, to a total of about $13 million. Hamilton proposed to convert the unpaid back interest to principal and to fund the total principal by an issue of interest-bearing securities, to the interest on which and to the redemption of which the government would permanently pledge part of its revenue.

The proposal not only was confined to the debt that had been contracted by the Continental Congress but also provided for the assumption by the federal government of the war debts owed by the states, which would add $25 million to the new national debt. In imitation of the British system by which Sir Robert Walpole had established his government's credit, the goal of the funding plan was not to retire the debt completely but to establish confidence that interest on government securities would be paid and that they could be sold or redeemed at or near their face value. When this situation prevailed, government securities could serve as collateral for private loans that expanded the credit available for business ventures.

Hamilton further proposed that Congress charter a Bank of the United

States with a capital of $10 million, one-fifth of which would be subscribed by the government, the rest by private investors. One of the bank's functions would be to make short-term loans to the government. The income of the Treasury, primarily from import duties, fluctuated seasonally, whereas to maintain the value of its securities the Treasury needed a reliable, consistent

(Courtesy of the National Portrait Gallery, Smithsonian Institution, Washington, D.C.)

Alexander Hamilton
by John Trumbull

source of cash. The bank's loans would serve this purpose. The government would deposit its money in the bank, which could also make its own private loans and issue bank notes that citizens could tender to the government at face value for the payment of taxes and other obligations. The notes of the Bank of the United States would be the principal currency in circulation.

Hamilton's conception of the government's responsibilities went beyond the management of its debts and finances. He sought, especially in his Report on Manufactures—submitted in December, 1791—to use federal power to shape the American economy. He wanted the United States to achieve the complex, internally balanced, self-sufficient economy toward which European nations were striving. Fearing that America's traditional trading partners would increasingly rely on their own and their colonies' resources and exclude American agricultural exports from their markets, Hamilton urged that the United States imitate this closed mercantilist system by developing the nation's industrial capacity to meet its domestic demand for manufactured goods, thereby diminishing dependence on Europe. His report proposed protective tariffs on some foreign manufactured goods, bounties for new American industries, and awards and premiums for improvements in productivity and quality. Such incentives would persuade capitalists that they could make greater profits from domestic manufacturing than from the traditional investments in shipping American agricultural products to Europe and selling European manufactures in America.

Not coincidentally, the features of Hamilton's proposals interlocked to foster one another. Holders of the public debt who stood to profit from the plan would lend their support to the federal government; the assumption of state debts would induce public creditors to look to the nation and not to the state for maintenance of the value of their holdings; relieved of their revolutionary war debt, states would have less justification for levying taxes of their own, whereas the federal government would have more reason to assert its powers through taxation; such federal taxes could promote the growth of manufacturing by raising the cost of competing imports; an excise tax on liquor would not only raise revenue from large-scale distillers but would also establish the federal government's direct authority over backcountry independent distillers and backcountry opponents of federal power; a stable federal revenue would secure the confidence of investors in the public credit—they could then devote some of their profits and some of the credit newly available through the Bank of the United States to investment in manufacturing; the development of an integrated economy of agricultural suppliers, American manufacturers, and American consumers would promote the consolidation of the Union through ties of commerce; thus the United States could, by national policy, hasten the day of its becoming a great power.

Although Hamilton had an almost visionary enthusiasm for his conception of national greatness and did not seek to profit personally from the implementation of his program, the grand design, like the earlier system of Sir Robert Walpole, had as its motive power the pursuit of self-interest. If Hamilton were correct, the United States could enhance its international security, its domestic prosperity, its cultural unity, and its political stability by exploiting the selfishness of private advantage for the ends of national policy. In fact, Hamilton believed, the nation could achieve these goals in no other way.

President Washington took no hand in the drafting of Hamilton's program. Although Washington managed his own business affairs astutely and amassed a fortune through a lifetime of land transactions, he was not expert in the complexities of public finance. His support for Hamilton's policies, however, was crucial to their enactment by Congress. Hamilton said that Washington "consulted much, resolved slowly, resolved surely." In August, 1790, after prolonged debate and by a narrow margin, most of Hamilton's proposals were enacted, followed by the legislation for the Bank of the United States in February, 1791.

Opposition to Hamilton's Program: Origins of the National Party System

Although almost everyone agreed that provision for the public debt was essential, Hamilton's plan excited strong, widespread opposition, which contributed to a lasting political division among the supporters of the Constitution. Some of the bases for opposition were highly specific. James Madison and his followers protested that most of the original holders of the public debt—people who had provided loans, goods, and services for the winning of independence, receiving the Continental government's paper money, loan office certificates, or promissory notes—had subsequently sold their claims to speculators for the fraction of the face value. Hamilton's plan would confer large profits on the monied men who now held the claims, while neglecting the patriots who had done most for the Revolution. Madison proposed to divide the government's repayment between the original and the ultimate creditors. Although congressmen joined Madison in commiserating with victimized widows, orphans, and veterans—denouncing greedy speculators—his alternative was too complex and entailed too much expense to attract much support in Congress.

The assumption of state debts aroused the opposition of congressmen from states that had contracted small debts or had paid off most of their debt since the war. Such states disliked the idea of now having to share in the cost of funding the debts of their less conscientious neighbors. To win support, the proponents of assumption had to add to the legislation federal grants to those states that would benefit least from assumption as well as special advantages for Virginia. Southerners, especially Virginians, were concerned by the fact that more than 80 percent of the holders of the national debt were Northerners and that most of the state debts were also in the North. Hamilton's system would increase the disparity of wealth and power in favor of the North. Hamilton obtained the additional votes needed to enact the funding and assumption plan by supporting the establishment of the national capital on the Potomac River in Maryland and Virginia, to take effect after a ten-year residence in Philadelphia.

Other bases of the resistance in Congress were broader concerns of principle, which became more urgent after Hamilton presented his plan for a national bank. To justify the demand for American independence, some proponents of the Revolution had argued that British liberty was being undermined by the manufacturing economy and the politics based on self-seeking (or, as Americans said, corruption) that Hamilton now proposed to import to the United States. Urban concentrations of population, great disparities in wealth, the dependent status of wage workers, a powerful central bank whose resources lessened the reliance of the executive on the voters and their representatives, discriminatory taxes that used the government's power for the benefit of a few at the expense of the many—all of these tendencies that made the British empire seem a threat to liberty would systematically subvert a republican form of government in the United States. Far from sharing Hamilton's fear that a solely agricultural America would be at the mercy of Europe, his critics, especially Thomas Jefferson, contended that America's crops and raw materials were the foundation of the more industrialized nations' well-being. This fact made the United States more stable and secure than its trading partners. Moreover, Americans' buying the bulk of their manufactured goods from Europe left the evils of industrial society far away. Americans could aspire to perpetuate the independent-minded, public-spirited citizenry essential for the survival of self-government exactly because Americans remained self-sufficient farmers free from the economic and political engines admired by Hamilton.

Although Hamilton won enactment of his program, it became, with the divergent opinions on America's foreign relations, the source of a basic division leading to competing political mobilization in rival parties, called Federalist and Republican. Political organizations, including long-standing two-party competition, were already well known in state politics, and many of these factions, or parties, were soon aligned in the new national party system. The Federalist and Republican parties, however, originated in Congress and among leading politicians. These men then encouraged a more general public alarm over governmental policy, which could best be influenced by systematic political cooperation. James Madison and Alexander Hamilton had collaborated in winning public ratification of the Constitution, and Hamilton had consulted Madison as he prepared his reports. Madison, however, became the parliamentary leader of opposition to Hamilton's system in the House of Representatives. Secretary of State Thomas Jefferson, who did not take office until March, 1790, soon became the central figure in the nascent party, though not publicly its spokesman. In the cabinet, Attorney General Edmund Randolph was an ally. In the Senate the adept political organizer from New York, Aaron Burr, could be used, if not trusted. In the House of Representatives the anti-Hamilton (or, by the time of Jefferson's resignation in December, 1793, the antiadministration) group was strongest, approaching a majority on some issues. Hamilton could count on a strong majority in the Senate, led by such able men as Oliver Ellsworth of Connecticut, Robert Morris of Pennsylvania, and Rufus King of New York. Representatives Fisher Ames and Theodore Sedgwick of Massachusetts and William Loughton Smith of South Carolina led pro-Hamilton members of the House, who controlled that body. Secretary of War Henry Knox allied with Hamilton in the cabinet.

For factions in the capital to become parties with national support, organized in even rudimentary networks, the concerns of the cabinet and Congress would have to become the concerns of influential men throughout the country and of voters who could change the composition of the House and, indirectly, the Senate, whose members were elected by state legislatures. One of the principal means of disseminating and intensifying these concerns was the partisan press, especially in Philadelphia after that city became the capital in 1790. The *Gazette of the United States*, edited by John Fenno, became the leading advocate of Hamilton's measures. Fenno dramatized and personalized his arguments by extravagant praise of Hamilton. To his critics, this was cause for alarm. George Washington was the most conspicuous example of the intimate connection between receiving fulsome adulation and possessing political power. Jefferson and Madison feared that the *Gazette of the United States* was exalting Hamilton similarly in order to make him the wielder of power that would overawe republican institutions. In 1791, to present the necessary warnings and to refute Fenno's support of the Hamiltonian program, Jefferson and Madison induced the poet and journalist Philip Freneau to undertake the editorship of a new paper, the *National Gazette*. In it Freneau denounced Hamilton's conspiratorial designs and praised Jefferson for fidelity to the principles of the Revolution. In practice, both editors were agents of the factions for which they spoke. They were responsible for organizing, clarifying, and exaggerating the opinions that would form one of the bases of party loyalty. Fenno's operations were supported partly by printing contracts from the Treasury Department and loans from Hamilton. Freneau received a clerkship in the State Department, which gave him an income with plenty of free time for his editorial labors. Hamilton wrote many of the attacks on Jefferson, published under pseudonyms, whereas Attorney General Randolph wrote defenses of Jefferson.

As Hamilton's financial program and other issues attracted more widespread opposition and support, an avowedly partisan press developed in
other cities, discussing not only local concerns but also the controversies
originating in the capital.

George Washington felt strong concern about the increasingly bitter divisions within his administration. Both Jefferson and Hamilton offered to resign, but the president hoped for a nonparty government that would help
attach the public to the Constitution. He wanted to keep Jefferson in office,
but he refused to believe that Hamilton or any significant number of Americans were guilty of conspiring to introduce monarchy. Washington had accepted the presidency with sincere reluctance. Part of his reluctance came
from the thought that, although his personal popularity might lend dignity
to the government, political controversy might undermine the popular esteem for him. To his distress, he saw this happening, as criticism of Hamilton and of monarchists widened to touch the president himself. Washington set great store by the reputation of respect for republican institutions
that he had established during the revolutionary war. In 1789 he feared that
accepting the presidency might look like ambition—reneging on the promise implied in his resignation of his commission—and he hoped to minimize
any such suspicion by serving only one term. In 1792, at his request, Madison wrote a draft of a farewell address, with which Washington hoped to
close his presidential term fittingly; but the growing political divisions, along
with crises in the economy and in America's dealing with England and
France, made Washington's continuance in office for a second term seem
imperative to Hamilton, Jefferson, Madison, and many others. Even as
Washington won reelection, however, the inchoate Republican Party gathered fifty electoral votes for Governor George Clinton of New York—as
well as four for Jefferson and one for Burr—in an unsuccessful attempt to
defeat the reelection of John Adams as vice president.

Having accepted a second term despite his own reluctance, Washington
was keenly sensitive to accusations that he was arrogating power to himself
and betraying his image as a civic-minded Cincinnatus who served only as
long as the public needed him. When a newspaper called him a king and
depicted him on a guillotine in 1793, Washington lost his temper in a cabinet meeting, which Jefferson recorded: "The President was much inflamed,
got into one of those passions when he cannot command himself, ran on
much on the personal abuse which had been bestowed on him, defied any
man on earth to produce one single act of his since he had been in the government which was not done on the purest motives, that he had never
repented but once the having slipped the moment of resigning his office,
and that was every moment since, that *by god* he had rather be in his grave
than in his present situation. That he had rather be on his farm than to be
made *emperor of the world* and yet that they were charging him with want-

ing to be a king. That that *rascal Freneau* sent him three of his papers every day, as if he thought he would become the distributor of his papers, that he could see in this nothing but an impudent design to insult him. He ended in this high tone." During his second term Washington, though still deploring parties and aspiring to preserve his position as a figure of national unity, became more and more a partisan, Federalist president.

The debate over Hamilton's program and the ensuing partisan rhetoric revealed that Americans had a source of political unity and authority at the national level other than respect for Washington. This was the United States Constitution. Despite the widespread opposition to its ratification, the document soon became an object of veneration and the appeal of last resort on controversial questions. Few men remained Anti-Federalists, and the developing parties of the 1790's had few significant continuities with the factions of the 1780's. The Constitution, almost everyone in political life agreed, defined the way to preserve an ever-vulnerable republican system of government. Contrary to the partisans' charges, Hamilton and the Federalists did not want to introduce monarchical tyranny; nor did Jefferson and the Republicans want to sabotage American unity and independence with anarchy or French revolutionary radicalism. In their deep disagreement, however, the two groups were appealing to a common source of authority for their claim to be patriots. They were constructing sharply divergent interpretations of the Constitution's ambiguous provisions.

For Hamilton, the main threat to American republicanism came not from the prospect of a tyrannical central government but from a weak federal government's inability to maintain its unity, solvency, and national independence. Thus, when Madison, Jefferson, and Randolph tried to persuade Washington to veto the bill establishing the Bank of the United States, on the grounds that the Constitution gave the federal government no such power, Hamilton disagreed. His defense of the constitutionality of the bank appealed to the last clause of Article I, Section 8 of the Constitution, which authorizes Congress to make laws that are "necessary and proper" for executing the powers vested in the government. In Hamilton's interpretation, which convinced Washington to sign the legislation, "necessary" meant not only essential for but also useful in or conducive to the execution of the government's duties. Since a bank would aid in collecting taxes, regulating trade, and providing defense—all of which the Constitution authorized—it was constitutional. This broad construction of the document's wording implied that the Constitution authorized an unlimited array of means whose use it did not specifically prohibit.

For Jefferson and the Republicans—at least until they took control of the federal government in 1801—the greatest threat to the republic was the use of what Jefferson called "props" for the government other than the freely given consent of the people. Such props would include officials' conspicuous military reputations, social and political rituals in imitation of European monarchies, concentrations of financial power aided by governmental policy, or displays of force through the taxing power, the judiciary, and other federal authorities. The Constitution, Republicans agreed, restricted the scope for abuses by confining the federal government to an essential minimum, keeping the remainder of governmental power at the state level, where it could be more closely supervised by the electorate.

The text of the Constitution could plausibly be construed along either of these lines. Its claim to delineate a dual sovereignty divided between federal and state governments and constituencies was theoretically ingenious and politically expedient but practically ambiguous. This ambiguity enabled the Constitution to function as a shared symbol of nationality and of successful self-government among people who deeply mistrusted one another's loyalty.

Despite their familiarity with state political factions, Americans were not accustomed to regarding as patriots those with whom they differed on fundamental questions of political principle, particularly when their opponents began to organize. Differences on immediate issues were quickly traced back to the basic issue of the American Revolution: the survival of liberty. Yet when differences were cast in these terms it was difficult to credit opponents with patriotic intentions or republican sentiments. Instead, it seemed self-evident that a faction which was pursuing dangerous measures must be a conspiracy—at best, to serve the self-interest of its members; at worst, to subvert the American Revolution. The Federalists and the Republicans tended to see themselves, not as conscientious rivals over questions of official policy, but as combatants, each party claiming to be the rescuer of American independence from internal enemies of the republic. This antiparty outlook and this apocalyptic interpretation of partisans' motives remained influential in political discourse long after parties were no longer new in national politics.

Westward Expansion: Settlers and Speculators

Americans of the nineteenth and twentieth centuries have often portrayed the economy and society of late eighteenth-century America as comparatively stable, traditional, almost decorous; yet, to people of the time the country seemed volatile, potentially explosive. Even without massive immigration—though the importation of slaves continued legally until 1808—the population was almost doubling every twenty years. Both the growth of population and the economic ambitions of Americans focused attention on the lands west of the Appalachian mountain chain. Anticipating the rapid extension of settlement between the Appalachians and the Mississippi River, many American investors, including George Washington, speculated in Western lands. They acquired claims to vast holdings, which they hoped to sell at a profit to other investors, even before actual migration began on a large scale. Opponents of Hamilton's funding and assumption measures contended that the national debt could be retired without recourse to Hamilton's federal "engine" simply by selling parcels of the public domain to speculators and settlers—so sure were the migration and the resulting revenue. Under the influence of bribes given to state legislators, the state of Georgia sold sixteen million acres to three Yazoo Land companies for $200,000—a vast tract of Georgia's Western lands in present-day Alabama and Mississippi. Robert Morris and his associates John Nicholson and James Greenleaf formed the North American Land Company, amassing claims to six million acres that they expected to resell at a large profit. Investors in the Potomac Company planned, with the help of a canal around the falls of the Potomac and a canal connecting the Ohio River network with the upper Potomac, to funnel much of the trade of the expanding West, from the Great Lakes to Tennessee, past the new national capital.

The vision and optimism of the speculators ran too far ahead of the actual settlements and purchases on which their hope for profits was ultimately based. Their market was soon impaired by the rising value of American government securities, which could be advantageously pledged in payment for land while they were depreciated but which became more expensive and less useful to speculators as the securities approached face value. Also, the outbreak of war in Europe in 1792 offered European capitalists more attractive returns on loans to belligerent powers than on purchases of American forests. Significantly, at the peak of speculative land values in the early 1790's, Washington, who had played this kind of game for thirty-five years and who needed money, was prudently selling some of his holdings while other men were still buying extensively. In 1795 the bottom began to drop out of the inflated market in Western lands. During the next fifteen years a wide array of speculators found themselves insolvent. Several, including Robert Morris, went to prison at the suit of their creditors.

Indian Affairs: Benign Policies, Brutal Realities

Although the migration to Ohio, Kentucky, and Tennessee was well under way during Washington's administration, the intensive settlement that would eventually match the speculators' vision depended on more than population growth. The West already had a population—the diverse Indian peoples, most of whom regarded the westward movement of whites with alarm. Indian leaders, especially Joseph Brant of the Mohawk and Alexander McGillivray of the Creek, hoped to confine white settlement within the narrowest possible limits, primarily near the major rivers. Britain and Spain, whose empires bordered the United States, also wanted to restrict American expansion. The British continued to occupy forts on territory ceded to the United States in 1783, acting as if Ohio were still British, and the Spanish in the Southwest encouraged Indians to confederate and whites to separate politically from the United States.

Washington, like many of his successors, announced a policy of equitable dealings and peaceful relations with the Indians. In 1791, he concluded a treaty confirming Indian title to most of the land granted by Georgia to the Yazoo Land companies. He urged Congress to define legal ways for the transfer of land from the Indians to whites, for the supervision of trade with Indians, and for the prevention of whites' attacks on Indians. Leaving out the question of the later governmental violations of treaties concluded during the Washington Administration, this policy confronted immediate difficulties. First, the goal of most Indians was not regional coexistence with whites under federal supervision but exclusion of whites from the Indians' ancestral lands. Second, the policy of coexistence was repeatedly violated by whites who settled on Indian lands. As one American officer reported, "The people of Kentucky will carry on private expeditions against the Indians and kill them whenever they meet them, and I do not believe that there is a jury in all Kentucky will punish a man for it." Third, the British and the Spanish encouraged the Indians to fight and provided them with arms and ammunition.

Early in 1790, attempting to exclude whites from the region north and west of the Ohio River, the Indians attacked, defeating Josiah Harmar's army at the Maumee River. In the autumn of 1791, General Arthur St. Clair, governor of the Northwest Territory, took the field with an ill-trained army. He fell into an ambush on November 4, 1791, losing more than nine hundred men killed and wounded. White settlers in Ohio withdrew to Cincinnati and Marietta. President Washington privately received the news of St. Clair's defeat while guests were dining with him. HIs courteous, formal demeanor remained unchanged until the guests had left and Mrs. Washington had retired. Then, alone with his secretary, Tobias Lear, Washington's emotions mounted into a rage as he said, "It's all over—St. Clair's defeated—routed;—the officers nearly all killed, the men by wholesale; the rout complete—too shocking to think of—and a SURPRISE into the bargain!" Remembering his parting words to St. Clair in Philadelphia, Washington now spoke in a torrent, throwing his hands up several times, his body shaking: "Yes, HERE on this very spot, I took leave of him; I wished him success and honor; you have your instructions, I said, from the Secretary of War, I had a strict eye to them, and will add but one word—BEWARE OF A SURPRISE. I repeat it, BEWARE OF A SURPRISE—you know how the Indians fight us. He went off with that, as my last solemn warning thrown into his ears. And yet!! to suffer that army to be cut to pieces, hack'd, butchered, tomahawk'd, by a SURPRISE—the very thing I guarded him against!! O God, O God, he's worse than a murderer! how can he answer it to his country;—the blood of the slain is upon him—the curse of widows and orphans—the curse of Heaven!"

St. Clair's defeat prompted the creation of the first congressional investigating committee, which reviewed the pertinent documents and blamed the outcome on army contractors who had failed to supply proper equipment. The government's Indian policy continued to entertain the prospect of a settlement by treaty until chiefs of the Six Nations, encouraged by the British, made clear in January, 1793, their insistence on an Ohio River boundary. Thereafter, despite some further negotiations, the administration concentrated on defeating resistance. Between 1790 and 1796 the Indian wars accounted for almost five-sixths of the federal government's operating expenses, eventually consuming a total of $5 million. To command in the West, Washington chose General Anthony Wayne, who reached Ohio in 1793. He carefully developed a trained, disciplined force, consisting of 2,000 U.S. Army soldiers and more than 1,500 Kentucky militiamen. In June, 1794, supported by British construction of Fort Miami on the Maumee River, 2,000 Indians gathered there. Wayne began the march against them in August and met a force of 1,300 Indians at Fallen Timbers, where he won a decisive victory on August 20, followed by the devastation of Indian towns

(Courtesy of The Henry Francis DuPont Winterthur Museum)

General Wayne Obtains a Complete Victory over the Miami Indians,
August 20th, 1794

and crops. The British were discredited in Indians' eyes by their refusal to fight the Americans, with whom they were officially at peace. Within a year Wayne used his new power to dictate the Treaty of Greenville, removing the Indians from the area that later became the state of Ohio, for which the United States paid $10,000.

Foreign Affairs: Internal Debate over Policies Toward France

The most difficult, divisive problem that confronted the Washington Administration was the conduct of America's foreign relations. For its security, as well as its pride in being a republic, the new nation needed to demonstrate that it was not a temporary aberration. Markets abroad were essential to the prosperity of its maritime carrying trade, its commercial farmers, and its producers of raw materials. The nation owed money to European creditors; Britons who had made loans to Americans before the Revolution still demanded payment. The eighteenth century had seen a series of European wars, which had extended to the overseas empires; wars that reached an unprecedented scale began during Washington's presidency. More so than many of its citizens desired, the United States was touched by events in other countries.

The greatest series of such events was the French Revolution. A sequence of bloody changes in the leadership of France, its transformation into a republic, and its war with other European powers forced the Washington Administration to make choices, both internationally and among American politicians who differed in their reactions to these developments. Although the early phases of the French Revolution attracted extensive sympathy in the United States, by 1793 the rise of the Jacobins, the Terror, and the expanding war on behalf of atheistic republican revolution alarmed many Americans without destroying the pro-French sympathies of others. More than thirty local political groups, partly imitating the Jacobin clubs, formed into Democratic societies and Republican societies, which were among the first community political organizations in the United States emphasizing national and international concerns.

Washington and the members of his cabinet agreed that the United States should stay out of the war that France had declared against Britain, Holland, and Spain in January, 1793. Hamilton and Jefferson disagreed, however, on how this should be effected. Hamilton and many other Federalists were appalled at the revolutionary violence in France and at the Frenchmen's assertion that they were the vanguard of similar revolutions throughout the world. In a private letter in May, 1793, Washington, discreetly omitting the name of the country, wrote that France's affairs "seem to me to be in the highest paroxysm of disorder . . . beacuse those in whose hands the G[overnmen]t is entrusted are ready to tear each other to pieces, and will, more than probably prove the worst foes the Country has." Hamilton argued early in April, 1793, that the Constitution authorized the president to proclaim neutrality and to enforce the policy against any Americans who might try to aid France. He wanted the United States to refrain from diplomatic relations with the revolutionary regime, giving France no grounds to invoke American aid under the terms of the 1778 treaty of mutual defense.

Jefferson did not want the United States to go to war, but he argued that since the Constitution gave to Congress the power to declare war, only Congress could declare neutrality. He wanted to delay a declaration of neutrality in the hope that the belligerent powers would grant more favorable terms of trade to Americans in order to keep the United States out of the war. Despite such calculations for American advantage, he believed that the survival of republicanism in France was essential for the security of republican government in the United States and for the future prospects of liberty elsewhere. In January, 1793, Jefferson expressed his regret that the executions in France had extended beyond "enemies" of the people to include friends of liberty, but he said of the Revolution, "Rather than it should have failed, I would have seen half the earth desolated." On March 12, 1793, Jefferson instructed the American minister in Paris to recognize the National Assembly as the government of France.

Washington accepted Jefferson's recommendation that the United States recognize the new regime, but he accepted Hamilton's interpretation of the president's authority to proclaim neutrality. In his April 22, 1793, proclamation he omitted the word "neutrality" but declared a policy of "conduct friendly and impartial toward the belligerent powers." Republicans, including James Madison writing under a pseudonym, denounced the proclamation as an unconstitutional aggrandizement of the executive and a betrayal of Americans' moral obligations to their fellow republicans in France. Madison argued that "every nation has a right to abolish an old government and establish a new one. This principle . . . is the only lawful tenure by which the United States hold their existence as a nation."

The divisions among Americans over the French Revolution and the European war grew more intense as a result of the activities of Edmond Genet, the first minister to the United States from republican France. Genet, a Girondist, was politically out of favor at home by the time he reached America, as the Jacobins were replacing and liquidating the Girondists; but to many Americans, including Jefferson, he was an attractive representative of the fight for republicanism in France, with which they sympathized. On April 8, 1793, Genet landed at Charleston, South Carolina, where he received an enthusiastic welcome and began a month-long trip to Philadelphia. In Charleston and at stops along his route, Genet made arrangements with American supporters for raising armies to liberate Louisiana and Florida from Spain, as well as Canada from Britain. These grandiose plans came to nothing, but they showed Genet's intention to secure

Americans' aid in France's wars, contrary to the policy of neutrality. The effusive public demonstrations of solidarity convinced Genet that his policy enjoyed more support than did Washington's. Jefferson, who asserted that 99 percent of Americans approved of the French Revolution, told Genet about the divisions within the cabinet and looked the other way when the French agent André Michaux sought to organize attacks on Louisiana and Canada.

Genet, in violation of Washington's proclamation, commissioned twelve privateering vessels to raid British shipping. Eighty British merchantmen were brought into American ports; they were condemned and sold—not by American admiralty courts, but by French consuls, for whom Genet claimed extraterritorial status. In July, 1793, Washington asked the Supreme Court to rule on the constitutionality of Genet's actions. The Court declined to do so. It asserted its equal status as a branch of government by refusing to act as counsel to the executive branch, confining itself to decisions in litigation. In 1794, in the case *Genet v. Sloop Betsy*, the Court ruled that Genet's consular courts were illegal and that any condemnation of prizes of war should take place in United States district courts, acting as admiralty courts. By August, 1793, Washington was ready to take action against Genet's operations. He prohibited the organizing of military units in America by belligerents. He forbade the privateers commissioned by Genet to enter American ports. The United States, however, had no navy and no army on its coast adequate to enforce these rules. Genet believed that he had sufficient popular support to defy Washington. He threatened to appeal "over Washington's head" to the pro-French sentiment of the American public. This threat was his undoing. Jefferson disassociated himself from Genet, and the government requested that France recall the minister. Since the Jacobins probably would have executed Genet, he was not forced to go home but was allowed to live in the United States as a private citizen.

Although Genet could not overthrow Washington, the controversy over his brief but excited tenure as minister clarified the deep division among Americans in their attitudes toward France. Washington could no longer aspire to preside over a people united in praise of him or over a nonparty government. In December, 1793, Jefferson resigned the secretaryship of state, to be succeeded by Edmund Randolph. Washington, during his second term, became decisively aligned with the developing Federalist Party, as his policies aroused more vigorous denunciation by Republicans.

Relations with Britain: Threats of War

The European wars did not give the United States the position of commercial advantage that Jefferson had imagined. On the contrary, the ports and the navies of the two main belligerents, France and England, both plundered the American merchant marine. Each stood to gain from trade with neutrals, but each also stood to gain from interrupting its enemy's neutral trade. France, beginning in 1793, confiscated cargoes in her ports. In June, Britain proclaimed a naval blockade of France, which became the basis for seizure of American cargoes headed there. In the autumn, when Britain undertook the conquest of the French West Indies, the government ordered the seizure of all ships trading with those islands—principally American— and kept its order secret until the concentration of ships for seizure was greatest.

Jefferson and the Republicans were troubled by the fact that 75 percent of American imports came from the British Empire and that most American exports went to Britain, even if the goods were subsequently re-exported to the Continent. Such a pattern of trade might make the United States dependent on British policy and susceptible to the monarchical influence of Britain's reactionary policies, the Republicans feared. They hoped to establish a more extensive trade with France—indeed, to force American trade into French channels in order to destroy the influence over American politics arising from commercial ties with Great Britain.

Jefferson and the Republicans imagined that they could use the weapon of American trade against Britain and without fear of British military action against the United States. The Republicans opposed expenditures for an American military establishment on the scale that Federalists favored. In response to raids on American commerce by Algerian corsairs, Madison recommended that the United States hire the Portuguese navy to do the fighting. Washington, though he and the Federalists deprecated war with Britain, believed that the British might attack America as an ally of France. Moreover, the British seemed to be encouraging the activities of the Barbary pirates to drive American shipping out of the Mediterranean. In February, 1794, Congress authorized the construction of six frigates but also, during the same year, voted bribes to the dey of Algiers for the protection of American vessels.

Few people in government doubted, in the early months of 1794, that the United States and Britain would soon be at war. Hamilton and some Federalist senators believed, however, that the United States could persuade the British that America did not intend to wage covert war under the pretense of neutrality. To this end, these men urged Washington to send a special minister to Britain, charged with concluding a treaty that would avoid war and would settle such points of controversy as the continued presence of one thousand British troops on United States territory and the terms of American trade with Britain and the British West Indies. The Republicans, clinging to Jefferson's belief in commercial coercion of Britain, passed a bill in the House of Representatives prohibiting American trade with Britain. The bill lost in the Senate only by the casting vote of Vice President Adams. The ensuing compromise, an embargo keeping American ships in port, was lifted when it proved detrimental to the trade of the Southern states. Washington decided to send a minister plenipotentiary to Britain and chose Chief Justice John Jay. Hamilton, whose attachment to Britain matched that of Jefferson to France, drafted Jay's instructions. Jay was to secure British withdrawal from the American West, reparations for British seizures of American merchant vessels, compensation for the slaves that the British army had removed from the Southern states during the revolutionary war, and a commercial treaty defining the Americans' trading rights with the British empire.

Jay wanted a treaty and not war with Britain. He did not go to London to issue ultimatums. Even if he had wanted to hold out the threatening possibility that the United States might join with neutral European nations to enforce trading rights, he could not have done so because Hamilton, on his own initiative, had already assured the British minister in Philadelphia that the United States would not join the Armed Neutrality. Hamilton and Jay hoped to get the best results by a friendly approach. The British were primarily concerned with preventing any American friendship with France and keeping Anglo-American trade open to offset British merchant marine losses, crop failures, and falling government revenues. Nevertheless, they were disposed to make few concessions to the United States at the expense of British interests, as wartime mercantilist policy defined those interests.

Jay secured very little beyond maintaining peace with Britain. The British agreed to remove their troops from American territory by June, 1796, and allowed Americans to trade with India. American vessels of seventy tons or less could trade with the British West Indies but could not take molasses, sugar, coffee, cocoa, or cotton to ports other than American. Since a small, single-masted sloop might measure nearly four hundred tons, this was a very limited concession. Other subjects of dispute—compensation for British spoliation of American commerce, British creditors' claims against American debtors, the location of the northwest international border—were referred to arbitration by joint commissions. Jay, who opposed slavery, did not even ask for compensation to slaveowners whose slaves had been freed by the British army. To secure these terms, Jay made a number of substantial concessions to Britain. He abandoned the American claim that neutrals had the right to trade freely with all belligerents, and he acquiesced in the British restrictions on neutral trade, including limitations on such commodities as naval stores and food. The treaty conceded Britain most-favored-nation status in American ports, thereby precluding American taxes and other legislation directed specifically against the British. The United States also conceded that it could not sequester money owed by Americans to Britons for private debts. Finally, the treaty guaranteed that American ports would not be open to the navies or the privateers of enemies of Britain; nor would prize vessels any longer be condemned in American ports.

The Federalists still had a commanding majority in the Senate; and, after removing from the treaty a prohibition on American export of cotton and the objectionable article on the West Indies trade, they were able to muster the two-thirds vote to ratify the treaty on June 24, 1795. Although the Senate undertook to deliberate in secret, Senator Stevens Thomson Mason of Virginia, an opponent of ratification, leaked a copy of the treaty, the terms of which were soon widely publicized. Jay's terms attracted bitter denunciation from Republicans: Mass meetings deplored the betrayal of American rights and national dignity; antitreaty petitions received many signatures. Workers in the port cities north of Baltimore were especially conspicuous in the protests organized by Republicans. The treaty was overwhelmingly unpopular among the political leaders of the Southern states.

Washington came near to leaving the treaty unsigned. He was especially provoked by learning, late in June, that the British had begun to seize American vessels carrying foodstuffs to France. In July, however, the British minister disclosed to the American government captured dispatches from the French minister in Philadelphia to his superiors. These convinced Washington that his secretary of state, Edmund Randolph, had sought bribes from the French. Washington decided to sign the treaty in order to assert that American policy was not subject to corrupt French influences. He feared that pro-French and anti-British sympathies among American politicians had already grown so great that only a treaty with Britain could forestall the degradation of the United States into a satellite of France. He required Randolph to execute the ratification before he revealed the captured documents to the secretary. When Randolph saw that his explanations did not convince Washington, he immediately resigned. Not until after the treaty went into effect did the British rescind the order for the seizure of American vessels.

Republicans decided to resist the implementation of the treaty in the House of Representatives by refusing to enact the legislation needed to carry its provisions into effect. They held the first congressional party caucus in order to mobilize their majority. Although this meeting did not produce consensus, it was an important innovation in disseminating a party policy and in seeking organized support. In March, 1796, the House called on the president to submit the documents pertaining to the negotiation of the treaty. This action implied that treaties need not be considered effective until the House approved them by its implementing legislation. Washington refused the request and asserted that the Jay Treaty was now the supreme law of the land. He cited as evidence of the House's error in its constitutional stance the fact that the Constitutional Convention had voted down a proposal to give the House a role in treaty making. In rebuttal to Washington, Madison argued what became the prevailing view of constitutional interpretation: that the specific opinions of the framers of the Constitution were not binding on subsequent interpretations of it. The House endorsed Madison's argument by a majority that included some Federalists.

To counteract the Republicans' defiance and to solidify Federalists' loyalty to the administration, Hamilton—who had been succeeded as secretary of the treasury by Oliver Wolcott, Jr., on January 31, 1795, but who remained an influential party leader—set out to stimulate and dramatize protreaty public opinion. With the support of businessmen who wanted increased trade and closer ties with England, public meetings and petitions voiced support for Washington and the treaty. At the end of April, 1796, the supporters of the treaty narrowly won a vote in the House in favor of implementing it. The aftermath fulfilled the expectations of those interested in American commerce. Exports to the British Empire increased 300 percent within five years. In the same period exports of American cotton rose from six million pounds to twenty million pounds. The rapid extension of this staple crop underlay the growth of a slave labor society in the Southern states. In 1796, British troops withdrew from the American Northwest, and the arbitration commissions in later years eventually settled the remaining issues.

The domestic agitation over the Jay Treaty promoted the coordination of party activities both in Congress and among the electorate, though the percentage of eligible citizens who voted remained small. Divisions over economic interests, the French Revolution, presidential power, sectional grievances, and competing visions of America's future came increasingly to be expressed through a partisan system. The Republicans enhanced the sophistication of their appeals to "the people"—that is, to many citizens whom the Federalists had not originally expected to have weight in matters of national policy. Newspapers, pamphlets, mass meetings, parades, local committees, and other techniques helped to expand the politically active population. The Federalists, though ultimately with less success, used similar methods on their own behalf.

Conspicuous in the denunciation of the Jay Treaty was bitter public abuse of President Washington. The Republican press charged him with affecting "the seclusion of a monk and the supercilious distance of a tyrant." He was called a "usurper" who was guilty of "political degeneracy" and who harbored "dark schemes of ambition." According to a writer in the *Philadelphia Aurora*, Washington had fought in the revolutionary war only for power and personal glory. Another accused him of military incompetence. He was even charged—correctly, as it turned out—with drawing his salary as president in advance. This meant, his critic said, that Washington intended to extract more than his allotted $25,000 per year from the Treasury—and he should therefore be impeached. Early in Washington's second term Jefferson had noticed that the president was "extremely affected by the attacks made and kept up on him in the public papers. I think he feels those things more than any person I ever met with." Politically, Washington's reaction to the criticism was to ally himself more fully with the Federalists. After the resignation of Randolph, the cabinet had only Federalists in it: Wolcott as secretary of the treasury, Timothy Pickering as secretary of state, James McHenry as secretary of war, and Charles Lee as attorney general. All of these men, as well as Washington, continued to be influenced by the advice of Hamilton, now an attorney in New York.

The Whiskey Rebellion and the Western Lands

The Washington Administration confronted a domestic challenge to federal authority during the summer of 1794, while Hamilton was still in the cabinet. The secretary of the treasury took advantage of the occasion to dramatize his conception of the federal government's power. The challenge consisted of violent resistance in four western counties of Pennsylvania to the collection of the federal excise tax on whiskey. Private distilling of whiskey was common in the West, partly because it made corn crops a more readily exchangeable and transportable commodity. The federal tax struck many Westerners exactly as Hamilton intended it should—as a direct assertion of their subordination to the federal government. Many western Pennsylvanians decided to resist. They threatened excise officers, robbed the

GENERAL GEORGE WASHINGTON.
Reviewing the Western army at Fort Cumberland the 18ᵗʰ of octob. 1794.

(Courtesy of the National Portrait Gallery, Smithsonian Institution, Washington, D.C.)

mails, stopped federal judicial proceedings, and seized United States soldiers who were guarding the home of an excise inspector. A general meeting threatened an attack on Pittsburgh.

Washington initially sent federal commissioners to the disturbed area; they were authorized to negotiate a peaceful settlement. Any federal use of force would have to rely on state militias called into federal service. Fearing more widespread defiance, the administration soon decided to use force. A thirteen-thousand-man army of militiamen from Pennsylvania, New Jersey, Maryland, and Virginia was mobilized under the command of Governor Henry Lee of Virginia. Contrary to the Westerners' threats, the federal units met no resistance. Some leaders of the resistance fled, and the followers remained quiet when the army arrived. About twenty men were arrested, of whom two were later convicted and subsequently pardoned by Washington.

The president agreed with Governor Lee and other Federalists that the Pennsylvania unrest did not arise from reluctance to pay taxes. It had been incited, Washington and his supporters charged, by the Democratic and Republican societies and by the inflammatory speeches of Republicans in Congress, who denounced the policies of the Washington Administration. Madison, Jefferson, and their supporters protested that the administration was using its role as executor of the law to discredit conscientious critics by unjustly linking them with lawbreakers in western Pennsylvania. These Republican complaints had merit. Hamilton had acted provocatively in the spring of 1794 by proceeding with prosecutions of delinquent distillers in distant federal courts after the law had been revised to allow remote cases to be tried in the closest state courts. When Hamilton explained that he was accompanying the militia in Pennsylvania because Governor Lee "might miss the policy of the case," it is likely that he was referring to this opportunity to demonstrate federal power—an opportunity he had orchestrated. Ultimately, Hamilton's eagerness to use federal force and Washington's denunciation of Republican provocateurs backfired, as their fellow Federalist, Fisher Ames, recognized. Ames said, "A regular government, by overcoming an unsuccessful insurrection, becomes stronger; but elective rulers can scarcely ever employ the force of a democracy without turning the moral force, or the power of public opinion, against the government." Washington's partisan interpretation of the Whiskey Rebellion helped establish him, in the eyes of the Republicans, as a thoroughgoing Federalist—a view that the Jay Treaty confirmed.

The volatility of western Pennsylvania exemplified a source of concern that had troubled American politicians since the Revolution—the political cohesion of such a large, diverse country. The controversies over Hamilton's financial program and the Jay Treaty disclosed severe sectional divisions between Northern and Southern states. The expansion of trans-Appalachian settlement raised the threat of separatism and unrest among Western settlers. The Federalists preferred that the Western lands be settled gradually and comparatively stably. To this end, the Land Act of 1796 required that federal land be surveyed before purchase and settlement, that it not be sold for less than two dollars an acre, and that purchasers not receive extended credit. The effect of these provisions was to confine purchasing of federal land primarily to land corporations.

The Mississippi River was the obvious natural channel for the exports of the West, but its southernmost banks were under the control of Spain, the possessor of Louisiana. For Mississippi River trade to be feasible, Americans would have to be allowed to navigate the river through Spanish territory and to deposit their products temporarily near the mouth of the river while the goods awaited export. At the invitation of Manuel de Godoy of Spain, Washington sent Thomas Pinckney to Madrid in May, 1795, to negotiate a treaty on this matter as well as on the questions of the border between the United States and the Spanish colony of Florida and the role of the Spanish in stimulating Indian resistance in adjacent American territory.

French military successes against Spain meant that Spain would have to make territorial concessions to France from its empire. These would include returning Louisiana to France. In doing so, Spain could still undermine the security of France's imperial position by weakening the defensibility of Louisiana. Thus Pinckney found Godoy ready to offer the United States generous terms. In the Treaty of San Lorenzo, October 27, 1795, Spain granted the privilege of navigation of the Mississippi and the privilege of deposit, recognized America's claim to the thirty-first parallel as the border of Florida, and promised not to incite Indians against the United States. Godoy evaded compliance with these terms until 1798 but left them as an encumbrance on French control of Louisiana thereafter.

Washington's Farewell Address: Three Lessons for the Young Nation

At the height of the scheming and political agitation in the presidential campaign of 1796—which turned on the choice of presidential electors and the attempts to influence the electoral college—Washington published his farewell address. In addition to declining to be considered for reelection, Washington sought to impress upon his fellow citizens three lessons that he considered crucial for the survival of the United States: The Union must be maintained by quelling sectional animosities; political parties threaten liberty by subordinating the people to factional leaders; and American interests are best served by avoiding intense attachments or intense aversions to other nations. Lacking the erudition and intellectual virtuosity of Hamilton or Jefferson, Washington also avoided the self-righteous dogmatism and immoderate enthusiasms to which the two younger men were susceptible. Washington asserted that the interests of the United States militated against exclusive attachment to one great power, even if that nation seemed to be the vanguard of liberty or the bulwark of civilization. Conversely, obsessive hostility toward any country clouded the pursuit of American interests by the preoccupation with the object of hatred.

Although most of the farewell address spoke in abstract terms—the president did boast of Pinckney's treaty and stressed the need to uphold the public credit—a reader could easily see that the address was in many respects a defense of Washington's policies as president as well as a condemnation of the behavior of his critics. Madison, who had helped with a draft in 1792, believed with other Republicans that the address was purely partisan and pro-British. Washington may have seen some vindication in the election of Vice President Adams as his successor; but the circumstances were not very edifying, considered in the light of Washington's admonitions. Newspaper polemics reached new levels of personal abuse, whereas partisans, not content with denouncing their enemies, betrayed their allies, too. Jefferson's supporters mistrusted their own vice presidential candidate, Aaron Burr. Since electoral votes were cast for individuals, without specifying the office, Hamilton hoped to manipulate the Federalist electoral votes so that Thomas Pinckney rather than Adams would emerge as president. New England Federalists were as determined to check Pinckney as Virginia Republicans were to check Burr. In the outcome of the double crosses, Adams was narrowly elected president, and his Republican opponent, Jefferson, received the second largest vote and became vice president. Although the party organizations were obviously rudimentary, the election luridly demonstrated how little weight Washington's farewell advice carried in practice; nor did posterity heed his counsel on sectional antagonism or on foreign relations.

Washington did not expect his advice to prevail. He wrote that he hoped only that in the future the memory of his words might "recur to moderate the fury of party spirit, to warn against the mischiefs of foreign intrigue, to guard against the imposture of pretended patriotism." At the time of his retirement, there were many grounds for satisfaction. The governmental institutions had survived changes in officials; partisans had not destroyed the government; and states had not left the Union. Indeed, Vermont, Kentucky, and Tennessee had joined it as new states. Nevertheless, Washington's address had a note of detachment, even pessimism, in it. He was eager to retire to Mount Vernon, to take with him intact his personal honor and his public reputation—leaving his fellow citizens and their posterity to endure the consequences of the illusions he vainly warned them against. He said of his warnings, "I dare not hope they will make the strong and lasting impression I could wish—that they will control the usual current of the passions or prevent our nation from running the course which has hitherto marked the destiny of nations." To Washington and his contemporaries, the course that nations had always run ended in the loss of their liberty and independence. The United States had a destiny no different from that of other countries; but he knew that, when it came, no one would be able to say that it was the fault of George Washington.

In 1799, resisting any hint that he should again be a presidential candidate, Washington wrote, "A mind that has been constantly on the stretch since the year 1753, with but short intervals and little relaxation, requires rest and composure." In retirement he still had many visitors, took an active interest in the crises of the Adams Administration, and accepted the nominal command of the special army established during the quasi-war with France. He censured the Virginia Resolutions against the Alien and Sedition Acts, urged Patrick Henry to come out of retirement as a Federalist candidate in Virginia, and rejoiced in the election of Federalist Virginians John Marshall and Henry Lee to the House of Representatives in 1798. Yet, despite the increasingly partisan role of Washington as an aegis for the Federalist Party—even including many eulogies of him in 1800—he remained an evocative symbol of American nationality. This stature grew even more conspicuous in the nineteenth century, after the alarms of the early national period had faded. The memory of Washington's unique strength of character and his providential achievements in the founding of the nation seemed to posterity to give promise that the United States enjoyed God's special favor. The historian George Bancroft wrote of him in 1858, "Combining the centripetal and the centrifugal forces in their utmost strength and in perfect relations, with creative grandeur of instinct he held ruin in check, and renewed and perfected the institutions of his country. Finding the colonies disconnected and dependent, he left them such a united and well ordered commonwealth as no visionary had believed to be possible."

Washington died as he had lived—practicing self-control, attending to details. In the early hours of December 14, 1799, he developed a severe inflammation of the throat, with labored breathing and much pain. During the day, he submitted quietly to a battery of medical treatments, including bleedings, blisters, and emetics; but he believed from the first attack that the disease was fatal. Finally, he said to his doctors, "I feel myself going. I thank you for your attention. You had better not take any more trouble with me; but let me go off quietly; I cannot last long." To his secretary, Tobias Lear, he said, "I am just going. Have me decently buried and do not let my body be put into the vault in less than two days after I am dead." When Lear did not reply, Washington asked, "Do you understand me?" Lear answered, "Yes, sir." Then Washington said, " 'Tis well." His last action, a few minutes later, was to take his own pulse as it fell.

Washington's Definitive Example: The Centrality of the Presidency

Like many subsequent presidents, Washington left office less popular and less influential than he entered it. Unlike other presidents, whom Americans have expected to be partisan, Washington lost some of his acclaim simply by developing a political affiliation. Compared, however, with the bitter experiences of his immediate successors—Adams, Jefferson, and Madison—Washington's presidency left him comparatively unscathed. The basic concern of the first president was to vindicate the proposition that republican institutions could function and survive. The specific tasks they faced seem much less complicated than those of many later presidents. The additional difficulty of the earliest chief executives was the uncertainty of maintaining the existence of the United States. In this undertaking no American could have inaugurated—or rather created—the office of president to such dramatic effect as did George Washington. His use of his personal reputation to promote his policies of public credit, expanding commerce, international neutrality, and the extension of westward settlement largely succeeded. Later presidents, pursuing different policies or facing concerns unimagined by Washington, would continue to emulate his use of the presidency. Hardly anyone could imagine a republican America pursuing any course of policy without a president of the United States taking the initiative. In that presumption of the centrality of the office lies Washington's most lasting governmental legacy.

Charles Royster

Bibliographical References
The most thorough biography of Washington is Douglas Southall Freeman, *George Washington*, completed by John Alexander Carroll and Mary Wells Ashworth, 7 vols., 1948–1957. More recent is James Thomas Flexner, *George Washington*, 4 vols., 1965–1972, which has been abridged in one volume under the title *Washington: The Indispensable Man*, 1979. For an excellent one-volume study, see Marcus Cunliffe, *George Washington: Man and Monument*, rev. ed., 1982. Garry Wills, *Cincinnatus: George Washington and the Enlightenment*, 1984, perceptively explores Washington's use of power and his public image. Valuable analyses of Washington's administration appear in John C. Miller, *The Federalist Era, 1789–1801*, 1960; in Forrest McDonald, *The Presidency of George Washington*, 1974; and in recent biographies of John Adams, Thomas Jefferson, James Madison, and Alexander Hamilton. An important work on the policy debates among political leaders is Drew R. McCoy, *The Elusive Republic: Political Economy in Jeffersonian America*, 1980. Curtis P. Nettels, *The Emergence of a National Economy, 1775–1815*, 1962, analyzes many complex developments. For the federal government's use of the military, see Richard H. Kohn, *Eagle and Sword: The Federalists and the Creation of the Military Establishment in America, 1783–1802*, 1975.

John Adams

JOHN ADAMS

1797–1801

On September 19, 1796, President George Washington published his fare-well address and revealed to the nation what he had decided privately months earlier, that he would retire from public life at the end of his second term. The news disappointed staunch Federalists, who hoped Washington would run again and thus avoid even the possibility that Thomas Jefferson might become president. It also delighted their opponents, who, not having to counter Washington's immense popularity, might be able to elect Jeffer-son president. Finally, it relieved Vice President John Adams (1735-1826), who wanted badly to be the Federalist candidate but who had, along with everyone else, to wait nervously until September to be certain Washington intended to retire after all.

Adams did not so much win the Federalist nomination in 1796 as inherit it. He had served Washington loyally as vice president for eight years, presiding quietly over the Senate, dutifully breaking tie votes in favor of Federalist economic and foreign policies when necessary (Adams broke twenty such ties, more than any other vice president in history). With the exception of Washington, no Federalist still active in national affairs rivaled his reputation with the public as an early and steady advocate of indepen-dence. No one still active, Federalist or otherwise, could bring with him to the presidency the long and successful experience in government and diplo-macy and the reputation as a legislator, essayist, and speaker that Adams could. If he was not loved by the people at large as was Washington, he was at least genuinely and widely respected for his service to the Revolution and the republic. In the minds of many Americans, and certainly in his own mind, Adams was Washington's heir apparent.

Lawyer, Revolutionary, Diplomat

Born in 1735 to a middle-class farming family in Braintree (now Quincy), Massachusetts, Adams' parents expected him to enter the ministry. He was graduated from Harvard in 1755 and taught school briefly in Worcester while he convinced himself that he would be far happier and much more successful disputing law before juries than dispensing piety from a pulpit. In 1758, he was admitted to the bar in Massachusetts and began practicing law in Braintree.

Public spirited and ambitious, Adams soon began writing essays for the Boston newspapers and was already established in a minor way as a public spokesman when the Stamp Act crisis vaulted him into politics and prominence. Resolutions denouncing the stamp tax that he prepared for the Braintree town meeting were well received and circulated throughout the colony. Soon after, he joined James Otis in Boston to challenge the constitutionality of the Stamp Act in court, and he found himself being drawn into popular politics in the capital and into the nascent political party forming around Otis, Sam Adams, John Hancock, and others. In 1768 Adams moved to Boston, and by the end of the decade his growing reputation as an opponent of British taxation and tyranny won for him election to the Massachusetts General Court.

Ill health forced his withdrawal from office for a while, but the Tea Act crisis brought him back into public view. In 1774, Massachusetts sent him to the First Continental Congress, where he urged a strong stand against English policy and opposed reconciliation on anything but colonial terms. Back in Massachusetts, he wrote a series of essays under the pseudonym of "Novanglus" refuting the Tory essays of Loyalist Daniel Leonard. The "Novanglus" essays circulated widely and began to build for Adams a "national" reputation in a nation not yet quite born. He returned to the congress after the war began, and in the spring of 1776 he was appointed to a committee to prepare a declaration of independence. Though Adams had little to do with drafting the declaration, he had much to do with wrestling Jefferson's text through an excited but nervous and often balky congress. In Jefferson's opinion, Adams was the declaration's "ablest advocate and defender" in the congress.

Adams began his diplomatic career in February, 1778, when the Continental Congress dispatched him to Paris to replace the discredited Silas Deane as a member of the American diplomatic team seeking French aid against England. For the next ten years, with only one brief hiatus during which he helped write Massachusetts' revolutionary constitution, Adams represented the republic abroad at Paris, Amsterdam, the Hague, and London on a variety of diplomatic missions: seeking recognition for the new nation, raising money, negotiating treaties of trade and alliance, and, most challenging of all, helping draft the Treaty of Paris, which finally brought the War of Independence, if not the American Revolution, to a formal close. In Paris, he acquired a healthy skepticism about French diplomats and a thorough dislike of Benjamin Franklin. Between 1785 and 1788, he served in London as the first United States minister to England. During his last two years abroad, he wrote *A Defense of the Constitutions of the United States of America*, which argued that bicameral (as opposed to unicameral) legislatures, the sharp separation of legislative, executive, and judicial functions in government, and a powerful executive with an absolute veto were all crucial elements of good constitutions. "The people's rights and liberties," he contended, could "never be preserved without a strong executive," for "if the executive power, or any considerable part of it, is left in the hands . . . of . . . a democratical assembly, it will corrupt the legislature as rust corrupts iron, or as arsenic poisons the human body." Such ideas would not be popular in America, he told Jefferson in 1787 (accurately, as it turned out), but he intended to publish his opinion anyway, "however unpopular it might be."

Adams returned home in 1788 and the following year won the vice presidency. It was not a particularly gratifying victory, since he received only 34 of the 69 electoral votes cast, and it placed him in a job he described halfway through his tenure as "the most insignificant office that ever the invention of man contrived or his imagination conceived." By 1796, then, Adams was determined either to move on to the presidency or, failing that, to retire to his law practice, his farm, and his family in Quincy.

The Campaign of 1796: No Electoral Mandate

The presidential campaign of 1796 was by modern standards, a curious one. Both candidates thought it demeaning and unseemly to plead for votes, so neither campaigned. In Adams' opinion, and Jefferson's too, public men should be called to office by an unsolicited electorate, very much as a minister was called to his pulpit by a congregation—a relaxed approach to presidential politics that would not survive Adams' presidency. Still, a campaign did take place in 1796, carried out mostly by newspaper essayists, editors, and political pamphleteers. Also, the election was expected to answer important questions. For example, what kind of government had the Philadelphia Convention of 1787 created? Or, put a little differently, where, precisely, was the limit of federal power with respect to the states? With England and France again at war, where did the best interests of the United States lie: as an ally of the revolutionary French Republic or as an ally in all but name of Great Britain? Or somewhere in between?

Jefferson and his backers believed that Adams, Hamilton, and the Federalists had already perverted the Constitution and increased the powers of the central government at the expense of the states to a dangerous degree during Washington's two terms. Should Adams win, they warned, this assault on the Constitution and on the liberties of all Americans would doubtless continue. Adams, Republican essayists insisted, was a monarchist at heart who would reestablish in American the principles of monarchial government if he could. He was therefore unfit to govern a free people, and for proof they pointed to his *Defense of the Constitutions.*

From Adams' point of view, the creation of an effective national government with its powers properly distributed among its branches, and the imposition of order on licentious state governments prone to truckle to the whim of popular majorities, had been two important purposes of the Constitution. Two-thirds of the states, he thought, had constitutions so defective that they were, "as sure as there is a Heaven and an Earth," bound to produce "disorder and confusion." For Adams, Jefferson's election promised not liberty but licentiousness, not an ordered and orderly republic but the chaos and injustice inevitably born of weak government.

The two men differed as well over foreign affairs. Jefferson looked upon the War of Independence as the beginning of a revolution that would secure for Americans new liberties. He considered the Revolution the first stage of an international movement that would topple monarchy throughout Europe as well as in America. Thus Jefferson and his Republicans welcomed the French Revolution and insisted that both America's revolutionary principles and its self-interest demanded close ties with France.

Adams and most Federalists, in contrast, looked on the War of Independence as the end of a revolution that had been fought, not so much to establish new liberties, as to preserve traditional ones. He thought of the Constitution as a means of securing these familiar liberties by returning order and authority to American national government. Neither America's principles nor its self-interest, then, dictated an alliance with the architects of the Terror in France or their successors. If forced to choose between embracing the tricolor or the union jack (and unlike arch-Federalists such as Timothy Pickering and Alexander Hamilton, Adams did not believe that the nation *had* to choose one or the other), he would have preferred the British, whose balanced constitutional system (the recent perversions of George III and his henchmen aside) Adams rather admired. A Jefferson presidency, he feared, would draw the nation into a disastrous war with England and weaken the republic, perhaps fatally.

In the end, the clumsy maneuverings of Hamilton probably had as much to do with the outcome of the election as the often hysterical debates conducted in the press. Even before Washington's farewell address, Hamilton hoped to find a way to prevent Adams' election without assuring Jefferson's. Adams was far too independent to work comfortably and closely with a man of Hamilton's arrogance and ambition. Hamilton eventually plotted to have Adams' vice presidential running mate, Thomas Pinckney of South Carolina, elected president, thus consigning Adams again to the limbo of the vice presidency. Since each elector cast two ballots, the scheme involved convincing a few Federalist electors to vote for Pinckney but not Adams. Presuming the Federalists won the election, Pinckney would have a few votes more than Adams and so would be president. He would, it was expected, accept with little protest Hamilton's advice on domestic and foreign affairs.

Inevitably, word of Hamilton's plot reached Adams. Angry about "treacherous friends" in his own party, he told his wife in December, 1796, that he was "not enough of an Englishman nor little enough of a Frenchman for some who would be very willing that Pinckney should come in chief." He predicted, however, that "they will be disappointed."

He was right. New England's eighteen Federalist electors, annoyed that Hamilton intended to steal the election from one of their own, voted solidly for Adams but gave no notes to Pinckney. South Carolina's eight electors voted for Pinckney but then cast all of their second-ballot votes for Jefferson. When the ballots were counted, Adams stood highest with 71 electoral votes, only two of which came from states south of the Potomac River. Jefferson stood second with 68 and so became vice president. Pinckney finished third with 59, and Jefferson's running mate, Aaron Burr of New York, polled only 30. Adams was president by three votes, a margin he found humiliating. Neither the Republicans nor his own pride would let him forget over the next four years just how narrow his victory had been. Unlike Washington, who had received every electoral vote in 1789, Adams was just barely president. He could hardly claim or even pretend, as Washington could, that he was president of all the people.

Adams as President: Under the Shadow of France

John Adams took the oath of office on Saturday, March 4, 1797. The new president was not a physically impressive man as he rose to deliver his inaugural address. Short and overweight, his hands occasionally trembling as the result of one of the vague illnesses that plagued him all of his life, he spoke with a lisp that made his words sometimes hard to follow. He praised Washington's policies and promised to continue them, and he tried to allay Republican-inspired fears that he might, by fiat presumably, alter the Constitution. He had, he insisted, no thought of making any changes in it "but such as the people themselves" might think necessary, and those only by amendment in the proper way. He hoped to "maintain peace . . . with all nations" and "neutrality . . . among the belligerent powers of Europe," and he professed (somewhat dishonestly) "esteem for the French nation" and (more truthfully) a determination to preserve Franco-American friendship by every reasonable means in his power, a pledge arch-Federalists thought uncomfortably Republican in tone. As the inauguration ended, a tired and relieved Washington told Adams, "Ay! I am fairly out, and you fairly in! See which of us will be happiest."

Adams began his term by trying to unite the nation and his own party behind his presidency. He offered a critical diplomatic mission to France to Thomas Jefferson, hoping to impress the French and to preempt Republican criticism of his foreign policy, but Jefferson refused the appointment. To foster unity in his own party, Adams kept Washington's cabinet officers: Timothy Pickering as secretary of state, James McHenry as secretary of war, Oliver Wolcott, Jr., as secretary of the treasury, and Charles Lee as attorney general. It was not, on the whole, a distinguished group. McHenry, for example, had been appointed only after a half dozen men declined to serve and Washington despaired of finding anyone more talented who would accept. Worse, most of the members owed their appointments and their influence in the party to Hamilton. McHenry and Pickering (and Wolcott more often than not) seemed determined to undermine the president's policies in order to implement Hamilton's in their place. McHenry went so far as to pass President Adams' queries to him on to Hamilton, who prepared replies that McHenry then passed back to the president as his own. At the head of a divided nation, a divided party, and a divided administration, Adams faced his first test as president.

Rarely in American history has a president been as completely preoccupied with a single issue throughout his term as Adams was with Franco-American relations. From his first day in office, the subject monopolized his time and destroyed his hopes for bipartisan support. It poisoned his already troubled relations with important leaders in his own party and crippled his attempts to earn the trust of his Republican opponents. Denounced throughout much of his term by the Jeffersonian left as a warmongering lackey of monarchist Federalists, and condemned by the Hamiltonian right as a cowardly panderer to American Jacobins, Adams followed his own independent policy, guided by his sense of integrity and his intuitive understanding of public opinion and the national interest. For four years no one, least of all Adams, knew whether his stubborn moderation in dealing with the French would succeed. In the end, when it did, Adams considered the results—enduring peace with France—the proudest achievement of his public life.

Even before Adams took office, it was clear that France and the United States were dangerously close to open war. Angered by President Washington's declaration of American neutrality (which helped England and hurt France), by the Jay Treaty (which did the same), and by Washington's recall of James Monroe as American envoy in Paris, the French reacted by ordering Monroe's replacement, Federalist C. C. Pinckney, out of the country. Shocked again by Jefferson's defeat in 1797, the French began to treat the United States in many ways as an enemy state. French naval vessels and privateers began to capture American ships and confiscate cargoes bound to or from English ports, especially in the West Indies. Americans serving in the British navy—even those who had been forced to serve against their will—were declared pirates subject to execution on capture. As more and more American cargoes were seized, many on meager pretexts, the two nations began to drift into war.

Adams called Congress into special session in May, 1797, to deal with the crisis. His opening message warned France "and the world" that Americans were "not a degraded people, humiliated under a colonial spirit of fear and a sense of inferiority," fated to be "the miserable instruments of foreign influence." He recommended some limited military preparations in case war came and, equally important in Adams' view, to establish American credibility overseas. After all, on the day he took office, the regular army numbered less than three thousand men and it had its hands full on the frontier. The navy, politely so called, barely existed, boasting only a few light revenue cutters, though three substantial frigates were under construction. Congress agreed to build twelve new frigates, to put the militia on alert, to strengthen coastal fortifications, and to arm American merchantmen trading to the East Indies and the Mediterranean.

The XYZ Affair

Having begun to prepare for war, Adams also asked the Senate to sanction a special commission to France to preserve the peace if possible. He proposed sending John Marshall of Virginia and C. C. Pinckney of South Carolina, both moderate Federalists very much in Adams' mold, and (over the shrill protests of Timothy Pickering and the brooding suspicions of other high Federalists) anti-Federalist Elbridge Gerry of Massachusetts. The Senate somewhat reluctantly agreed. Congress adjourned in mid-July and the president and nation settled back to await the outcome. Everything depended on the commissioners' reception in France.

Early in March, 1798, Adams learned that not only had the ruling Directory of France refused to receive the commissioners officially but also that Talleyrand, the foreign minister, had demanded a bribe of £50,000 sterling and a substantial loan for France as his price for merely beginning negotiations.

Talleyrand did not yet know (though he was about to learn that whereas diplomacy in Europe might customarily be conducted by gentlemen in the privacy of their chambers, diplomacy in a popular republic could be conducted very differently. In the United States the most sensitive diplomatic communications might even appear in the press and be hotly debated in the finest townhouses and the rawest frontier taverns if there were votes to be won as a result. Talleyrand also did not understand (though he was about to learn this, too) that new nations tend to be extraordinarily sensitive about their national honor and downright starchy about insults to the flag—and the United States in 1798 was still a very new nation.

After Secretary of State Pickering replaced the names of the French agents who carried Talleyrand's demands to the American commissioners with the letters X, Y, and Z, Adams sent the commission's dispatches to Congress. The Senate ordered them published in April, 1798, and the nation exploded with anger. Their publication, wrote Charles Francis Adams, "was like the falling of a spark into a powder magazine." Even some Republicans now denounced France and applauded C. C. Pinckney's reply to the

PROPERTY PROTECTED, a la Françoise.

(Courtesy of the Lilly Library, Indiana University, Bloomington, Indiana)

insulting demand for money: "No! No! Not a sixpence!" Adams, who normally walked the streets of Philadelphia without the public much noticing or caring, suddenly drew cheering crowds when he attended the theater or appeared in public. "Adams and Liberty" became a popular slogan, and overnight public opinion turned on France and rallied behind the president and the party that had long been suspicious of the French Revolution and that had warned that a French alliance was not in America's interest. The XYZ affair, as it came to be called, carried Adams and the Federalists to heights of popularity neither would ever know again. Almost as angry as the people he led, Adams promised Congress that he would "never send another minister to France without assurances that he will be received, respected and honored as the representative of a great, free, powerful and independent people."

The Half-War with France

Protecting American commerce from French attack was the first priority. To that end, Adams asked Congress to create a department of the navy, to buy or build another twenty warships as soon as possible, to permit merchant ships to arm against French attack, and to abrogate all existing treaties with France. He also wanted the navy and American privateers authorized to prey on armed French ships (but *not* on unarmed vessels).

Many Federalists in Congress and out, such as Fisher Ames and Stephen Higginson, almost eager for a grand patriotic war, were pleasantly surprised by Adams' strong words. They assumed that he now saw the justice, the utility, and the inevitability of the war they were certain must come.

They could not have been more wrong. What Adams wanted was to force France to negotiate with the United States yet again, but this time on equal terms. The key to his plan was a fighting navy strong enough along the Atlantic coast and in the West Indies to neutralize French pressure on American commerce and to make the price of French belligerence at sea high enough that Talleyrand would seek a diplomatic end to the conflict. The Federalist majority in Congress, however, looked on the XYZ affair, the public rage it fostered, and the full war they expected to follow as a heaven-sent opportunity to destroy their Jeffersonian opponents by branding them traitors and as a chance to rid the country (as one of them put it) of "democrats, mobocrats and all other kinds of rats." Hamilton's allies in Congress and the cabinet pushed through a program of military preparation that went well beyond Adams' carefully measured response to French provocations. Congress approved raising a ten-thousand-man army and enlisting another fifty thousand in a provisional army that could be quickly mustered into service following a declaration of war or a French invasion. Without consulting the president, the Federalist majority adopted a new series of taxes on houses, land, and slaves to pay for it all.

Adams had not asked for a large army to fight a declared war; he wanted a strong navy to prevent one. Yet he dared not veto the army bill. National unity, or at least the appearance of it, was crucial to Adams' plan. With the nation already engaged in an undeclared war with France at sea, he could not permit the angry brawl between the president and Congress that a veto would trigger.

Adams' lukewarm enthusiasm for the new army soon grew cooler. Many Federalists who were dissatisfied with Adams' leadership saw the army as a way to raise their preferred leader, Alexander Hamilton, to military glory and possibly to the presidency. Washington had converted success on the battlefield into a presidency. Perhaps Hamilton could too. Washington was the only possible man for commander in chief of the new army. Even Adams saw that, and he promptly offered him the post. The aging general, one of the few prominent Federalists who understood that Adams' goal was to establish peace rather than to promote a war and who thoroughly approved, accepted on two conditions. Happily retired at Mount Vernon, he did not want to take command in the field unless dire national emergency (presumably a French invasion of the South aimed at raising a slave rebellion) made his presence with the army absolutely essential. Also, he insisted he be allowed to name his own subordinate officers. "If I am looked at as the Commander in Chief, I must be allowed to chuse such as will be agreeable to me," he wrote to Secretary of War McHenry.

Washington, however, who had been privately lobbied by Hamilton and his supporters, including (unknown to Adams) Secretary McHenry, eventually insisted that Hamilton become his second in command and therefore, in effect, field commander of the army. He threatened to resign if he did not get his way. By now, Adams despised Hamilton. He is, he wrote to Abigail Adams in January, 1797, "a proud Spirited, conceited, aspiring Mortal always pretending to Morality, with as debauched Morals as old Franklin." As President, however, Adams had little choice. Washington's resignation would divide the nation and turn a good part of the public against the administration. Angrily ("You crammed him down my throat," Adams complained later), he consented to Hamilton as the army's ranking major general.

The Alien and Sedition Acts

In the meantime, Congress laid plans to suppress enemy aliens and French sympathizers in America, to shield the government from divisive criticism during the war that was doubtless only months away, and to restrict the growth of the Republican party. The Sedition Act of July, 1798, made libelous or false statements about public officials of the United States, or any statement fostering sedition or contempt for the government, federal crimes punishable by fine and imprisonment. Republicans denounced the law and warned that Federalists thought virtually all dissent seditious and all criticism treasonable. In the hands of partisan judges and prosecutors, they predicted, the law would be used to suppress the kind of public debate over men and measures that was essential in a free republic. Some of their fears were borne out as the editors of important Republican newspapers were prosecuted under the Sedition Act and several were jailed. Yet no Federalist editor went to prison for printing charges about Vice President Jefferson (presumably shielded from criticism by the law too) that were as false and malicious as any leveled at Adams.

The acts moved Jefferson and Madison to introduce resolutions into the Virginia and Kentucky legislatures, arguing that the Constitution was, properly understood, a compact among sovereign states that were competent to judge for themselves whether federal laws were or were not constitutional. Jefferson went further, claiming that states could nullify federal laws they deemed unconstitutional.

The president had not asked for the Sedition Act, but he had no real objection to it either. For a public man, he was remarkably thin-skinned, and he would recall for years the pain and humiliation newspaper attacks on him produced. In his anger, he found it difficult to distinguish between partisan attacks on his integrity and seditious attacks on the presidency and the nation. "The profligate spirit of falsehood and malignity" in the press, he told the people of Boston at the time, threatened "the Union of the States, their Constitution of Government, and the moral character of the nation."

New alien laws, passed in the same session of Congress, gave Adams the power to expel enemy aliens during wartime and dangerous aliens in peace-time and increased the time an immigrant had to live in the United States before becoming a citizen from five years to fourteen. There is no need, said Harrison Gray Otis, summing up Federalist thought on the matter during an earlier debate over naturalization, "to invite hordes of wild Irishmen, nor the turbulent and disorderly of all parts of the world, to come here with a view to disturb our tranquility," especially, he might have added, when those Irishmen and their like voted Republican with alarming consistency once they became citizens.

The summer and fall following Congress' adjournment in 1798 was the worst time of Adams' presidency. His wife, Abigail, fell sick, and Adams, afraid she was dying, stayed with her in Quincy and conducted such affairs of state as he could by mail. In early October he had to humble himself and agree to have Hamilton command the army under Washington. His plan to make the army acceptable to voters of all parties by appointing some prominent Republicans to high positions in it failed when Washington and Congress combined to thwart him. Congressional Federalists argued that Jacobins and Republicans (synonymous terms in their opinion) could not be trusted to lead troops against their French friends—or against American rioters and rebels if it came to that. Of Washington's refusal to accept Republicans as staff officers, a still bitter Adams wrote years later, "I was only Viceroy under Washington and he was only Viceroy under Hamilton." As the officer corps filled up with Federalists—and there were a lot of them, so many that eventually the new army had one commissioned officer for every seven men—the army began to resemble not so much a national force as a Federalist one.

Since Adams was in no particular hurry to enlist men for Hamilton to command, he delayed serious recruiting until 1799, well after the passions and inflamed patriotism of the XYZ affair had cooled. In 1798, the ostensible reason for creating the army (fear of a French invasion) had disappeared altogether when Lord Nelson's fleet defeated the French at the Battle of the Nile. Adams thought there was "no more prospect of seeing a French army here than there is in Heaven." As the possibility (it had never been a probability) of invasion receded month by month, more and more voters began to agree.

Hamilton, however, hoped to use the army for more than simply repelling invaders and helping the British destroy the French Revolution, attractive though the idea was. He also dreamed of launching, in alliance with Britain, an invasion of Spanish America and of attaching Florida and Louisiana to the United States. When this scheme was presented to Adams (by third parties), he replied that the United States did not happen to be at war with Spain just then, so it was improper for the president even to receive such a proposal, much less act on it. Hamilton also thought it likely that the army would have to suppress insurrection in states such as Virginia, known to be teeming with unrepentant Jeffersonians who might take up arms to resist the Alien and Sedition acts and the collection of federal taxes.

Adams thought Hamilton's immediate fears groundless, but he did not entirely dismiss the possiblility of serious dissent. The large standing army, commanded exclusively by Federalists, and the resulting high taxes that Hamilton thought essential to preserve "domestic tranquility," Adams believed would be very likely to destroy it. If people are forced to pay for "a great army . . . without an enemy to fight," Adams told McHenry in October, 1798, there was no telling what might happen. The public, he warned Theodore Sedgwick early the next year, had so far "submitted with more patience than any people ever did to the burden of taxes, which has been liberally laid on, but their patience will not last always!" Americans had, after all, an uncomfortable amount of practical experience in subverting governments and overturning constitutions; they had done it twice in the last twenty-five years, once by convention and once by rebellion. When Jefferson and others argued in 1798 that laws clearly repugnant to the Constitution were not laws at all, and that they might be nullified by the states, they were speaking the language of revolution, the same language that had justified colonial resistance to the Stamp Act and the Intolerable Acts and had finally laid the groundwork for independence. Few who had lived throughout the Revolution could have missed the resemblance.

By the end of 1798, protests over high federal taxes were increasing and petitions demanding relief were reaching Congress and the president. In Northampton County, Pennsylvania, three militant tax protesters were jailed for refusing to pay. A local auctioneer named John Fries then led a mob that captured a Federal marshal and forced him to release the jailed men. Hamilton seemed almost happy at the news: Perhaps at long last his army would have someone to fight and a rebellion to suppress. President Adams, calling on the rioters to disperse, sent the army in to restore order. The troops, however, found order already restored and no one to fight. Fries and two others were promptly arrested, tried, and convicted of treason. When they were sentenced to hang, they appealed to Adams for pardons, which he granted against the unanimous advice of his cabinet. Breaking three men out of jail, Adams reasoned, hardly amounted to treason. Also, hanging Americans for protesting taxes that Adams himself thought high and ill advised seemed neither just nor politic. Besides, when dealing with dissent, Adams preferred, if he could, to remove its causes rather than to treat its consequences. Events at home and abroad soon made it possible for him to do just that.

Peace Negotiations with France

By the summer of 1798 it was clear to Talleyrand that his attempt to obtain money from the American envoys and France's attempt to bludgeon the United States into a friendlier foreign policy had not only failed but also had driven the United States close to open alliance with England. The English were already accepting American vessels into their convoys and offering to lend the United States cannon to help fortify its coast. The last thing France needed in 1798 was another declared enemy. Talleyrand began to signal his desire to reopen negotiations. American ships being held in France were released. French privateers in the West Indies were reined in, and French courts there were ordered to stop condoning on the thinnest of grounds the seizure of American cargoes. Some of the most notorious judges involved were recalled to France.

In July, Talleyrand let Elbridge Gerry, the only American envoy still in France, know that any new negotiator Adams might wish to send to Paris would be respectfully received. He even claimed that the demand for a bribe had been instigated by underlings without his knowledge or approval—a lie John Adams found it as convenient to pretend to believe as Talleyrand found it prudent to tell.

In October, 1798, Gerry returned to America and reported to Adams Talleyrand's eagerness to negotiate. At the same time, letters from William Vans Murray, American minister to The Hague, came in reporting the same. Shortly thereafter, Adams told his cabinet that although he was still thinking about a declaration of war, he was also considering sending a new peace commissioner to France.

By February, 1799, the president had made up his mind to try negotiations again. Talleyrand's messages had much to do with his decision, but so did conditions at home. Anger over the Alien and Sedition acts and the army taxes was on the rise and might get out of hand, and public opinion was beginning to turn against England. The English, too, were seizing American ships, and English admiralty court judges in the West Indies were condemning American cargoes just as enthusiastically as their French counterparts. Republican papers sarcastically recounted these "evidences of British amity." In February, 1799, the *Philadelphia Aurora* reported that in the last six months of the previous year, England had seized $280,000 worth of American goods, $20,000 *more* than France. Also, only the English stopped American ships routinely and hauled off able-bodied seamen to serve in the British navy, claiming that they were British nationals. Some doubtless were; others were not. Then, in November, 1798, HMS *Carnatic* stopped the American warship *Baltimore* en route to the West Indies and removed five crewmen as suspected British deserters. This act was a violation of American sovereignty (and honor, Republican papers happily pointed out) so raw that even Secretary of State Pickering, England's strongest advocate in Adams' cabinet, had to protest. By early 1799, then, to a growing number of Americans it was by no means as clear as it had been that the English were friends and the French enemies.

On February 18, Adams regained control over foreign policy, which had been slipping by inches out of his hands and into the war Federalists' hands since the XYZ affair. At the same time, although he certainly did not intend to do so, he destroyed what remained of Federalist Party unity and probably his own chance for reelection. Without consulting his cabinet, he sent the Senate a brief message, which Vice President Jefferson, then presiding, read: "Always disposed and ready to embrace every plausible appearance of probability of preserving or restoring tranquility, I nominate William Vans Murray, our minister resident at The Hague, to be minister plenipotentiary of the United States to the French Republic."

The Senate was stunned. Astonished Republicans were puzzled, since they were still convinced that Adams lusted after a war. Federalist senators, expecting war and believing it necessary, were outraged. When the House of Representatives heard the news, wrote one eyewitness to the scene, "the majority acted as if struck by a thunderbolt."

High Federalists thought the proposal madness, but moderate Federalists rallied to Adams. John Marshall liked the idea, as did Benjamin Stoddart (secretary of the navy and the only cabinet member not left over from the Washington Administration), Charles Lee, and Henry Knox. Most important of all, Washington, to whom Adams wrote explaining what he had done and why, approved—or at least he did not publicly disapprove. Nothing, however, could be done without Senate consent and militant Federalists there were determined to block new negotiations. Adams unbent far enough to add two more men acceptable to the Senate to the peace commission, but he hinted that if the Senate refused to consent to *any* commissioners, he might resign, leaving Thomas Jefferson as president. The Senate promptly approved a three-man peace commission.

Rumors that the peace might be saved turned into a growing hope that it would be and then into popular insistence that it must be. Adams, however, would not be rushed. Just as public bawling about avenging the nation's honor after the XYZ affair could not impel him to declare war, so now he would not be driven to conclude a peace "that will not be just or very honorable" by, as he put it, a "babyish and womanly blubbering for peace." "There is not much sincerity in this cant about peace," he told Washington. "Those who snivel for it now were hot for war against Britain a few months ago, and would be now if they saw a chance. In elective governments, peace or war are alike embraced by parties, when they think they can employ either for electioneering purposes." Presidents must lead, Adams believed, not follow either popular whim or party preference. Their function under the Constitution was to hold to the course they thought best to prevent the republic's changing direction with every shift in the public mood. The House of Representatives should reflect popular views, but all presidents should—

and this president *would*—stand above all that.

Adams delayed sending the commission overseas for eight months, until he received "direct and unequivocal assurances" from the French government that it would be properly dealt with and, not incidentally, until several more American warships had been launched, increasing the nation's strength on the seas and its credibility at the bargaining table. At last, in November, 1799, the peace commission sailed for France. Months of intrigue by Hamilton, Pickering, and others to get Adams to change his mind, to stop the peace and save the war *somehow*, had failed. Adams held to his decision. They never forgave him for it.

The Campaign of 1800: Republican Slurs and Federalist Infighting

In May, 1800, a Federalist congressional caucus nominated Adams for reelection and C. C. Pinckney for vice president. A Republican caucus chose Jefferson and Aaron Burr. There followed eight months of brutal campaigning. Federalist writers and clerics denounced Jefferson as an atheist, a libertine, and a Jacobin whose election would trigger an epidemic of rape, riot, and infanticide across the land. Republicans countered that Adams was a monarchist, an aristocrat, and an enemy to the Constitution. It was rumored in Republican circles that he had intended to reestablish aristocracy in America by marrying one of his children to one of George III's, and that he had planned to become King John I of North America. Only Washington's threat to kill him if he tried it, the rumor went, had saved the republic. Other reports had Adams sending Pinckney to Europe to procure four mistresses, two for himself and two for the president. (If true, Adams quipped, "Pinckney has kept them all for himself and cheated me out of my two.")

Jefferson presented himself in the election as the defender of states' rights against overweening federal power, as the protector of civil liberties against the authors of the Alien and Sedition Acts, and as the advocate of fiscal responsibility against the profligate spending of tax-happy Federalists. Adams found these issues hard to handle. He knew by now that the Sedition Act had been a mistake, but his party had passed it, and had recently refused to repeal it, and he had signed it into law. He opposed a larger army and high taxes, but his party had championed both, and he had signed the resulting laws. He could not deny that federal spending during his term had nearly doubled or that taxes had soared, and he *did* think federal law and government were, and ought to be, superior to state law and government.

Adams, however, distanced himself from the more militant Federalists. It was obvious by election time that he wanted to avoid a declared war with France and to end the undeclared war at sea. Also, the Federalist majority in Congress, uneasily eyeing the coming election, had voted to begin reducing the army early in 1800. All that helped, but the nation did not learn that

Adams' peace commission had reached an accommodation with France until the last days of the campaign, after nearly all the electors had already been chosen.

Finally, Adams had to fend off not only Jefferson but also a powerful segment of his own party. In May, he asked Secretaries McHenry and Pickering for their resignations on grounds of gross disloyalty to the president. When Pickering refused, Adams fired him. Hamilton and his allies understandably looked on another term for Adams as a disaster almost as great as a Jefferson presidency. They asked Washington to run again, and when he refused, they tried to arrange the election of Pinckney. Hamilton wrote a venomous pamphlet, intended only for influential Federalists and electors, denouncing Adams as unfit to govern. Republican editors got hold of a copy, printed it, and gleefully wondered aloud when Hamilton would be indicted under the Sedition Act.

Yet, with all his problems, Adams made a fight of the election and came close to winning. Much of the party's old leadership abandoned him, but the rank and file did not. The pivotal state was South Carolina, Pinckney's home state and the only Southern state with a vigorous Federalist tradition, but Republican campaign managers so skillfully distributed promises of federal patronage to the state legislature (which chose South Carolina's electors) that its eight votes went to Jefferson.

By December, Adams, who had just moved the government to the still uncompleted Capitol at Washington, knew he had lost. When the electoral votes were tallied, Jefferson and Burr each had 73 (thus they tied for the presidency), whereas Adams had 65, Pinckney, 64, and John Jay, 1. Four years earlier thirteen different men had gotten electoral votes. By 1800, the two national political parties so dominated presidential politics that no one but candidates they endorsed got any votes. (The lone vote for Jay was deliberate, cast so that Adams and Pinckney would not tie for the presidency if the party won.)

Bitter and exhausted, like Washington before him, Adams longed to be free of the incessant, vicious, partisan wrangling that seemed to him now virtually part of the presidency. Yet he wanted badly to be reelected as a vindication of his first term and a public endorsement of his judgment, integrity, and character. He blamed Hamilton for his defeat and humiliation, and the end of Federalist rule.

As Congress wrestled over whom to declare president, Jefferson or Burr, and as it prepared for the inauguration to follow, Adams carried out his final duties as president—signing a new judiciary act and appointing John Marshall as chief justice of the Supreme Court were the two most important. Then, at four in the morning on inauguration day, he boarded a public stagecoach heading north. Somewhere near Baltimore, as Jefferson took his oath of office in the Capitol, John Adams' public career ended.

He retreated to Quincy, to farm and read (at last there was time enough), to write occasionally about history or law, and to correspond with friends. Not for thirteen years did his pain, humiliation, and anger fade enough to permit him to write again to his old enemy and older friend, Jefferson. As the years passed and the nation changed around him, he remained proud of his presidency and convinced that it had been a success. He would be happy, he said in later years, if his gravestone bore only this: "Here lies John Adams, who took upon himself the responsibility of the peace with France in the year 1800." He died on July 4, 1826.

Adams in Retrospect: "A Self-Made Aristocrat"

Throughout his public life, Adams displayed an almost cynical understanding of how and why men and governments do what they do. "I have long been settled in my opinion," he told Jefferson in 1787, "that neither Philosophy, nor Religion, nor Morality, nor Wisdom, nor Interest, will ever govern nations or parties against their Vanity, their Pride, their Resentment or Revenge, or their Avarice or Ambition. Nothing but Force and Power and Strength can restrain them." As the foundation for the foreign policy of an infant republic in a world of monarchies, Adams' ideas had much to recommend them. As the foundation for policy and governance in a popular republic, they left much to be desired. His continued belief in them explains to some extent why as president he had more success in dealing with foreign adversaries than with his fellow countrymen.

He was, wrote historian Gilbert Chinard, "a self-made aristocrat." As such, he never completely understood the democratic strain in the American Revolution, and he never accepted fully its implications. As time and generations passed, the author of *A Defense of the Constitutions* seemed more and more alien to the increasingly democratic and populist mainstream of American thought, until in the minds of Americans Adams' memory was all but completely overshadowed by Washington and eclipsed by Jefferson.

Robert A. Becker

Bibliographical References

Good book-length accounts of John Adams' presidency are Stephen G. Kurtz, *The Presidency of John Adams: The Collapse of Federalism, 1795–1800*, 1949, and Ralph A. Brown, *The Presidency of John Adams*, 1975. For a brief but lively account, see John C. Miller, *The Federalist Era*, 1960, chapters 12–14. On Franco-American relations, see Alexander DeConde, *The Quasi-War: The Politics and Diplomacy of the Undeclared War with France, 1797–1801*, 1966. Manning J. Daur, *The Adams Federalists*, 1953, focuses on the party. Page Smith, *John Adams*, 2 vols., 1962, is the most thorough biography. Peter Shaw, *The Character of John Adams*, 1976, is a controversial one. For John Adams' writing, see Charles Francis Adams, ed., *The Works of John Adams*, 10 vols., 1856. The correspondence of Adams and Jefferson in Lester J. Cappon, ed., *The Adams-Jefferson Letters*, 2 vols., 1959, is fascinating.

THOMAS JEFFERSON

1801–1809

The third president of the United States was the first to gain office by successfully challenging an incumbent. The orderly transfer of authority from John Adams to Thomas Jefferson was a novel success for the new American constitutional system. Jefferson was the only president to be followed by two trusted and loyal friends, James Madison and James Monroe. This "Virginia dynasty," lasting a full six presidential terms, remains unique in American history.

When Jefferson took office, the United States had more than 5.3 million inhabitants and extended from the Atlantic to the Mississippi and from the Great Lakes to the northern boundary of Florida. When Jefferson retired, the population had grown beyond eight million people, and American territory extended to the crest of the Rocky Mountains; indeed, the United States now pretended to have some claim to the Oregon Country on the Pacific Ocean. While Jefferson was president, Robert Fulton, with the backing of Jefferson's political friend Robert Livingston of New York, succeeded in introducing steam navigation on the Hudson River. Eli Whitney, having failed to realize a fortune on his celebrated cotton gin, nevertheless prospered with a contract from Jefferson's War Department for manufacturing rifles with interchangeable parts in Springfield, Massachusetts. Native talent was continually being augmented by gifted immigrants, such as the radical English scientists Joseph Priestley and Thomas Cooper and the gifted architect Benjamin Latrobe, who helped design the public buildings of the new city of Washington.

A Child of the Enlightenment

With most developments in American society Jefferson was happily and deeply sympathetic. An optimistic child of the Enlightenment, he especially valued education, scientific inquiry, mechanical invention, and voluntary organizations for the improvement of mankind. He believed that government should not tax people to do these things for them but rather should create a climate in which such good things would be done at the people's initiative. Jefferson's maxim, "That government is best which governs least," was therefore not intended to encourage radical individualism but rather to encourage the widest and fullest possible participation in society.

Like many of the democratic heroes of the United States, Jefferson started life in the first rank of society. His father, Peter Jefferson, had worked hard and effectively to build an estate of nearly ten thousand acres around Albemarle County, which he had helped create. Peter was married to Jane Randolph, whose many-branched family was as wealthy and powerful as any in Virginia. He flourished as a tobacco planter, surveyor, militia officer, and justice of the peace. Thomas was born April 13, 1743, into a world, not of dignified leisure, but of bustling, wilderness-clearing, slave-trading, Indian-fighting activity. Among his father's associates were men who already yearned for the virgin lands of the Ohio Valley. Westward expansion, something closely associated with Jefferson until he retired from the presidency, was a family inheritance.

Educated in the local schools of two Anglican clergymen until he was seventeen, Jefferson rode down to the provincial capital of Williamsburg in 1760 to complete his liberal education and learn the law at the College of William and Mary. Such was his precocity that he soon found himself a regular guest at the table of the acting governor, Francis Fauquier. There, too, were Jefferson's favorite teachers, Dr. William Small from Edinburgh and the kindly and erudite lawyer George Wythe. Before he was twenty-one, Jefferson was accustomed to seeing the world through the eyes of learned, active, and powerful men.

Peter Jefferson had died in 1757, when Thomas was fourteen, and from then on Thomas took little interest in his family but much in his studies and in his friends. After six years of study in Williamsburg, he settled into the life of planter and lawyer and was reasonably successful at both occupations. In 1769, he won election to the House of Burgesses, where he quickly joined the majority there defending colonial rights against the supposed incursions of ministerial authority from England. In 1772, he married a wealthy widow, Martha Wayles Skelton, by most accounts an attractive and intelligent woman as well as a fine musician. She died only ten years later in 1782, leaving Jefferson with two daughters, Martha and Maria (Polly). Several other children had been stillborn or died in infancy.

A National Leader: From the House of Burgesses to the White House

Marriage added greatly to Jefferson's responsibilities, and so did the growing crisis between England and her colonies in America. The young burgess from Albemarle became familiar to radicals throughout the colonies through his fiery pamphlet of 1774, *A Summary View of the Rights of British America*. The next year he attended the Continental Congress in Philadelphia, where his draft of "Causes for Taking Up Arms" was too strong for most of the other delegates but where his literary talents were fully recognized. This led to his appointment to the committee that drafted the Dec-

In CONGRESS, July 4, 1776.

The unanimous Declaration of the thirteen united States of America,

(Courtesy of the National Archives, Washington, D.C.)

Declaration of Independence

laration of Independence. Though Congress made a few changes in it (which seemed much more significant to Jefferson than to most subsequent readers), the document remained an example of Jefferson's remarkable style, both for the force and felicity of its general philosophical statements and for the almost reckless élan with which the crimes of George III were cataloged.

Though established as a national leader, Jefferson left the Continental Congress in September, 1776, preferring to be closer to his wife and children. For three years he worked tirelessly in the Virginia legislature, collecting all the laws of the colonial era and, with Wythe and Edmund Pendleton, forging a new legal code appropriate to a liberal planter's republic. He then served as governor for two terms, 1779–1781, a period which unfortunately coincided with a sustained British invasion of the state. Jefferson was as helpless to prevent the marches and raids of Lord Cornwallis' army as other Southern governors had been. Still, some Virginia politicians tried for a time to blame Jefferson for the inability of the militia to turn the British away. Later, Generals Washington and Rochambeau, not Jefferson, received the credit for finally defeating the British army in Virginia.

Retired from office with some feeling of relief, Jefferson wrote the only book he ever published in his lifetime, *Notes on the State of Virginia*, a work about the geography, products, and social and political life of eighteenth-century Virginia.

The death of his wife left Jefferson temporarily despondent and aimless. Also, perhaps, it made him willing to serve away from home again. Seventeen eighty-three found him once again in the Continental Congress where he was chiefly responsible for the new nation's system of weights and measures. As chairman of a committee on western lands, he also drafted an elaborate ordinance for the development of western territories into eventual statehood. His draft included the provision that after a few years no more slaves could be introduced into the West, a provision that failed to secure the needed support of nine states in the Congress. Before Congress finally acted to create the Northwest Territory, Jefferson had departed for Paris, initially to help John Adams and Benjamin Franklin with commercial negotiations and then, in 1785, to replace the aging and homesick Franklin as United States minister to France.

In Paris Jefferson tried hard to strengthen commercial relations between France and the United States, but the feebleness of the Congress under the Articles of Confederation and the increasing ineffectiveness of the government of Louis XVI made such changes impossible. From a personal point of view, however, this was a very satisfying period. Jefferson's five years in Europe introduced him fully to the best minds, architecture, wines, and amenities of France. He was a close observer and, to a degree, even an unofficial adviser in the first stage of the French Revolution.

Back in the United States at the beginning of 1790, he accepted President Washington's invitation to become secretary of state. Within a year, however, he had begun to organize opposition to Alexander Hamilton, who as secretary of the treasury functioned as a sort of prime minister under Washington. Since Washington usually supported Hamilton, Jefferson eventually found his position untenable. At the end of 1793, he resigned after completing a report on American trade that indicted the British for unfair trading practices and urged closer ties with the chief ally of the United States, France. Jefferson then enjoyed three years of retirement in which he especially concentrated on building his mansion at Monticello. He still kept up a full political correspondence and became John Adams' chief rival for the presidency in the election of 1796. The Constitution as originally adopted did not anticipate the existence of political parties. Members of the electoral college voted for two candidates for president. The one receiving the greatest number of votes, if a majority, became president, and the one with the next highest number, vice president. Under this system in 1796 John Adams, a Federalist, was chosen president and Jefferson, a Republican, was elected vice president. While conscientiously presiding over the Senate during the next four years, Jefferson kept his political activities well concealed. They included writing the defiant Kentucky Resolutions of 1798, which asserted the right of the states to nullify acts of Congress—in this case, the Alien and Sedition acts, which were intended to silence or remove from the country critics of the Federalist Party.

The election of 1800, in which Jefferson challenged the incumbent Adams, took place in a heated partisan atmosphere. Jefferson and the Republicans campaigned against Adams and the Federalists by portraying them as threats to the very notion of republican liberty. They had suppressed freedom, taxed heavily, and created a dangerous military establishment, the Republicans charged. The people responded with wide support for Jefferson and his vice presidential candidate Aaron Burr, but again the voting in the electoral college produced an unintended result. The electors still did not distinguish between candidates for president and vice president and cast the same number of votes for Burr as they did for Jefferson. The Constitution dictated that the election was to be decided in the lame duck House of Representatives that had been elected in 1798. Many Federalist members in the House thought Burr the lesser evil and a man with whom they could work and cast their votes for him. After many ballots prolonged a stalemate well into February, 1801, a group of border state Federalists withdrew their support from Burr, and Jefferson was finally elected. Two years later, Congress, led by Republicans fearful of a repetition of the dangerous confusion of 1800, passed and the states quickly ratified the Twelfth Amendment to the Constitution, which provided for separate balloting for president and vice president.

The new president was close to his fifty-eighth birthday, but he still stood erect and lean, well over six feet tall, with red hair and a ruddy complexion. Always wise in his diet and drink and conscientious in taking exercise, Jefferson enjoyed exceptionally good health until his very last years. He had broken his right wrist in France and never quite recovered complete control of his right hand, but its effect on his violin playing was worse than on his writing. Otherwise, his only physical problem was an occasional severe migraine, which had a way of striking and prostrating him at times when he could scarcely afford to leave his work. Indeed, Jefferson was so industrious that the headaches may have been the way his system forced him to rest from time to time.

A Federalist Legacy of Peace and Prosperity

As John Adams' successor, Jefferson began his first term with several important assets. The United States was at peace with all the major powers, revenues exceeded expenditures, and trade was at an all-time high. So, too, were personal incomes. A good case can be made for saying that Jefferson inherited a strong and prosperous nation because the policies he had systematically opposed had nevertheless served the nation very well. In any case, Jefferson began his term in a conciliatory and generous mood. He came to his inauguration on March 4, 1801, dressed in homespun, as George Washington had done twelve years earlier. Although he owned a handsome carriage, he chose to ride to the Capitol on horseback, emphasizing the fact that he was an ordinary citizen whom his fellow citizens had elected chief magistrate. "We are all Republicans, we are all Federalists," he asserted; the previous quarrels had represented mere differences of opinion and not fundamental differences of principle. Repeating ideas on foreign policy that had appeared in Washington's Farewell Address, he called for friendship with all foreign nations, "entangling alliances" with none. Disarming critics who charged that he would sell out to the French, Jefferson promised that he would not restore the Alliance of 1778. Furthermore, he was determined to continue the nation's profitable trade with England. He urged a harmony of interests in the Republic, though he did assert the primacy of agriculture by describing commerce as "her handmaiden."

Jefferson enjoyed the advantage of having two devoted, loyal, and highly intelligent friends serve in his administration through its full eight years: James Madison as secretary of state and Albert Gallatin of Pennsylvania as secretary of the treasury. His other appointees were reasonably able and represented unavoidable political considerations. Thus his secretary of war, Henry Dearborn, came from the Maine district of Massachusetts and his attorney general, Levi Lincoln, came from Worcester, Massachusetts. Robert Smith, secretary of the navy, was from Maryland. Most of these men, and especially the trio of Jefferson, Gallatin, and Madison, were extremely attentive to the important details of administration.

Jefferson grasped instinctively that he was both chief administrator for the government and head of its majority party; he performed the latter role shrewdly and with masterful informality. Abandoning the formal levees held every week when Congress was in session by his predecessors—they were excessively monarchical for Jefferson's taste—the president entertained congressmen and members of the small diplomatic community in a series of dinner parties. Even there he abandoned protocol, letting each guest scramble for his seat at the table. Still, these were hardly potluck affairs; Jefferson had a fine French chef and a cellar of excellent wines. He had no taste for public oratory but a splendid gift for conversation. In the give-and-take around the president's dinner table, Jefferson quite pleasantly did most of the giving, and his ideas unfailingly filtered into the two chambers of Congress.

Reducing to Government's Reach: The Judiciary Act of 1802

With such promising men and methods at his disposal, Jefferson was, at the outset of his administration, still chiefly concerned with reducing, not expanding, the sphere of government. Economy and retrenchment were his paramount goals, and they required that something be done about the Judiciary Act of 1801. After losing the election of 1800, in an effort to retain control of the judicial branch, the Federalist lame ducks in Congress passed a bill greatly expanding the number of judgeships in the federal system. Besides its partisan purpose, the law wisely anticipated the future growth of the nation and the increasing need for federal courts. It also relieved the justices of the Supreme Court from riding circuit, and as these justices were likely to be men of advanced years, this change was both prudent and merciful. Just before leaving office, Adams appointed loyal Federalists to the new judgeships. The federal judiciary had thus become, as John Randolph of Virginia quipped, "a graveyard for decayed politicians."

With Jefferson's encouragement, the new Congress passed the Judiciary Act of 1802, which essentially repealed the act of 1801 and abolished all the new posts. Secretary of State James Madison further struck at the opposition by declining to deliver a number of certificates of appointment to office that Adams had made out the last night of his presidency and left for his successors to deliver. One of these made William Marbury a justice of the peace for the District of Columbia. Upon failing to obtain his commission, Marbury sued, asking the Supreme Court to issue a writ of mandamus ordering Madison to deliver it. In the celebrated case of *Marbury v. Madison*, the Court found that, although Marbury was entitled to have his commission, the Court could not force Madison to deliver it, for the section of the Judiciary Act of 1789 that empowered the Supreme Court to issue writs of mandamus under its original jurisdiction was unconstitutional. Although Jefferson and Madison were naturally pleased that Madison did not have to deliver to Marbury his commission, they found very unpalatable the Supreme Court's asserting the right of judicial review—that of nullifying an act of Congress on the ground that it violated the Constitution.

Besides the Judiciary Act of 1802, the Seventh Congress, Jefferson's first, passed other measures that pleased a majority of Americans. With the end of Adams' Half-War with France in 1800, the Federalists had reduced the army and navy, but the Republicans cut them further. Also, with trade flourishing and customs receipts mounting, they declared that internal taxes were no longer needed and eliminated all of them, including a very controversial one on distilled liquor. The income from land sales alone permitted the government to meet all of its current expenses and to reduce the national debt significantly as well. It had as a further source of funds the income from the sale of its stock in the Bank of the United States. Even though Jefferson had argued against the constitutionality of the bank when it was chartered in 1791, the institution flourished and expanded during his presidency, and it saved the Treasury considerable sums by transferring funds from one part of the country to another at no charge.

War with the Barbary Pirates: To the Shores of Tripoli
    There was one small exception to the general pattern of reduced federal activity under Jefferson's presidency. In 1801, the pasha of Tripoli declared war on the United States by the customary device of having his agents chop down the flagpole in front of the U.S. Legation. Such a declaration meant that warships of Tripoli would attack American merchant shipping in the Mediterranean, taking ships and cargoes as prizes and holding their crews for ransom. For several years the Federalist administrations had paid subsidies and ransoms to three other North African potentates to protect

(Courtesy of the Library of Congress, Washington, D.C.)
Decatur's Struggle with the Algerines

American shipping and rescue its sailors. Now Tripoli was, in effect, demanding a generous payment. In the 1780's, Thomas Jefferson had advocated development of a powerful American navy, in no small part to relieve the United States of the necessity of paying blackmail to the piratical princes of the Barbary Coast. Without seeking authorization from Congress, President Jefferson dispatched a small fleet to the Mediterranean to protect American ships and, if necessary, attack the Tripolitans. Like his predecessors, Washington and Adams, Jefferson tended to disregard the clear prescription of the Constitution that the president make foreign policy with the advice and consent of the Senate. The war with Tripoli went badly through 1805 when, as a result of a combination of American naval pressure and diplomatic skill, the pasha was induced to sign a peace treaty, although the United States was required to pay $60,000 for the release of American prisoners.

Peaceful Expansion: The Louisiana Purchase

Jefferson presided over an era of peaceful growth in the western territories of the United States. He eased out the old Federalist governor of the Ohio Territory, Arthur St. Clair, who had made many enemies by his indifferent administration and by his opposition to the admission of Ohio to statehood. Following his removal, Ohio became a state in 1803, adding strength to the Republican majorities in Congress. Meanwhile, Congress had authorized a government for the Indiana Territory, and Jefferson appointed William Henry Harrison, son of a former governor of Virginia, to be its governor.

About the same time a series of events occurred that led to the greatest achievement of Jefferson's presidency and to the single largest addition to American territory, the Louisiana Purchase. In 1763, Bourbon France had reluctantly transferred Louisiana to Spain as compensation for her loss of Florida. A succession of French ministries in the 1780's and 1790's pondered various schemes for reoccupying Louisiana but found none practical. By 1800, however, the king of Spain considered the area a burden rather than an asset. Its only purpose for him was to protect Mexico by offering a buffer against the notoriously expansionist English and Americans. By the secret Treaty of San Ildefonso (1800) Spain retroceded Louisiana to France, which promised in another document that the territory would not be alienated to a third power.

In 1802, news of the retrocession reached Jefferson, followed by the more alarming news that the Spanish governor had used the transfer as an excuse to close the Mississippi to American commerce. Worse still, Jefferson learned that Napoleon Bonaparte had sent a great fleet and army under General Charles Leclerc to reconquer the former French colony of Haiti, which had been the world's foremost producer of sugar before rebellious

(Courtesy of the Library of Congress, Washington, D.C.)

Map of the United States of America, 1819

blacks succeeded in overturning their former masters. After he had reestablished French rule and slavery in Haiti, Leclerc was instructed to occupy Louisiana.

Jefferson responded by alerting his western military commanders to the possibility of war with France in the Mississippi Valley. He also set in motion a plan he had first conceived as a member of the Articles of Confederation Congress in 1783: an expedition of expert observers and mapmakers to explore the uncharted trans-Mississippi West. This expedition, to be led by two veteran frontiersmen, Meriwether Lewis of Virginia, Jefferson's private secretary, and William Clark of Kentucky, when first projected by the president was intended as a reconnoitering of foreign and potentially enemy territory. At about the same time, Jefferson advised his representative in Paris, Robert Livingston, to inform Napoleon that the United States could not tolerate France's control of access to the Gulf of Mexico through the Mississippi River. The United States could accept moribund Spain's control of Louisiana and the mouth of the Mississippi, at least for a time, but with the French at New Orleans, the United States would be forced to seek a firm alliance with Great Britain and then attack Louisiana as soon as the next European war started. Livingston added, however, that the United States was prepared to buy New Orleans from France and thereby remove the major cause of future strife.

Livingston's threats would have been wasted on Napoleon had his campaign in Haiti succeeded, but it failed: The blacks, partly armed by British and American traders, fought ably, and Leclerc's men suffered dreadfully from tropical diseases. Though the French general succeeded by treachery in capturing the black leader, Toussaint L'Ouverture, other leaders arose and eventually drove out the French.

Having lost one army in Egypt and another in the West Indies, Napoleon decided to pursue his ambition closer to home. He determined to concentrate his efforts on the defeat of Great Britain, the perennial and formidable enemy of France. Without a single French soldier to defend it, Louisiana was no longer of any value to him, but he badly needed money. He therefore offered to sell the whole territory to the United States for $15 million, then a considerable sum of money. James Monroe, sent by Jefferson to help with negotiations, joined Livingston in accepting the emperor's offer. President Jefferson and Congress ratified their agreement and voted money for the purchase as quickly as possible. Recalling his belief in a strict construction of the Constitution and noticing that the document nowhere authorized the executive to purchase territory from foreign governments, Jefferson had at first suggested to his cabinet that it might be wise to propose an amendment specifically granting that power. Madison, however, pointed out that amendments, like laws, could not operate *ex post facto*. To propose an amendment would be virtually to admit that the purchase had been unconstitutional. Thus the Jeffersonians became self-conscious broad constructionists.

The Louisiana Purchase was enormously popular in the United States, but a remnant of Federalists, led by Timothy Pickering of Massachusetts, opposed the purchase bitterly, and with a degree of merit often overlooked. The territory, opponents pointed out, was not Napoleon's to sell. Why pay $15 million to an international swindler for stolen goods? If we had any right to Louisiana at all, it would have been better simply to occupy it and defy the French tyrant. Furthermore, the people who actually lived in Louisiana had not been consulted, and therefore the United States had no right to annex them unless they were willing to be annexed, according to the principle of the right of self-government so central in the Republican creed. In fact, Congress had, on Jefferson's advice, set up a special military government for Louisiana, which, though it treated the inhabitants fairly enough, allowed migrants from the older United States to move in and take control. Slavery was confirmed, which pleased the creole planters, but the African slave trade stopped, which angered some of them. Louisiana thus became another market for the surplus slaves of the upper South and especially valuable for Virginia, the largest and most populous of the slave-selling states.

Pickering now wrote a number of private letters proposing that the states without slavery explore the possibility of joining with Canada and the maritimes in a new and free confederation. None of his friends thought such a scheme feasible, including the strong-minded George Cabot of Massachusetts, the most influential member of the so-called Essex Junto. From that time to this, however, rumors have abounded of a New England secessionist conspiracy, waxing and waning from the time of Pickering's letters of 1804 down to the Hartford Convention of 1814.

Signs of Disunion: The Burr-Hamilton Duel and the Impeachment Trial of Samuel Chase

Many Federalists, though opposed to disunion, were again willing in 1804 to unite with Aaron Burr in hope of regaining political power. Burr, when he realized that he would be replaced as Jefferson's candidate for vice president, sought that year to be elected governor of New York as a base from which to run for president. During his campaign, Alexander Hamilton, horrified at the proposed alliance between Federalists and Burrites, privately spread his opinion that Burr was a man of talent but no scruples. Burr subsequently lost the race for governor, although less because of Hamilton's comments than the strong tide in favor of Burr's former Republican allies that year. Nevertheless, Hamilton's remarks had found their way into print, which led Burr to challenge Hamilton to a duel in which he shot and mortally wounded Hamilton. Although his political career had come to an end, Burr completed his term as vice president.

With Burr no longer a viable candidate, the Federalists never found a serious challenger for the presidency in 1804. Some tried to gather votes for Charles Cotesworth Pinckney of South Carolina, but he had neither a program nor a network of supporters required for an effective campaign. Moreover, Jefferson had become extremely popular. Frugality in government, peace with foreign powers, general prosperity, and especially the Louisiana Purchase all served to heighten Jefferson's appeal. Even former president and Federalist John Adams allowed it to be known that he favored the Virginian's election. Only Connecticut, Delaware, and two electors from Maryland gave their votes to Pinckney; Jefferson carried the rest of New England and even his rival's home state of South Carolina.

During the period between the election and Jefferson's second inauguration, the Republicans proceeded with the impeachment trial of Federalist Samuel Chase, an associate justice of the Supreme Court. It was, in fact, with this trial that Jefferson's fortunes as president began to change. Earlier the Federalists had been quite helpless to prevent the Senate's removal of John Pickering, a United States district court judge in New Hampshire, for that old Federalist was mentally incompetent and should have resigned. Since he was unwilling to do so, neither the Constitution nor the Judiciary Act prescribed a legal method of his removal.

Impeachment is limited to cases involving high crimes and misdemeanors, yet the House drew up a bill of impeachment for Pickering and the Senate mustered more than the needed two-thirds vote in 1804. Pickering was unable to appear in his own defense, nor did he send anyone to appear for him. Once again the Jeffersonians were proving far less scrupulous about the letter of the Constitution than they had been when out of power. The impeachment of Samuel Chase, however, was quite a different matter from that of Pickering. Although Chase had been an intensely partisan Federalist, accustomed to insulting Republicans from the bench, he had not lost his reason and was quite able to defend himself in a legal proceeding. A team of outstanding lawyers joined in his defense. With Burr presiding and John Randolph leading the prosecution for the House of Representatives, Chase received a fair and full trial before the United States Senate. Had he been found guilty and removed from office, the subsequent history of the United States might have been quite different, for after removing one partisan judge, Congress might more easily have removed others. The Senate, however, would not supply the needed two-thirds vote on a single one of the charges against Chase. One reason was a continuing respect for the independence of the judiciary. Chase had clearly been guilty of bad manners, arbitrary conduct, poor taste, and partisan harangues in his courtroom. Yet none of these was in violation of federal statutes, and the Constitution makes no provision for removing unpleasant or even bungling judges. Chase had perhaps disgraced the bench, but he was no criminal.

Jefferson's Second Term: Optimistic Beginnings, Unforeseen Difficulties

If Jefferson felt any personal disappointment over Chase's acquittal, no trace of it appeared in his buoyant second inaugural address. He congratulated his countrymen on the success of pure Republicanism. "The suppression of unnecessary offices, of useless establishments and expenses, enabled us to discontinue our internal taxes," he declared, and then, warming to his theme of frugality, he continued, "It may be the pleasure and pride of an American to ask, what farmer, what mechanic, what laborer, ever sees a tax-gatherer of the United States?" Yet, thanks to good management, the day would soon dawn when all the debts of the federal government would be retired and the Treasury would enjoy a surplus. Would it not then be timely, "by a just repartition among the states, and a corresponding amendment of the constitution," to spend such surpluses on the improvement of "rivers, canals, roads, arts, manufactures, education, and other great objects within each state." Turning toward Native Americans, Jefferson declared that he had regarded them "with the commiseration their history inspires." He would continue his policy of introducing the domestic and agricultural arts of the United States among them and like his predecessors and successors would work to assimilate the Indians into the large and growing American society. The address also contained a brief affirmation that the federal government should not meddle in religious institutions, and a rather surprising claim that, though a forebearance against libel and falsehood had been in itself a good thing, allowing truth to drive out error, nevertheless, "no inference is here intended, that the laws, provided by the State against false and defamatory publications, should not be enforced; he who has time, renders a service to public morals and public tranquility, in reforming these abuses by the salutary coercions of the law." The address ended with an appeal to the American people to sustain good government and with a dignified appeal to "that Being in whose hands we are, who led our forefathers, as Israel of old, from their native land, and planted them in a country flowing with the necessaries and comforts of life."

Jefferson's second term would end on a far more somber and uncertain note than his first term, but one can hardly blame him for his optimism on March 4, 1805. Indeed, the prosperity of the United States would continue until Jefferson himself curtailed it in 1808. A major source of American prosperity throughout the years 1793–1812 was the neutral carrying trade during the French Revolution and Napoleonic Wars, which, for all its risks and inconveniences, expanded American opportunities for foreign enterprise—and attracted foreign capital to the United States—far more than was possible when all of Europe was at peace. A European peace did hold from 1801 until early 1803, and the trade of the United States declined somewhat as a result; but with the resumption of the European war, foreign trade again grew and in 1804 actually flourished under a most unusual condition: None of the belligerents placed any serious obstacles in the way of American involvement in the carrying trade. When the warring powers later undertook to prevent the United States from contributing significantly to their enemies' prosperity by trading with them, Jefferson and Madison tried to defend what had been the status quo of 1804, but this proved impossible.

Unaware of the difficulties into which European events must soon plunge him, Jefferson in 1805 pressed for further national triumphs. The Lewis and Clark expedition, launched in the spring of 1804, carried the American flag over the Rockies to the mouth of the Columbia River in 1805. Although failing to find the waterways that Jefferson hoped would link the upper Missouri to the Pacific, the expedition convinced Jefferson and his successors that the United States should span the continent. Before the return of Lewis and Clark, Zebulon M. Pike led an unsuccessful search for the source of the Mississippi River. In 1806–1807 he conducted a second expedition into the Spanish Southwest and brought back important information about that area. East of the Mississippi, Jefferson turned his attention to East and West Florida. They pointed, in George Dangerfield's useful simile, like a pistol aimed at New Orleans and the gateway to the heartland of North America. He urged his diplomats in Europe to persuade Spain that further retention of the Floridas was both costly and futile. They were of no use to Spain and belonged naturally to the territories already owned by the United States. Finally, Jefferson allowed the commercial terms of Jay's treaty with England to expire, trusting that the increased size and strength of the United States would enable him to secure a new treaty considerably more favorable to United States interests.

At first, negotiations over Florida went badly. Jefferson asked Congress for a secret appropriation of $2 million for the purchase of Florida. He then sent a public message to Congress taking a hard line against Spain, threatened Spain through diplomatic channels, and quietly suggested to Napoleon that if Spain could be influenced to sell Florida, the money could wind up in Paris. Napoleon and his agent Talleyrand took the position that they could not help the United States at this time because Spain was unwilling to sell, yet they left the impression that something might be done later. The following year—1806—Jefferson sponsored and Congress enacted a total embargo of American trade with the independent black nation of Haiti. This was partly to foster the goodwill of Napoleon, who still hoped to reconquer the former French colony, and partly in response to the racial attitudes of many congressmen. Even after currying favor with Napoleon, the Jefferson Administration still did not acquire East or West Florida; the former was annexed only in 1810 and the latter in 1819.

Conflicts with Britain

The British, far from becoming more tractable during their new war with France, swiftly became more hostile to the United States than they had been at any time since 1783. The reason was the huge increase of American shipping after 1803. The British had encouraged American trade in the late 1790's because the United States was then engaged in an undeclared naval war with France and was in effect a British ally. In 1804, far from being at war with France, the United States was carrying a great deal of its shipping, as well as that of its reluctant ally, Spain. Bound by recent custom from attacking American merchant shipping, Britain saw more and more trade pass into American hands. Indeed, the demand for American shipping grew so rapidly that there were not enough ships and sailors to meet it. Foreign ships therefore transferred to American registry, and foreign sailors, including many Englishmen, took service on American ships.

By the summer of 1805, many Englishmen had come to resent the way the United States raked in profits while they bore the cost of protecting the Atlantic from the aggressive French emperor. Neutral rights were all very well; the American contribution to French prosperity was, however, profoundly unneutral.

Throughout the French Revolution and Napoleonic Wars, Britain had adhered to her unilaterally proclaimed Rule of 1756, which held that no trade normally prohibited in times of peace would be allowed—even in the hands of neutrals—in time of war. This rule was interpreted to mean that American vessels could not carry cargoes from the French West Indies to France since that trade had been proscribed before the war. Britain's Admiralty

Court, however, modified this rule in 1800, when considering the case of an American merchant ship, *Polly*. If an American ship bought French colonial goods, carried them to the United States, and paid duties on them there, they might then reexport them to Europe, where the British would regard them as American goods and not subject to seizure under the Rule of 1756. This practice of the "broken voyage" was liable to fraud. American ships often sailed directly from the West Indies to Europe, pretending by means of forged papers to have completed a broken voyage via the United States.

In 1805, the British Admiralty Court in the case of the American merchantman *Essex* rejected the broken voyage concept and reasserted the Rule of 1756 in its full vigor. British ships again claimed as prizes of war American vessels laden with French goods. Showing some discrimination, they seized only sixty American vessels, far fewer than they had in a similar crisis in 1793. Still, the use of British sea power to regulate American trade was galling, and no relief could be expected from Europe. In 1805, Horatio Nelson led his British fleet to a decisive victory over the combined fleets of France and Spain at the Battle of Trafalgar. Nelson died gloriously, and Napoleon remained from then until the end of his career a military threat only on land. Not since the days of Sir Francis Drake and Sir John Hawkins had Englishmen felt so superior, or acted so arrogantly, on the high seas. Now to prevent French goods sailing for Europe on American ships, they stationed their own warships just outside the major harbors of the United States where they boldly stopped and searched American merchantmen. Once at New York Harbor an American ship refused to stop for a search by HMS *Leander*. *Leander* fired what was supposed to be a warning shot across the American ship's bow, but the shot struck and killed a sailor.

British commanders on the blockading ships looked for British sailors as well as French merchandise on American ships. Service in the British navy was hard, and the pay was poor. Many British tars had been drafted by a system little better than kidnaping. By the thousands they jumped ship and took berths on American merchantmen, where the service was easier and safer and the pay better. No matter how inhumanely they were recruited or treated, however, such men were deserters in time of war. England could not tolerate their loss, for if a few thousand desertions were winked at, the number would soon reach tens of thousands, and England's mighty fleet would stand unmanned.

To stop this drain on their manpower, ships of the Royal navy stopped and searched American vessels, seized any deserters who were discovered, punished them, and returned them to service. Shorthanded British captains, however, often took not only deserters from the Royal Navy but also American citizens of English birth and Englishmen who had not served in the navy and had taken out papers applying for United States citizenship. Occasionally, they even seized native Americans. Americans differed over whether the United States should tolerate British searching of its ships for deserters. Those Federalists who were most sympathetic to Britain's struggle against Napoleonic France were inclined to allow the indignity. A large minority would tolerate the Rule of 1756 in its application against the French tyrant, but few could stomach British blockades of American harbors. The guns of *Leander* had given the United States grounds for war.

Jefferson wanted war even less than did his few remaining Federalist opponents. He was no pacifist, as he had most recently proved in fighting Tripoli. In the present crisis, however, Jefferson was above all an opportunist. Even with a galling semiblockade, American shipping enjoyed in 1806 its most profitable year ever. Warfare would increase the costs of government, reduce revenue, and yield no certain advantage in return. Convinced of the proposition that free ships make free goods (and free sailors), Jefferson and Madison decided to negotiate. They sent William Pinkney, a moderate Federalist lawyer from Baltimore, to assist the regular minister to England, James Monroe. Madison drew up instructions, which were expertly reasoned but hopelessly one-sided, demanding all possible advantages for American trade while offering the British nothing but goodwill in exchange. Departing from these instructions, Monroe and Pinkney negotiated a treaty in which England, although explicitly recognizing the right of American ships to carry cargoes from the West Indies to Europe if they had first stopped and paid a tariff in an American port, conceded nothing material on the matter of impressment. When the treaty reached the United States early in 1807, Jefferson refused even to submit it to the Senate for its ratification. Had the Senate learned the full contents of the agreement, along with the explanations of Monroe and Pinkney, it might have accepted the treaty.

Not long after, on June 22, 1807, the only new frigate commissioned under President Jefferson, the USS *Chesapeake*, under the command of Commodore James Barron, was sailing down Chesapeake Bay on her maiden voyage when the British frigate *Leopard* insisted on searching her for deserters from the Royal Navy. Barron quite properly refused, but his ship was in such poor order and his crew so little trained that he could offer no resistance when *Leopard* opened fire. After sustaining three dead and eighteen wounded and firing one shot for the sake of honor, Barron surrendered. The *Leopard*'s officers then removed four sailors from the *Chesapeake* and departed. At Halifax the British convicted and hanged one of these men. The other three, Americans who had volunteered to join the British navy, were also convicted but pardoned on the understanding that they would resume their service.

The British foreign secretary, George Canning, disavowed *Leopard*'s actions on the grounds that his government had never claimed the right to stop and search ships of the United States Navy. Canning also offered repa-

rations for the dead and wounded. Even so, Jefferson might have had a declaration of war had he summoned Congress immediately and asked for one.
The president, however, waited until October to summon Congress, while
strengthening shore defenses, sending a number of stiff notes to the British
government, and closing American ports to British warships. The latter
move curtailed the warships' effectiveness markedly by forcing them to go
either to Halifax or to Bermuda for supplies. Jefferson declined to accept
the apologies and reparations offered by Canning unless Britain agreed to
do much more. He wanted it to punish Admiral Berkeley, who had ordered
the affront and had since been transferred to another part of the world, and
to promise to desist from all forms of impressment. Canning refused to
negotiate further until the ban on British warships had been lifted. The
question of reparations for the *Chesapeake* dragged on until 1811; by the
time it was settled, other aggravations had made it seem a negligible matter.

Commercial Warfare: The Ill-Conceived Embargo

In the closing months of 1807, the United States found itself pressed by
both Britain and France in a wholly new and uncomfortable way. After the
defeat of Trafalgar, Napoleon had conceived the plan of ruining the British
by cutting off all their trade with the continent of Europe. In his infamous
Berlin Decree of November 21, 1806, Napoleon declared the British Isles
under a state of blockade, which he enforced by confiscating any ship found
in European harbors carrying British goods. The British retaliated early in
1807 by extending their blockade to all European ports complying with the
Berlin Decree. When Napoleon completed his "continental system" by
bringing Russia into it, the British added Orders-in-Council, which declared
that no nation might trade in Europe unless its ships first secured a license
and paid duties in England. Napoleon's Milan Decree of December 17,
1808, then declared that any ships obeying the British orders would be
confiscated.

Before the British and French had completed their measures for destroying each other's trade, Jefferson asked Congress to activate a limited Non-
Importation Act first passed in 1806 but suspended during the Monroe-
Pinkney negotiations. The act, aimed entirely at England, barred a number
of importations that Americans could live without. Jefferson next persuaded
Congress to adopt the Embargo Act, one of the most extraordinary acts in
the history of American legislation. Not merely prohibiting trade with Britain and France, the Embargo Act required all American ships to stay at
home and prevented the exportation of all American commodities. Although, in a way, a logical response to the *de facto* commercial warfare that
the two greatest powers in the world had turned against the United States,
unfortunately, it did more harm to America than it did to France and England. Hundreds of American ships sat idle and deteriorating in their har-

bors, the shipbuilding industry ceased, sailors were thrown out of work, New England fishermen lost their markets, and farmers lost outlets for their surplus grain, salt meat, and livestock. Tobacco and cotton planters, perennially short of cash, also suffered, but their commodities at least kept fairly well, and their chief capital—their slaves—continued to appreciate in value. Napoleon used the Embargo Act as an excuse to seize $10 million worth of American shipping.

As 1808 wore on the act produced numerous complaints at home, but Congress supported the administration in a series of acts that served to make the ban more effective. It placed coastal shipping under strict controls and heavy bonds. It increased the size of the army and used small army detachments to patrol the long Canadian border where Americans were smuggling goods overland that they could not get out by sea. It also increased the "mosquito fleet" of gunboats, too small to challenge British warships but low in cost and useful for catching the small sailing craft that specialized in smuggling. After a trial of fourteen months, just before he retired from the presidency, Jefferson signed the act repealing the embargo. He also signed a new Non-Importation Act, which prohibited trade with France and Britain, but he promised to restore it with whichever power withdrew its decrees against neutral shipping. Since the new act permitted trade with all other nations and allowed American ships to return to the high seas, prosperity began to return.

Jefferson's handling of the nation's relations with France and England not only had been strongly criticized by the Federalists but also had alienated some of the members of his own party as well. One of the most important was John Randolph of Virginia. Randolph had been a loyal Republican throughout the president's first administration, chairing the powerful House Committee of Ways and Means in the interests of retrenchment and economy. In the 1790's, Randolph had been an ardent supporter of the French Revolution, believing, with many other educated Americans, that its cause was that of human freedom. By 1806, however, the self-proclaimed Napoleon Bonaparte, ruled France by naked power and was launched on the conquest of Europe, whereas the British, however high-handed and selfish, were fighting for liberty. Randolph accordingly shifted his sympathies to Britain. He was highly displeased that Jefferson and Madison, although they detested Napoleon, were quite willing to cooperate with him if they could gain advantages for the United States by doing so.

Randolph, supported by a small faction of the Republican Party called "Quids," turned even more strongly against Jefferson over the so-called Yazoo land claims. In 1795, the Georgia legislature had sold to the Yazoo Land Companies several million acres of its western lands in an area later ceded by Georgia to the United States. The next legislature rescinded the sale on the ground that it had been made fraudulently. Jefferson arranged a compromise settlement of the matter that would have satisfied Georgia and the Yazoo investors, many of whom were Northern Republicans whose support he sought. Randolph blocked the necessary legislation in Congress, charging that Jefferson had abandoned the states' rights principles of his party and become in essence a Federalist. The Yazoo claims were not settled until after Jefferson left office.

Internal Opposition: The Burr Conspiracy

In the meantime, Jefferson became involved in an imbroglio with his former vice president, Aaron Burr. Burr, thoroughly discredited because of his political machinations in New York and his killing of Alexander Hamilton in a duel, embarked on a scheme, the exact nature of which has never been clearly known. He visited the English minister to Washington, Anthony Merry, and proposed a plan for creating an independent Louisiana under British protection. Merry forwarded this proposal to his government with an enthusiastic endorsement; sager heads advised against plotting with Burr and soon recalled Merry to England. Meanwhile, Burr had been to see the Spanish minister with quite a different appeal. To forestall a planned invasion of Mexico, Burr proposed a coup d'état against Jefferson right in the District of Columbia. He would engage to organize this with the help of money from Spain. No money was forthcoming, but Burr went on seeing people and making daring proposals. In Washington, Philadelphia, and especially in the new towns of the trans-Appalachian West, Burr built up a network of committed friends, most of whom believed that he was planning an expedition against Mexico.

By the early months of 1806, Jefferson had heard from many western correspondents warning him of Burr's activities. These Westerners cared nothing for the rights of Spain in Mexico, but they did fear a secession plot, centered in New Orleans, where many citizens still grumbled at the American annexation. Such fears were plausible: From the earliest days of the United States there had been Americans of independent minds and great ambitions who had believed that the Mississippi Valley, including its great tributaries, the Ohio and Missouri, must someday be the seat of an empire quite independent from the Eastern states. Jefferson himself had contemplated such a separation with equanimity in the 1780's, but his views were now quite different.

In August, 1806, Burr concentrated a force of sixty to eighty armed men and ten boats on an island in the upper Ohio River. As the expedition descended first the Ohio and then the Mississippi, Jefferson sent word to his Western commanders that Burr was leading an illegal expedition and should be arrested. Evidently, Jefferson had become convinced that such action was necessary on receiving an urgent warning from his military authority at New Orleans, General James Wilkinson, who later became the government's most important witness at Burr's trial. Burr and Wilkinson had plotted together in Philadelphia and later in New Orleans. Wilkinson, as it was

E.Gridley Sc.

A.BURR, ESQ.

(Courtesy of the National Portrait Gallery, Smithsonian Institution, Washington, D.C.)

later learned, had been a well-paid spy for Spain at various times. He collected more Spanish gold by pretending to save Mexico from Burr's military invasion. He then posed as protector of the United States, claiming that he was saving Louisiana from the menacing Burr. Whatever Burr may actually have had in mind, he knew that it would not work with Wilkinson now against him and a warrant out for his arrest. He tried to reach sanctuary in Florida by traveling overland but was recognized, arrested, and sent to Richmond to stand trial for treason.

A grand jury, with John Randolph as foreman, found ample grounds for indicting Burr, and he came to trial in August, 1807. Jefferson's attorneys gathered an enormous amount of evidence, but much of it was contradictory. To this day no one really knows exactly what Burr had in mind or even if he knew himself. The trial did reveal that Jefferson was something less than an absolute civil libertarian, for he had published the government's case against Burr in advance of the trial and prejudged him guilty. Ironically, the Republican Judiciary Act of 1802 established procedures by which Jefferson's political enemy, John Marshall, sitting as a circuit court judge, presided at Burr's treason trial. In instructing the jury Marshall narrowly defined treason as an overt act against the United States observed by at least two witnesses, and the jury found that Burr's guilt had not been proved. In the course of the trial Jefferson invoked executive privilege by declining to answer Marshall's subpoena to appear as a witness. Jefferson, sorely disappointed at what he regarded as yet another instance of reckless Federalist obstruction to good government and believing Marshall's conduct on the bench to have been criminally wrong, sent the record of the trial to the House of Representatives, hinting that it might find grounds for the chief justice's impeachment. He also suggested amending the Constitution to make federal judges removable. Nothing came of these ideas.

Jefferson could at least take pleasure in the loyalty to the Union exhibited by almost all Westerners during Burr's scheming, arrest, and trial. Meanwhile, it was still possible to convict Burr for the lesser charge of violating the neutrality laws, which he had admitted doing while denying the charge of treason. Burr, however, jumped bail and fled to Europe where he spent several years trying to sell chimerical schemes to the British and French governments. In 1813, he returned quietly to New York where he prospered modestly as a lawyer until his death in 1836.

As the time for the election of 1808 approached, Jefferson decided that he would not run for a third term. Despite the failure of his foreign policy and the unpleasantness of the Burr conspiracy, no widespread political reaction occurred against the president and his party. Although the Republicans failed to duplicate their sweep of 1804, they still easily elected their candidate, Jefferson's friend James Madison, with 122 electoral votes compared to only 47 for the Federalist candidate, Charles Cotesworth Pinckney. They also retained comfortable majorities in both houses of Congress. Only in New England did the Federalists reestablish strong party organizations and win control of state governments.

Following the precedent of Washington and John Adams, Jefferson retired completely from public life at the end of his presidency. Returning to his beloved Monticello, he spent the last seventeen years of his life in "philosophical serenity," but in great financial difficulty. He always answered queries from Madison and Monroe fully and cordially, but he made no effort to influence them. The chief fruits of his long and active retirement were a philosophical correspondence with his ancient friend and sometimes foe, John Adams, and the founding of the University of Virginia. Jefferson and Adams both died on July 4, 1826, as citizens throughout the United States were celebrating the fiftieth anniversary of American independence. Jefferson had planned a small and elegant monument to himself at Monticello. Its inscription identified him as author of the Declaration of Independence and the Virginia statute for religious freedom and as founder of the university.

(Courtesy of the Library of Congress, Washington, D.C.)

MONTICELLO

Jefferson's Record as President

Significantly, Jefferson did not list any of the public offices he had held. This was in part modesty, but it was also an expression of his lifelong fear of government's tendency to become too powerful and hence tyrannical. This fear, along with his urbane but retiring manner—he was never comfortable in public meetings—kept Jefferson from being one of the nation's most striking chief executives. The best and worst deeds of his administration— the Louisiana Purchase, the prosecution of Burr, and the enforcement of the Embargo Act—were all responses to major crises thrust on Jefferson and the nation. Otherwise, it was his wish that government should encourage constructive voluntary activity, and the years of his presidency were happily marked by the founding of new banks, the digging of canals, the laying of roads, the expansion of industries, the introduction of new inventions, the founding of schools, and the growth of population. Slavery, unfortunately, was spreading rather than declining, especially because of the acquisition of the sugar-growing province of Louisiana and the rapid spread of cotton as a major crop for export. Jefferson did sign, with satisfaction, an act that closed the international slave trade at the earliest moment the Constitution permitted, January 1, 1808.

Jefferson's style and methods were too subtle to be imitated, but he was a better president than the bare record suggests. Ideally, an American president must be the boss of a national political party, a ceremonial and ideological leader capable of reaffirming and adapting national values and ideals, and a tough-minded executive able to run the government and delegate authority to competent and honest subordinates. Very few of our presidents have done as well in each of these categories as Thomas Jefferson.

Robert McColley

Bibliographical References

The imposing *Papers of Thomas Jefferson*, 20 vols., edited by Julian P. Boyd, 1950–1982, have reached only to 1791. The presidency is represented in *The Writings of Thomas Jefferson*, 10 vols., edited by Paul L. Ford, 1892–1899, and *The Writings of Thomas Jefferson*, 20 vols., edited by A. A. Lipscomb and A. E. Bergh, 1903. Among biographies, Dumas Malone, *Jefferson and His Time*, 6 vols., 1948–1982, is outstanding; Merrill Peterson, *Thomas Jefferson and the New Nation*, 1970, is the best in a single volume. The astigmatic but penetrating views of the Adamses are in Henry Adams, *History of the U.S. During the Administrations of Jefferson and Madison*, 9 vols., 1891–1893. More straightforwardly critical is Leonard Levy, *Jefferson and Civil Liberties: The Darker Side*, 1964. Noble E. Cunningham, *The Process of Government under Thomas Jefferson*, 1978, reveals how the administration functioned. Drew R. McCoy, *The Elusive Republic*, 1980, is an ideological study of Jefferson's foreign policy; more conventional studies include Bradford Perkins, *The First Rapprochement*, 1955, and *Prologue to War*, 1963; Burton Spivak, *Jefferson's English Crisis*, 1979; and Clifford L.

Egan, *Neither Peace nor War*, 1983. David Hackett Fischer, *The Revolution of American Conservatism*, 1965, takes a fresh look at post-1800 Federalists, Thomas P. Abernethy explores *The Burr Conspiracy*, 1954, and Richard E. Ellis probes the problem of courts in a democracy in *The Jeffersonian Crisis*, 1971.

JAMES MADISON

1809–1817

No man ever came to the presidency with better credentials than James Madison. Most of his friends believed that Madison was among the most brilliant men in America. Indeed, Thomas Jefferson once spoke of him as "the greatest man in the world," by which he meant that his friend was second to none in his intellectual abilities. By the time he became president, his place as a great American statesman was already assured.

Madison was born on March 16, 1751, at Port Conway, Virginia, the home of his maternal grandparents, but he grew up at the Madison home in Orange County, Virginia. After preparatory training by tutors, he entered the College of New Jersey (Princeton) in 1769. He was graduated two years later and remained for an additional year's study.

Madison first entered politics as a young delegate to the Virginia convention of 1776, which drafted the state constitution and declaration of rights. After serving as a member of the state assembly and governor's council, in 1780 he became a delegate to the Continental Congress. There he played a major role in creating the public domain out of the Western lands and worked to defeat Spain's efforts to close the Mississippi River to American commerce. Returning to Montpelier, his home in Virginia, at the end of the revolutionary war, he was elected to the state house of delegates where he helped complete the disestablishment of the Anglican Church. During the turmoil that followed the Revolution when the upper classes felt threatened by uprisings of the discontented poor farmers and workers, such as Shays' Rebellion in Massachusetts, it was Madison who sought, more actively than any other American, to replace the inadequate Articles of Confederation with a constitution providing for a stronger central government. The federal convention of 1787 was in a real sense Madison's handiwork, from its seedling moments in a commercial conference of delegates from Maryland and Virginia in 1785 to the actual gathering of the constitutional framers two years later. On the convention floor he was an able debater, and his Virginia Plan, introduced at the outset, gave the delegates a working draft of a plan of government that with many changes eventually became the Constitution. Madison's journal of the proceedings not only made him the ultimate authority on the Constitution but also preserved a record for history. He also played a major role in the struggle to secure state ratification of the new Constitution, producing along with John Jay and Alexander Hamilton a superb body of essays interpreting and explaining the Constitution, published as *The Federalist*.

The Jefferson-Madison Philosophy

Madison served in the first four Congresses under the new Constitution, where he proposed the first ten amendments to the Constitution—the Bill of Rights—in 1791. He was also instrumental in forming the political faction that grew into the Democratic-Republican Party, which opposed Alexander Hamilton's Federalist policies. Working with Jefferson, Madison was, in fact, the most visible public opponent of Hamilton's program of funding the public debt, creating a national bank, and expanding American armaments. In 1797, Madison retired from Congress and returned to Montpelier. At home he kept abreast of political developments and as coauthor with Jefferson of the Virginia and Kentucky Resolutions of 1798, which asserted the right of the states to nullify acts of Congress they considered to be unconstitutional, supplied a rallying point for the political opposition to Federalist programs.

When Jefferson became president in March, 1801, Madison, as expected, became secretary of state and served his chief for the next eight years as both a loyal party supporter and principal foreign policy adviser. The sorest trials faced by Jefferson and Madison grew out of the Anglo-French War that had begun in 1793. No problems were more vexing than those involving overseas trade. American maritime commerce had expanded rapidly, partly in response to the opening of lucrative wartime commodity markets. The British navy challenged this growth by impressing seamen from American ships on the ground that they were British citizens, and seizing ships bound for European ports under the control of France. Napoleon countered by seizing American vessels in the Caribbean or en route to British ports. The existence of hundreds of captured American vessels and thousands of impressed seamen testified to the weakness of the United States, if not its actual failure to have established itself as a true nation. No truly independent power could possibly accept such insults to its sovereignty.

Yet both Jefferson and his secretary of state acted with restraint when a declaration of war against either England or France would have been fully justified. On the one hand, as dedicated republicans, they believed war was the worst evil that could befall a nation. Wars meant large armies and navies, huge expenditures, and the loss of life. Peace, on the other hand, allowed government to maintain a low tax structure, even the retirement of the national debt and, for the most part, minimal interference in the life of the average citizen. In early agrarian times, American voters enthusiastically supported the Jefferson-Madison philosophy.

As Jefferson neared the end of his second term, he was urged by his supporters to stand for reelection but he declined, helping to set a two-term tradition that stood until Franklin D. Roosevelt successfully ran for a third term in 1940. Jefferson used his influence to secure the nomination by the Republican congressional caucus for his good friend and secretary of state, James Madison. The Federalist candidate was Charles Cotesworth Pinckney of South Carolina. Madison defeated him easily, receiving 122 electoral votes to 47 for Pinckney. Six votes went to Vice President George Clinton, the candidate of a small number of disaffected eastern Republicans.

Madison as President: Inherited Conflicts

The new president was not physically impressive. Slender and only about five feet, six inches tall, he had a high forehead and a face so wrinkled by early middle age that he appeared to be much older. Madison, however, had considerable fame and he brought great political experience to the presidential office. Moreover, when he assumed office on March 4, 1809, he inherited a popular and generally unified political party from Jefferson.

The administration had reduced federal expenditures and lowered taxes, which contributed to Jefferson's and his party's wide acceptance. Yet, beneath the surface, factions had begun to form in the Republican Party. For the most part, in his last months in office Jefferson ignored the problem and tried to avoid any issue that would create discord. He had not been able to escape every confrontation, however, especially one with dissident senators from his own party. One of his last official acts was the nomination of his former secretary, William Short, as minister to Russia. The Senate's 31–0 vote against confirming Short's appointment was not only the most mortifying event of Jefferson's final days as president but also a warning to his successor not to risk similar humiliation; the senators would not accept a continuation of Jefferson's policy of rewarding enemies and neglecting friends.

In choosing the members of his cabinet, consequently, Madison was circumspect. Although wishing to make the able, Swiss-born Albert Gallatin his secretary of state, Madison was intimidated by the threat of Senate rejection into retaining him as secretary of the treasury, the post he had held under Jefferson. Similarly, bowing to pressure from Senate Republicans who professed to be his friends, he offered the State Department post to Jefferson's navy secretary, Robert Smith, brother of Senator Samuel Smith of Maryland. A worse choice could hardly be imagined. Congressman John Randolph gave the nomination backhanded approval by remarking that Smith knew "how to spell," but he neglected to add that Smith did not know how to write a dispatch or state paper. The president himself had to write most of his diplomatic correspondence. Finally tiring of Smith's incompetence, in 1811 Madison dismissed him and named his old friend and fellow Virginian James Monroe secretary of state. Madison replaced Smith in the

Navy Department with Paul Hamilton of South Carolina. For secretary of war he chose Dr. William Eustis of Massachusetts, and he kept Caesar Rodney as attorney general.

Anglo-American Discord: False Hopes for Resolution

The chief problem facing the new president was the continuing dispute with Britain and France over American's right as a neutral on the high seas. Just before he took office, Congress repealed Jefferson's Embargo Act, which had banned carrying foreign goods in American ships, and replaced it with a law—the Nonintercourse Act of 1809—that forbade all trade with England and France but permitted a resumption of commerce with either power if and when it ceased to violate American maritime rights. This new piece of legislation pleased neither the war hawks (the Western and Southern congressmen who favored war with England and the annexation of Canada and the seizure of Florida from Spain) nor the New England commercial classes, who wanted peace and unrestricted commerce with all nations. The situation seemed to change, however, when David Erskine, the British minister in Washington, hinted to Secretary of State Smith that he had the power to revoke the detested orders in council, under the authority of which the Royal Navy attempted to halt American trade with French-controlled Europe. Erskine, who had married an American, was perhaps overly zealous in his efforts to achieve an Anglo-American accord, whereas Madison was too eager to believe that Great Britain was suddenly ready to do what justice required. The president was undoubtedly influenced by the need to unclog American ports of their stockpiles of grain and cotton in order to bolster the prices of these commodities and end the agricultural depression. Furthermore, with foreign commerce at a standstill, income from import duties, the chief source of revenue for the federal government, had almost stopped. Consequently, Madison welcomed Erskine's overtures and accepted his assurances that the orders in council would be revoked. In return, under the provisions of the Nonintercourse Act, Madison issued a proclamation declaring that Americans could resume trading with England. Madison's achievement was acclaimed across the nation: Even the Federalist newspapers in Boston gave the president credit. Tough-talking congressmen from the Southwest grew silent, scores of ships loaded cargoes destined for British ports, and for a few weeks Madison basked in glory.

Madison's glory proved short-lived, however. When the British foreign secretary, George Canning, learned of Erskine's action, he repudiated it and ordered Erskine home. Erskine's instructions had stipulated that British concessions were dependent on American agreement to the right of the Royal Navy to intercept American ships bearing raw materials and goods for France. As historian Henry Adams has noted, Canning probably realized that such a brazen affront to American sovereignty would eliminate all chance for an accord.

The Madisons were enjoying a summer vacation at Montpelier when an express rider from Washington arrived with word of Canning's action. Madison was forced to issue a humiliating counterproclamation repudiating his earlier one and acknowledging that nothing had changed. Not only did Canning recall Erskine but he also rubbed salt in the wound by appointing as the next minister to Washington Francis James Jackson, the devious diplomat who earlier, as minister to Denmark, had spoken of peace to the Danes a few hours before the British bombarded their capital.

From the time Madison learned of Canning's rejection of the Erskine agreement, one could convincingly argue, the United States was set on a course for war with England. In a matter of weeks the winds of diplomacy had forced American ships back into port and whipped up a storm of public outrage against Britain. "The late conduct of the British ministry has capped the climax of atrocity towards this country," observed the *National Intelligencer*, a Washington newspaper published by Madison's friends.

After learning from Secretary Gallatin that the new British minister appeared to have "nothing to say of importance or pleasant," the president decided to delay his return to Washington for a while. When he finally arrived there in late September, he had an interview with Jackson that was painfully short. In a subsequent conversation with the secretary of state during which the nature of Jackson's instructions was discussed, a shouting match took place, ending with the exhaustion of American patience and Madison's refusal to have any further dealings with Jackson. His recall was sought early in January, 1810.

Testing the British and the French: Macon's Bill No. 2

War talk revived, although the military forces of the United States remained on a peacetime footing. Unwilling to accept the idea that a large military establishment gives strength to a nation's diplomacy, Madison adhered to the republican belief that in a time of crisis the militia could do America's fighting. Great Britain showed its contempt for American public opinion by leaving its ministry in Washington vacant after Jackson left. Meanwhile, Napoleon matched the British for arrogance by issuing the Rambouillet Decree in March, 1810, calling for the confiscation of all American ships in French-controlled ports that had violated the Nonintercourse Act. In doing so, the French emperor was ordering his navy to operate exactly as the British government had stipulated in its instructions to Erskine—but now France was going to seize the Yankee ships as prizes of war.

Madison, despite his generally antiwar disposition, was coming to believe that war was unavoidable. When, in 1810, the well-intentioned Pennsylvania Quaker George Logan prepared to undertake a private peace mission to England, Madison applauded Logan's motives but cautioned him, "Your anxiety that our Country may be kept out of the vortex of war, is honorable to your judgment as a Patriot, and to your feelings as a man. But the question may be decided for us, by actual hostilities agst. us or by proceedings leaving no choice but between absolute disgrace and resistance by force."

In the meantime, Gallatin worked with Nathaniel Macon, chairman of the House Foreign Affairs Committee, to draft legislation that would open the sea lanes to American ships but close all ports in the United States to belligerent vessels. Gallatin's object was to revive trade and increase lagging customs income so sorely needed by the federal Treasury. Although Macon's first bill failed in the Senate, Macon's Bill No. 2 passed and became law in 1810. Disarmingly simple, it repealed the Nonintercourse Act and removed all restrictions on American commerce, but, holding "up the honor and character of this nation to the highest bidder," the law stated that if England would repeal her orders in council, the United States would reimpose nonintercourse with France, and if France would withdraw her obnoxious decrees, the United States would reimpose nonintercourse with England.

Although Madison believed that the American people approved of Congress's action and of his relatively passive role in the management of the nation's foreign affairs, the Federalists, at least, were highly critical of the president's performance. Samuel Taggart, congressman from Massachusetts, observed, "Jefferson by a system of intrigue and low cunning managed the party. Madison is a mere puppet or a cypher managed by some chiefs of the faction who are behind the curtain." The radical Republicans, noted Taggart, overlooked French provocations while castigating England. "Because France burns our ships, confiscates our property, and imprisons our seamen they want to fight Great Britain."

Madison considered Macon's Bill No. 2 to be a poor successor to earlier legislative efforts to protect American rights on the high seas. "The inconveniences of the Embargo, and non-intercourse, have been exchanged for the greater sacrifices as well as disgrace, resulting from a submission to the predatory systems of force," he wrote William Pinkney, the American minister to London. Madison knew that the new law favored Britain, implicitly acknowledging her control of the seas. "She has now a compleat interest in perpetuating the actual state of things, which gives her the full enjoyment of our trade and enables her to cut it off with every other part of the World," he told Pinkney. Napoleon, however, might "turn the tables on G. Britain" by announcing France's resumption of trade with the United States if the United States would renew nonintercourse with Great Britain, the president observed.

Madison proved to be a good prophet. On learning of the new American law, Napoleon instructed his foreign minister, the duke of Cadore, to write a letter to John Armstrong, the United States minister to France, stating that France was prepared to revoke its decrees effective November 1, 1810, and calling on the United States to issue a proclamation reopening trade with France alone unless the British revoked their orders in council. Madison was informed of the emperor's action while on a summer vacation in Virginia. A decent interval would be needed to discover whether Great Britain intended to follow suit, but meanwhile Madison felt relieved. Napoleon's action, he said, "promise us at least an extrication from the dilemma of a mortifying peace, or a war with both the great belligerents." Even so, Madison's position remained precarious. If Napoleon was insincere and had to be denounced as a liar, England would have no reason to change its policy. The result would be disastrous for American commerce and agriculture, for it would create a de facto monopoly for the British.

Assuming that the revocation of the French decrees was genuine, on the day following the date on which they were set to expire, Madison issued a proclamation reinstituting nonintercourse with Great Britain under the terms of Macon's Bill No. 2. Napoleon, however, then issued new decrees against American shipping in French ports, decrees equally as damaging as the earlier ones. In his annual message to Congress, Madison had to acknowledge that France had acted in bad faith and, in effect, admitted that nobody in Washington knew the true situation in Europe.

Annexation of Florida

During this time, developments on the Southern frontier in that part of West Florida adjacent to the Mississippi River required a response from Madison. Following the purchase of Louisiana, Jefferson had quietly tried, without success, to purchase the region from Spain. In the fall of 1810, however, Americans in Baton Rouge revolted and asked to be annexed to the United States, and Madison quickly issued an executive order transferring all of West Florida to the Territory of Orleans, although the area east of the Pearl River was not effectively organized until 1812.

Federalists in Congress denounced the West Florida "invasion" as unconstitutional. Americans in the Southwest, on the other hand, were not satisfied because they wanted all of Florida. The territory still in Spanish hands was a refuge for runaway slaves and a base from which hostile Indians mounted raids across the border. Besides, control of the rivers flowing through Florida into the Gulf of Mexico would give the farmers in the region easy access to outside markets for their products. Responding to their wishes, in January, 1811, Madison sent a secret message to Congress asking for authority to order a temporary occupation of East Florida if the Spanish would agree to it, or in the event of "an apprehended occupancy therefore by any other foreign power." After demurring for a while, Congress gave Madison such authority.

Although Madison was mainly concerned with foreign affairs, important domestic problems arose that also claimed his attention. In 1811, the charter

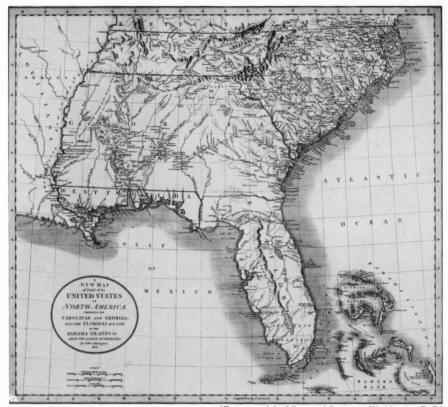

(Courtesy of the Library of Congress, Washington, D.C.)
The Southern United States with East and West Florida

of the Bank of the United States would expire. As a congressman, Madison had strongly opposed Congress's chartering of the bank in 1791, claiming that its action was unconstitutional. As president, though, he recognized the government's need of the bank to carry on its business efficiently. Despite Secretary Gallatin's pleading, however, so much Southern rhetoric had been spent excoriating the bank that Senate Republicans from Virginia and Maryland felt obliged to lead a drive to kill the institution. The recharter bill was defeated by the tie-breaking vote of Vice President George Clinton. Finding himself powerless in the situation, Madison was forced to watch the bank's dismantling.

Meanwhile, dispatch ships arriving from Europe during the spring and summer of 1811 brought no news of change in British or French policy. The president ordered the American minister to London, William Pinkney, home without naming anyone to take his place. Nevertheless, shortly after, Augustus J. Foster appeared in Washington as Jackson's replacement as British minister. The only important news he brought was that the orders in council would remain in force until Napoleon withdrew his decrees in a verifiable manner.

Although having nothing to say about the French decrees, the new French minister in Washington did inform Madison that the emperor would not interfere if the Americans should seize the rest of Florida. Madison had already sent two American emissaries to East Florida with authority to take possession of the territory if conditions were favorable. By August, one of them, General George Mathews, a former governor of Georgia, reported that the area was ripe for plucking and that the price would be low—"two hundred stand of arms and fifty horsemen's swords," as he estimated. Still, Madison held back, apparently willing to recognize a *fait accompli* but not eager to order an invasion.

Acknowledging the urgency of the international situation, Madison moved the date for convening the forthcoming session of Congress forward thirty days. As the congressmen drifted into Washington, the British minister reported hearing talk of war, but he discounted it as more American hyperbole. Henry Clay, he noted, "talked to me of war as of a duel between two nations, which, when over, would probably leave them both better friends than they had ever been before." Another congressman, Robert R. Livingston, was far more blunt, warning Foster that he had only thirty days in which to pack and leave for home.

In his State of the Union message to the belligerent congressmen, Madison spoke with more confidence than he had in many months. Knowing that newspapers across the country would print his message in full, he wanted to make his case with the American people. The president reported that the British had been asked to match the French by withdrawing their hated orders in council but the Royal Navy had replied by an even "more rigorous execution" of the obnoxious orders. British naval vessels hovered off the American coast in a provocative fashion, and an American frigate had fired on a vessel of the Royal Navy simply to maintain "the honor of the American flag." The existing state of British-American relations, said Madison, had "the character, as well as the effect, of war on our lawful commerce."

Without saying so explicitly, Madison pointed out that Britain had pushed America as far as it could go. Yet the British minister so misperceived Madison's true feelings that he sent a message to London implying that the president was merely bluffing. Keep the orders in council, call the president's bluff, and the Republicans will lose the next election, counseled Foster.

Tippecanoe: Pretext for the War Hawks

Madison's message was being read at crossroads and in courtrooms across the land when a dramatic incident in the Indiana Territory helped build support for war. On November 7, 1811, General William Henry Harrison's troops beat back an Indian attack near the confluence of the Wabash and Tippecanoe rivers with heavy losses for the warriors led by The Prophet, brother of Chief Tecumseh. Frontier rumors connected the Shawnee leaders with British officials in Canada, leaving a conviction in the minds of most Americans that the attack had been inspired by redcoated Englishmen. While the young war hawks in Congress rattled sabers for the folks back

(Courtesy of the Library of Congress, Washington, D.C.)

The Battle of Tippecanoe

home, the secretary of state talked with the House Foreign Affairs Committee frankly about the prospects for peace. When he finished, one member concluded, "The present session will not be closed without *arrangement*, or an actual war with Great Britain." With only token opposition, the House approved bills increasing the army from six thousand men to an authorized thirty-five thousand regular troops supported by fifty thousand militiamen.

Before he would move to use these new troops, however, Madison waited for the return of the sailing vessel *Hornet*, which was bringing dispatches from the American chargé d'affaires in London. If they should reveal that the American government's recent actions had brought about no change in the British orders in council, Madison was ready to abandon all hope of peace. Still, in the spring of 1812, Republican antiwar views and Madison's indecisiveness combined to dampen the war fervor in Washington. Some angrily accused Madison of being more concerned about his reelection than about the issue of war or peace. As one Federalist congressman put it, "There is not a doubt entertained but the great pole star in the view of which he shapes all his measures, is his reelection to the presidency for the next four years."

Madison's attention was diverted from the imminent threat of war with England by disconcerting news of events in East Florida where in March 1812 General Mathews reported that with a tiny American expedition he had seized Fernandina, at the mouth of St. Mary's River in the northeast corner of Florida, and had forced the Spanish commandant's surrender. Mathews requested instructions on what to do next. Instead of praising his action, however, the State Department rebuked the general, and Madison described his action, in a letter to Jefferson, as having been taken "in the face of common sense, as well as his instructions." Madison rightly thought that the Florida invasion placed his administration "in the most distressing dilemma." His actions repudiated by the American authorities, Mathews was forced to abandon his conquest while Madison turned his attention back to European affairs.

The government continued anxiously to await the return of the *Hornet* and news from England. Before its arrival, however, Madison learned that Spencer Perceval had the prince regent's support to become the new prime minister, which meant that no important change in British policy could be expected. "It appears that . . . they prefer war with us, to a repeal of their orders in Council," Madison wrote Jefferson. "We have nothing left therefore, but to make ready for it." When the *Hornet* finally arrived in late May, the dispatches it carried revealed that indeed nothing had changed. The orders in council remained in effect. Only a cancellation of those orders would have prevented war. Even though Madison believed, "that war contains so much folly, as well as wickedness, that much is to be hoped from the progress of reason; and if any thing is to be hoped, everything ought to be tried," he now thought that all the peaceful options had been tried, leaving war as the only way to protect the nation's rights and honor.

Congress, acting as if it knew what Madison intended to do, voted to extend a sixty-day embargo, designed to keep American ships at home in case a war started, to ninety days so that merchant vessels on the high seas might have time to reach an American port in safety. Members of the Republican Party in Congress had already caucused and voted unanimously to support the president for reelection. He thus felt assured that they would vote for a declaration of war should he request it. Presciently, on May 25, Jefferson wrote Madison, "Your declaration of war is expected with perfect calmness, and if those in the North [the antiwar New England Federalists] mean systematically to govern the majority it is as good a time for trying them as we can expect."

Madison, with the aid of Secretary of State Monroe, evidently worked on the president's war message to Congress for a week before he delivered it. The president wanted to present an unassailable argument, for he anticipated trouble from the New England Federalists and yearned for vindication in the forum of public opinion. His message was delivered to the clerk of the House of Representatives on June 1 and read at a secret session of Congress. Stripped of its rhetoric, the president's message declared that by virtue of Britain's actions in impressing American citizens into the Royal Navy, interfering with American trade, and inciting the Indians on the frontier, a state of war between the two countries already existed and Congress's duty was to recognize that fact officially. The House voted for the war resolution 79 to 49, but in the Senate the division appeared so close that votes had to be rounded up until the last minute. Although the antiwar Federalists stood firm, to the president's great relief the vote for war was 19 to 13. Madison signed one declaration of war on June 18. A few days later Augustus Foster, the British minister, called on Madison before departing for home. He subsequently recalled that in this last interview the president said he considered "that the war would be but nominal." Several months later, Washington learned that two days before the United States declared war Castlereagh had relented and told Parliament that the orders in council were being repealed. Reports of the British turnaround made some members of the administration hesitate to support the declaration until Madison let it be known that it was too late to undo Congress's action. Henceforth, hot lead and cold steel would decide the matter.

War with Great Britain

As the fighting began, earlier predictions that Canada would quickly fall to the American invaders, and become a bargaining chip at the diplomatic tables proved to be exceedingly optimistic. General Henry Dearborn's army moved so slowly that his planned capture of Montreal turned into a fiasco. Even worse, General William Hull, after crossing the Detroit River into Upper Canada and advancing timidly toward Fort Malden, lost his nerve and withdrew to Detroit where he surrendered to the British without firing a single shot. Hull was later court-martialed and sentenced to be shot, but because of his fine revolutionary war record, Madison pardoned him. American attacks on Canada at the western end of Lake Ontario also failed when militiamen refused to cross the Niagara River into Canada. At first the navy gave a good account of itself, winning a number of single-ship duels with British vessels, but the British preponderance of ships was so great that by the spring of 1813 the American navy was bottled up in port and the British had blockaded the American coast.

In the presidential election in the fall of 1812, following these military failures, Madison was challenged by DeWitt Clinton of New York, an antiwar Republican running with Federalist support. Even though the Republicans put Elbridge Gerry of Massachusetts on the ticket with Madison, the president carried only one New England state and garnered fewer than half the electoral college votes of the Middle Atlantic states, but he swept the South and West and received a total of 128 electoral votes to 89 for Clinton. New England's antiwar votes and its leading newspapers' harsh criticism of his administration bewildered Madison: He could not conceive of citizens placing pecuniary interest above patriotism.

Madison Begins a Second Term: A Beleaguered America

In his inaugural address following his reelection, Madison restated the nation's war aim as the restoration of American independence, but by the winter of 1812-1813 only an extreme patriot could have claimed progress in that effort. The Canadian invasion had failed on all fronts, the Royal Navy had clamped a tight blockade on American ports, and America's ally France was mired in an invasion of Russia and could do nothing to ease British pressure on the United States. Gallatin scrounged for funds to pay for weapons, blankets, uniforms, and food for the armies. In the face of so many problems and battlefield defeats, Secretary of War Eustis left the cabinet. His replacement, John Armstrong, former minister to France, started off badly by choosing the ill-starred James Wilkinson to command another Canadian invasion. After a short skirmish at Chrysler's Farm, on the north side of the St. Lawrence River, Wilkinson retreated. Commodore Oliver Hazard Perry's victory on Lake Erie and William Henry Harrison's triumph at the Battle of the Thames River in upper Canada in October, 1813, helped restore flagging American morale. When the Russian czar offered to act as a mediator in peace talks, Madison accepted and appointed three commissioners, led by Secretary of the Treasury Gallatin, to meet with the British at a neutral site.

The fighting continued, however, and developments in Europe left the Americans in an even more precarious position. After his great victory at Dresden in August, 1813, Napoleon began the long retreat that ended with his surrender to the British at Waterloo. The peace that followed in Europe released fourteen British regiments for service in the American theater. Britain continued to fight even though it had abandoned the practices of impressment and blockade that had originally led to war. Now with the best army in the world, the British decided on a series of attacks in North America that would end the war once and for all.

Totally inexperienced in military matters, and lacking an assertive character, Madison relied on his cabinet and a growing horde of generals to provide the leadership required to stop the British offensive. Unfortunately, problems plagued both the military effort and the cabinet itself. The American militia, despite all rhetoric, was no match for the well-trained British regulars. Furthermore, as England escalated its war effort, American commerce was swept from the seas and customs receipts, the main source of federal revenue, declined dramatically. With Gallatin's departure on the peace mission to Europe, William Jones, who had replaced the incompetent Paul Hamilton as secretary of the navy, assumed the extra burden of running the Treasury Department, and under his leadership financial crises were solved by expedients that offered only short-term relief. In the War Department, Secretary Armstrong, harboring presidential ambitions, made his decisions with an eye toward the 1816 election and consequently became an increasing liability to the administration.

When the American peace mission reached Europe, it soon discovered, as Gallatin reported from London, that British public opinion favored a continuation of the war. "They thirst for a great revenge," he observed, "and the nation will not be satisfied without it." With the American oceangoing navy shrunk to a single ship of the line, the venerable *Constitution*, the British were free to navigate at will along the Atlantic coast. Raids on American ports brought prize money that the Royal Navy crews shared, leading British sea captains to cast covetous eyes on Baltimore, New Orleans, and other depots of American commodities that would bring high prices in Europe. Thus in the British strategic planning for 1814, a major objective was the Chesapeake Bay region, where an attack on Washington in retaliation for the burning of York (Toronto) in 1813 was planned to accompany a raid for plunder on Baltimore.

The British plan for 1814 also included a pincers movement, with the northern prong striking at Lake Champlain and the southernmost one directed at New Orleans. A courageous American defense at Plattsburgh, New York, thwarted the British army coming down from Canada, however, and logistical delays hampered the New Orleans expedition. Meanwhile, a combined British army-navy task force moved up Chesapeake Bay toward the capital and Baltimore. The sudden appearance of the British fleet in rendezvous off Tangier Island near the mouth of the Potomac River forced the president to seek counsel in preparing a hurried defense of the capital. On July 2, he chose General William H. Winder to command a motley collection of regulars, marines, and gunboat crews totaling fewer than two thousand. On paper at least, some fifteen thousand militiamen were also armed and available for duty.

The British Take Washington: The Burning of the White House

The British commanders delayed their assault until August 18, but even with the extra time General Winder had still done little to thwart their plans. Confusion and incompetence were the order of the day: Monroe took the field with a small band of dragoons, Armstrong proved utterly incapable of issuing a sensible order, and Winder became *hors de combat* after falling off his horse. The British landing party continued toward the capital, panic broke out in Washington, and Madison took off on horseback with some of his staff and cabinet members. In the ensuing melee, Dolley Madison made her famous flight to the suburbs with most of the White House silver, some prized velvet curtains, a small clock, and a huge portrait of Washington loaded on a wagon driven by a faithful black servant.

Winder returned to action but the militia were overwhelmed at Bladensburg, Maryland, and the meager defense forces disappeared. Unmolested, the British troops walked into a nearly deserted Washington on August 24. During the next twenty-four hours, they managed to burn the White House, capitol, and several other public buildings, while the retreating Americans destroyed the navy yard. From different vantage points the president and his wife viewed the glowing sky. Their intended rendezvous at a plantation house near McLean, Virginia, thwarted by delays in the president's party, they were finally reunited at Falls Church, Virginia, the next day.

(Courtesy of the Library of Congress, Washington, D.C.)
The Taking of the City of Washington in America
Wood Engraving by G. Thompson

That same day, August 25, a freak tornado struck Washington, adding to the devastation wrought by the British. Finding little of value to plunder, the British troops returned to their ships that night. Only two days after the enemy's initial attack, Madison returned to Washington, though not to the blackened White House, which he never again occupied. The president instead took up quarters in a relative's house on F Street and looked for a place to hold a cabinet meeting. William Wirt, a fellow Virginian, who saw the president at this time found the sight distressing. "He looks miserably shattered and woe-begone," noted Wirt. "In short, he looked heart-broken."

With the British fleet and troops still somewhere below the city, Madison assembled his cabinet to decide on a course of action. When the president expressed to Secretary Armstrong his disappointment at the collapse of the capital's defenses, Armstrong took affront and soon resigned amid rumors from Baltimore that Senator Samuel Smith had taken charge of that city's defenses. Reports from Richmond, Philadelphia, and elsewhere that the people's reaction to the news of the British attack on the capital was one of defiance rather than depression helped to restore the administration's morale. Only in certain parts of New England, it seemed, did the leading citizens think that Madison got the drubbing he deserved. Early in 1814, resolutions were already circulating at a number of town meetings calling for an end "to this hopeless war" and abandonment of a wartime embargo on trade. Madison tried to mollify the dissidents by convincing Congress on April 14 to repeal the embargo. Only half satisfied by this concession and goaded by the high Federalists, the Massachusetts legislature sent out a call for a general convention, to meet at Hartford, Connecticut, in December for a discussion "by any or all of the other New England states upon our public grievances and concerns." To secede or not secede from the Union was in the minds of some extreme Federalists, the main question.

The news was not all bad, however. Along with the information that Baltimore had repelled a British attack, Madison had learned of the beginning of negotiations between British and American diplomats in Ghent, Belgium. Castlereagh, who had turned down the czar's mediation offer, agreed to talk directly with the American envoys. On the other hand, the country's financial condition remained precarious. The Treasury held large quantities of private banknotes, mostly from Southern institutions, which Northern bankers would not accept, and Boston financiers refused to buy Treasury notes unless they were heavily discounted. To keep the army paid and fed, as well as to prevent the bankruptcy of the federal government, would be no mean feat. Madison had to find some way to keep an army in the field in order to keep England at the negotiating table.

In September, 1814, with the smell of burnt furniture still in the air, the Madisons moved to John Taylor's Octagon House on New York Avenue, not far from the ruins of the White House. While his wife worked at decorating the house and attempted to create a pleasant atmosphere there, the president sent Congress, reassembled in temporary quarters in the patents and post office building, a message full of foreboding. If "the negotiations on foot with Great Britain" should lead to something concrete, he stated, money would be needed to implement "a return of peace." In view of what had happened in the last month, however, intensive hostilities seemed more likely than peace. In either case, the nation's Treasury needed an immediate infusion of cash, for it held only $5 million at the start of the fiscal year in July. Failure to find "pecuniary supplies" and provide for an adequate military force, Madison warned, would threaten "our national existence." The full extent of the financial crisis was revealed later when Acting Treasury Secretary George W. Campbell explained that a shortfall of some $50 million could be expected during the coming year unless Congress found a way to raise the money. Congress decided that the Treasury Department needed a more resourceful head and suggested to the president Gallatin's friend, Alexander J. Dallas for the post. Madison, accordingly, nominated Dallas on October 5, and the Senate confirmed the nomination the next day.

Despite the serious interference of the war with the nation's commerce, the government continued to derive a substantial part of its income from the tariff, especially after Congress raised the rates. Also, in spite of the aversion to such sources of taxation as "unrepublican," near the end of the war some revenue was raised through an excise tax and a stamp duty. Congress also tried, with indifferent success, to levy a direct tax on the states, which it had no power to enforce. Two-thirds of the cost of the war was met by loans. As a result, by the end of the conflict the national debt amounted to well over $100 million. Although the nation's financial situation was grim indeed, in his State of the Union message in December, 1814, Madison managed to note a ray of hope in the military situation to the south. General Andrew Jackson's Tennesseeans, he reported, had scored a victory over the Creek Indians at Horseshoe Bend, Alabama, which eliminated the possibility of a successful alliance between that tribe and the British. Almost as Madison's message was read, Jackson's forces repulsed a British attack on Mobile, which American forces had seized in 1813. In a matter of weeks, reports of a British expeditionary force in the West Indies, probably headed for New Orleans, brought Jackson to Madison's attention this time as the logical leader of the Southern port's defenses.

Meanwhile, the negotiations at Ghent, Madison learned early in October, were continuing, although the British were confident that they would prevail after Napoleon's downfall. They demanded the exclusion of American fishermen from British territorial waters, pressed for the cession of part of Maine to Canada, and urged the creation of an Indian barrier state in the West south of the Great Lakes. British negotiators also sought some agreement on naval vessels on the Great Lakes, fixing the northern boundary of the United States at the source of the Mississippi, and an acknowledgment of the British right to use that river. Although some of these demands had the stamp of British arrogance, Madison seemed to be encouraged by the progress of the talks. In any event, he decided to make the British peace terms public. A storm of opposition arose from Republican newspaper editors, who screamed that the propositions called for abject surrender, while the party's patron saint at Monticello ticked off the demands one by one and concluded: "In other words . . . she reduces us to unconditional submission."

New England Separatists: The Hartford Convention

In New England, the November, 1814, elections seemed to indicate that a majority of voters there still favored a policy of appeasement toward England and whatever additional action the Hartford Convention, which was soon to convene, might endorse to restore the region's prosperity. Madison looked back at the actions of the New Englanders and saw a pattern of behavior very close to treason itself—smuggling to avoid the embargo, a refusal to send the state militia forces to fight when Canada was invaded, insults to recruiting officers, and niggardly support for the anemic federal Treasury. He hoped that these actions represented the views of only a minority of the people of the region.

Besides the official delegations from Massachusetts, Connecticut, and Rhode Island who gathered at Hartford in December were three informal representatives from New Hampshire and Vermont. The delegates decided to hold their sessions behind locked doors. As Henry Adams has noted, this "excess of caution helped to give the convention an air of conspiracy." Although Madison decided against trying to interfere with the convention's deliberations, as a precaution he sent a loyal recruiting officer to Connecticut to observe the situation and instructed him to ask for aid from neighboring states if overt acts of treason should occur. Some of the extremists among the delegates, such as Timothy Pickering of Massachusetts, talked of preparing the way for "the separation of the northern section of the states" from the rest of the Union. More moderate Federalists, such as Harrison Gray Otis, whom Madison had known from their days together in Congress, played a moderating role and prevented any radical action. The convention proposed seven amendments to the Constitution intended to limit Republican influence and protect the interests of their section. After three weeks the delegates adjourned but voted to meet again if the Congress did nothing to satisfy their grievances in which event they would presumably recommend a more extreme course of action.

With the approach of Christmas, 1814, Madison appeared to have little to celebrate. Ghent and Hartford were ominously silent, while in Washington the president's party chieftains bickered over ways of carrying on the war in 1815. Not the least of Madison's worries came from rumors out of the South. Some of Wellington's Waterloo veterans, it was reported, were on board British vessels waiting for the winds to carry them to New Orleans. There the townspeople were at odds with General Andrew Jackson over his preparations for the city's defense. So dark were the American prospects that Timothy Pickering gloated, "From the moment the British possess New Orleans, the Union is severed."

Dramatic Reversals: Victory at New Orleans, a Peace Treaty at Ghent
The new year soon brought a dramatic change in Madison's and the nation's fortunes. First came the breathtaking reports brought by an express from the South. New Orleans was saved! Jackson's men had swept the British invaders from the field, inflicting twenty-six hundred casualties to a mere handful for the defenders. The manner in which the British retreated meant they would not try another attack. Church bells tolled their joyous refrain as well-wishers called at the president's house to offer congratulations. At the same time a stagecoach from Hartford unloaded three delegates from the secret convention ready to hand the president their demands, but the delirium created by Jackson's victory left them no stomach for the business. In an ill humor, they trudged off to await a better opportunity.

Their opportunity never came, for ten days after the news of Jackson's victory at New Orleans a messenger arrived in Washington with the preliminary peace treaty from Ghent. The war was over, if the Senate ratified the treaty, and the nation had lost not an inch of territory nor conceded a major right to the enemy. Unsolved matters of fishing rights off the coast of Canada and boundaries were left to the future arbitration of special commissions. Since the nadir of the American cause had been reached a few months earlier, this unexpected news appeared to be something of a miracle. Torchlight parades and banners extolling the president testified to his sudden popularity in every section of the country save one. Madison saw two of the Hartford delegates at a social gathering shortly after and was mildly amused by their obvious embarrassment. Suddenly, what New England thought or did was of little or no concern to the president.

The scenario for Madison's final years as president seemed to have come from the pen of a guardian angel. On February 18, 1815, he sent Congress a special message with his version of the war's origin and end. "The late war, although reluctantly declared by Congress, had become a necessary resort to assert the rights and independence of the nation," he declared. Ignoring the militia failures, the inept military leadership, and the constant search for dollars as he exulted in the outcome, Madison observed, "The Government has demonstrated the efficiency of its powers of defense, and . . . the nation can review its conduct without regret and without reproach."

In his eagerness for national unity, Madison even glossed over the wartime dissent of New England. No sign of vindictiveness was evident in his retrospective view of "Mr. Madison's War," as the high Federalists on Beacon Hill chose to call it. Madison must have read the public letter sent from a Boston meeting of Republicans with particular pleasure. It thanked him for "maintaining the honor of the American Flag against those who had arrogantly assumed the Sovereignty of the Ocean." Of all the accolades Madison received, however, none could have been more welcome than Jefferson's. "I sincerely congratulate you on the peace; and more especially on the éclat with which the war closed," Jefferson wrote. With peace restored, Jefferson hoped his old friend would push hard for a return to Republican principles, particularly in the field of foreign affairs, where Americans had so much to learn. "We cannot too distinctly detach ourselves from the European system, which is essentially belligerent," Jefferson advised, "nor too sedulously cultivate an American system, essentially pacific."

Never had the blessings of peace been so apparent to Madison as in the days that followed. The nation's mood was euphoric, and more than one observer realized that something fundamental had happened in America as a result of the war. With the peace and with the licking administered the British at the Battle of New Orleans, the young republic had proved something to itself. A sense of nationhood, which even Washington's administration had failed to nourish, began to flower. Returning to his adopted land after the diplomatic mission, Gallatin perceived the change. The people, he observed, "are more American; they feel and act more like a nation."

One of the first manifestations of the surge in national pride was the Mediterranean expedition dispatched to attack the Barbary pirates of North Africa. The American warships devastated the pirate vessels. So thoroughly did they accomplish their task that the dey of Algiers sued for peace and promised to promptly free the American prisoners he was holding for ransom. Further action at Tunis and Tripoli brought a similar response, ending in a complete American triumph. Henceforth, the American flag was respected by the Barbary pirates who had for decades contemptuously extracted an annual tribute from the United States Treasury.

The new nationalism that followed the war also found expression in domestic policy. Madison, in a sharp reversal of his earlier advocacy of states' rights and a federal government of strictly limited power, called for a strong military establishment, a uniform national currency, a tariff that would protect new American industries, a federally subsidized system of roads and canals, and a national university. The experiences of the war amply justified Madison's request for a stronger military establishment, and Congress responded by authorizing an army of ten thousand men and appropriating $8 million for the construction for fifteen new naval units. While emphasizing the basic financial soundness of the nation, the president conceded that some alternative to the inadequate state banks was needed to provide for a stable public credit and a uniform national currency and expressed a willingness to support a bill chartering a Second Bank of the United States.

When a bill creating such an institution with a twenty-year charter passed

Congress, Madison promptly signed it into law. How much the political parties had reversed themselves was evident as Republicans pushed the bank bill forward while Federalists, who had pleaded for the First United States Bank in 1791, made an earnest but feeble effort to defeat it. When Congress passed another measure appropriating $1.5 million to pay for the bank's charter, and all future dividends on government-owned stock in the bank to create a permanent fund to support the construction of roads and canals, Madison vetoed it, but only on constitutional grounds. He believed that a constitutional amendment was required to enable Congress to exercise such power.

To protect new industries established just before and during the war from the competition of cheap foreign, and especially British goods, being dumped on the American market, Congress passed and Madison signed a protective tariff bill that maintained or increased the wartime duties.

Madison's proposal for a national university, which was to be repeated by John Quincy Adams when he became president, was in both instances ignored by Congress.

Madison enjoyed his final year in office as Congress, under the leadership of Henry Clay and John C. Calhoun, worked through his legislative program. He spent a leisurely summer and fall at Montpelier, looking forward to the election of his successor. The Republican congressional caucus had selected his choice, Secretary of State James Monroe, as the party's candidate. The Federalist candidate was Rufus King of New York. His party badly weakened by its near treasonous opposition to the war, King carried only three New England states with a total of 34 electoral votes to 183 for Monroe. The succession of presidents from Virginia—the "Virginia Dynasty"—would continue.

Madison's last months in Washington were marked by a civility and popularity he had rarely known during forty years of public service. A veritable procession of well-wishers called at the temporary presidential residence on Pennsylvania Avenue. In his valedictory State of the Union message in early December, 1816, Madison described the chief achievement of his eight years in office in a single sentence: "I have the satisfaction to state, generally, that we remain in amity with foreign powers." All the travail of two wars with England, the quasi-war with France during the Adams Administration, the battles with the Barbary pirates, and the long squabble with Spain over the Mississippi River and Florida was subsumed in Madison's terse announcement. America was at peace with the world. Taking the Constitution as the palladium of American liberty, Madison predicted the continuation of "a Government pursuing the public good as its sole object" and one "whose conduct within and without may bespeak the most noble of all ambitions—that of promoting peace on earth and good will to man."

John Adams was one of the two Americans who best understood

Madison's feelings as he left the presidency. "Notwithstanding a thousand Faults and blunders," Adams wrote Jefferson, Madison's "administration has acquired more glory, and established more union, than all his three predecessors . . . put together." The former president's gracious remarks undoubtedly reached Montpelier, and for the next decade when Madison visited with Jefferson (who kept up a lively correspondence with Adams) there was a mingling of thoughts of self-congratulation among the three founding fathers. Only they understood all the difficulties a president faced, and only they knew how much America had needed the sense of nationhood it finally achieved in 1815.

Madison in Retirement

Madison's achievements of eight years in the presidency can be succinctly summarized as having given the nation a stronger loyalty to the idea of republican government and a full awareness of American nationhood. As the Madisons traveled homeward in 1817 only one problem remained as a stain on American independence: slavery. Up to 1817 Madison's energies had been devoted to preserving independence and the civil liberties it guaranteed to the American people. As a Virginian, a slaveholder, and a planter, it was beyond Madison's capability to shape a solution for the slavery issue that was beginning to crystallize. In his retirement, which lasted for another nineteen years, Madison worried more about political threats to the Union—nullification and later secession—than about the corrosive effects of slavery on the national character. Until his dying day, Madison never claimed that slavery was right—only that its abolition was beyond his power.

During the remainder of his life, Madison experienced his share of trials and triumphs. The dissolute conduct of his stepson, John Payne Todd, was a constant problem as Madison tried to shield the young man's shady character from public view. Madison once estimated that he had spent more than $20,000 trying to keep Todd out of jail or other scrapes. Family matters aside, Madison's health remained as fragile in retirement as during his active days. His medicine chest must have taken up a large part of his living quarters at Montpelier, where he alternately tended to his aged mother, watched as Dolley lost her good looks and comely figure, and wrote checks to cover Payne Todd's indiscretions.

Despite a reduction in his standard of living (his salary of $25,000 annually while president had no equivalent in farming income later), in retirement Madison and his wife were still noted for their hospitality. Famous visitors and ordinary citizens who called at Montpelier always found a dining table loaded with a variety of meats, vegetables, sweetcakes, breads, cider, and wine. During his last years, the expenses outran income and Madison was forced to sell some slaves—an experience common to many planters after the 1819 panic—which he excused by saying that the blacks were simply going from his plantation to that of a relative. At Jefferson's urging, Madison became involved in the founding of the University of Virginia and served briefly as its rector. His remarkable friendship with Jefferson ended when black crepe shrouded Monticello in 1826. Madison spent his last decade arranging personal papers, with an eye toward creating a legacy for the nation and for Dolley Madison, for he realized that the cash value of his notes of the federal convention alone would provide a financial cushion for his widow.

When Madison became ill in June, 1836, well-meaning friends and relatives suggested that drugs might prolong his life until the Fourth of July, so that he might expire on Independence Day as had Adams, Jefferson, and Monroe. Madison dismissed the suggestion outright. He looked on July 4, 1776, as the beginning of a new era and saw no value in an artificial reminder of one of mankind's most glorious moments. He died on June 28, 1836.

Robert A. Rutland

Bibliographical References

Despite many shortcomings, Irving Brant's *James Madison*, 6 vols., 1941–1961, is valuable for its originality and sympathetic treatment. The best short biography is Harold S. Schultz, *James Madison*, 1970, which is factually sound and full of important insights. Standing somewhere in between these works are Ralph Ketcham's readable *James Madison: A Biography*, 1971, and Robert A. Rutland, *James Madison and the Search for Nationhood*, 1981. A meritorious work is Merrill Peterson, *James Madison: A Biography in His Own Words*, 1974.

Although the tendency in Henry Adams' classic *History of the United States: During the Administrations of Jefferson and Madison*, 9 vols, 1889-1891, is to regard Madison as a failure as an administrator, there is much merit and sound information in this interpretive work. Madison's political thought is central to the theme of Drew R. McCoy, *The Elusive Republic: Political Economy in Jeffersonian America*, 1980, and Madison's role in the formation of one of the great political parties is recounted in Noble E. Cunningham, Jr., *The Jeffersonian Republicans: The Formation of Party Organization 1789-1801*, 1957. Virginia Moore's *The Madisons*, is rather uncritical but contains valuable information on Dolley Madison and the complex genealogy of the Payne and Madison families. Two works by the late Adrienne Koch deserve a place in any library. Her *Jefferson & Madison: The Great Collaboration*, 1950, and *Madison's "Advice to My Country"*, 1966, are books written with profound scholarship and affection.

For the specialists, J. A. C. Stagg, *Mr. Madison's War: Politics, Diplomacy and Warfare in the Early American Republic 1783-1830,* 1983, offers monumental research and a forthright view of Madison as a wartime president. Conover Hunt-Jones, *Dolley and the "Great Little Madison",* 1977, emphasizes Madison's interests in architecture and decoration, with additional essays on his intellectual pursuits.

James Monroe

JAMES MONROE

1817–1825

The day began auspiciously for a new administration and a new era. March 4, 1817, inauguration day for President James Monroe, dawned mild and radiant. Some five to eight thousand citizens witnessed the simple yet impressive ceremony. It was held outdoors, on the steps of the so-called Brick Capitol, a temporary structure for Congress located on the present site of the Supreme Court. Everywhere there were signs of the steady progress that had been made since British troops left the nation's capital in fiery ruins. The newly renovated President's House, soon to be called the White House, would be ready for occupancy in six months, and the Capitol would be usable in December, 1819.

The Virginia Dynasty

The vision of the American republic rising from the ashes of war formed an appropriate backdrop to Monroe's inauguration. The new president was the last of the generation of revolutionary heroes to head the nation, a member of what John Quincy Adams called a special "race of men." He was also the last of the three great members of the Virginia Republican dynasty to lead his country in the early years of the nineteenth century.

Born of Scottish and Welsh ancestry in Westmoreland County, Virginia, on April 28, 1758, Monroe came from a family of modest estate. With the support of his mother's brother, however, an influential member of the Virginia ruling aristocracy, Monroe entered William and Mary College in 1774. In Williamsburg, he was swept up in revolutionary activity, joined the Third Virginia Infantry, and in the fall of 1776 was fighting with Washington's army in New York. His military record was distinguished, and at the Battle of Trenton, he was severely wounded in a daring charge that succeeded in capturing the enemy's cannons.

Monroe emerged from the fighting with the rank of major, the esteem of General George Washington, and the fixed ideal of serving the worldwide cause of liberty. He thoroughly identified the principles of the Revolution with "free republican government," and he considered the success of America's republican experiment essential to the spread of liberty everywhere. He therefore turned to the study of law as preparatory to a career in politics.

Significantly, his teacher and mentor was the wartime governor of Virginia, Thomas Jefferson, and thus began a lifelong association that brought social and intellectual, as well as political, rewards. It was also Jefferson who introduced Monroe to James Madison. Monroe's friendship with these men was occasionally strained, but it endured and, as president, he continued to solicit their advice.

Beginning in 1782 with his election to the Virginia House of Delegates, Monroe began a political career in which success and accomplishment were punctuated by periods of disappointment. He served as a delegate to the Continental Congress in 1783, where he sought to strengthen the Confederation government and to uphold the rights of the West to navigate the Mississippi River. Nationalism and expansionism would continue to be keynotes of his political thinking. He also attended the Virginia ratifying convention (he was a moderate opponent of the Constitution) and then, in 1790, was elected to the United States Senate.

A Precocious Diplomat

In 1794, Monroe, who was now identified with the Republican Party, was appointed by Washington as minister to France, but he was soon recalled by the president for being overly pro-French. The political tide was flowing in a Republican direction, however, and Monroe soon reentered public life, first as governor of Virginia in 1799 and, in 1803, as President Jefferson's special envoy to France to conclude the Louisiana Purchase agreement.

Monroe's triumph in France was not followed by further success as minister to England and envoy to Spain. When a treaty with England was not even submitted to the Senate for ratification, Monroe returned to the United States in late 1807, his political fortunes temporarily impaired. Yet the growing crisis with England again brought a need for his services, and after a short period as a state legislator and governor, he returned to national office as Madison's secretary of state. Monroe's experience and skill proved so valuable that during the War of 1812, he also took over the War Department when its previous occupant proved woefully incompetent.

By the time Madison's presidency drew to a close, Monroe's record of public service made him the Republicans' heir apparent. It came as little surprise that in March, 1816, the Republican congressional caucus nominated him. With the Federalist Party moribund, Monroe won an overwhelming presidential victory with 183 electoral votes against only 34 for his opponent, Rufus King.

The Virtues of Nonpartisanship

The president-elect was an impressive figure, both in height (he was about six feet tall) and bearing. His clothing resembled revolutionary-period fashion, often a dark coat, knee-length pantaloons, and white-topped boots.

His hair was cut short in front, powdered, and gathered in a queue behind. It was, however, his plain, honest, and virtuous character that most struck contemporaries. As Adams noted, Monroe did not possess brilliance, but rather "natural prudence and good sense, a tact, and a knowledge of men, which eminently fitted him for a successful politician." Somewhat slow and cautious in forming judgments, he was firm and energetic in upholding them. Others reached a conclusion more rapidly, another cabinet member observed, "but few with a certainty so unerring."

Monroe had his imperfections. Overly sensitive to criticism and given to brooding over alleged slights, he never won the kind of passionate devotion that some presidents have. Yet his modesty and warmth were major assets and account for his continued popularity in the midst of heated controversy.

The country that Monroe now headed was, under the beneficent sway of peace, undergoing a period of rapid change that would, in a few short years, make the world of his birth appear as quaint as Rip Van Winkle's phlegmatic Dutch community. Settlers poured into the West, advancing the frontier and adding six new states to the Union between 1812 and 1821. Planters and farmers in the South rushed into more fertile lands, spreading slavery in their wake. In the North, particularly in New England, the pace of industrialization quickened as capital flowed into manufacturing. Meanwhile, a revolution in transportation was under way, primarily involving the construction of canals but also embracing steam navigation and river and road improvements. Jeffersonian agrarian ideals inevitably faded, but the national pride and prosperity that immediately followed the War of 1812 helped ease the strains of adjustment to these new conditions.

Monroe's political philosophy admirably suited this period of transition. He was not a Jeffersonian ideologue, but rather a pragmatic and moderate nationalist ready to adjust Republican limited government principles to the demands of commerce, communications, and manufacturing. A more doctrinaire president would likely have added to, rather than muted, the difficulties of post-1815 America.

Monroe's inaugural address established the "liberal and mild tone" of his administration. Following Republican tradition, he celebrated the intelligence and virtue of the people, pledged "economy and fidelity" in government, and promised to discharge the national debt. Monroe also added new emphases to Republican doctrine. He endorsed the "systematic and fostering care" of manufacturing and spoke of the "high importance" of internal improvements, the construction of roads and canals, which he wanted to "bind the Union more closely together." Finally, he underlined the need for a large-scale program of fortifications and the improvement of the militia and navy.

Monroe's thinking about political parties and the presidential office constitutes one of the most fascinating aspects of his administration. More than any president except Washington, Monroe scorned political parties and acclaimed the virtues of nonpartisanship. He believed that political parties were neither necessary nor desirable in a free society. Indeed, he considered them a "curse" and thought government should be based instead on the people's "virtue."

Monroe recognized that the elimination of parties would have to take place gradually. In the meantime, he had no intention of reviving Federalism by appointing Federalists to office. For the present, the country needed to depend on its friends, Republicans, whose loyalty would be jeopardized if former enemies received political favor, but Monroe hoped that the effects of peace, the spirit of "moderation," and the absence of great political excitement would eventually bring an end to parties.

Monroe sought to place his administration on "national grounds," and his search for unity and harmony was most conspicuously demonstrated in his famous tour of the East and Northwest in the spring of 1817, and, two years later, of the South. Everywhere—from Baltimore to Portland, from Detroit to Pittsburgh—Americans hailed the new president with a burst of "National feeling" and demonstrations of respect for the Union and its "republican institutions." It was during his visit to Boston that the phrase "Era of Good Feelings" originated to become a label for the two terms of Monroe's presidency. The expression captured the patriotic hopes of its president that Americans would "all unite" to secure the success of self-government.

Monroe has generally been considered a weak president, content to drift with outside events and to follow the lead of Congress. Only in the realm of foreign policy has his more active contribution been acknowledged. This picture has some validity. He was, by temperament and circumstance, a less activist president than Jefferson or Andrew Jackson.

Yet Monroe was a surprisingly effective and able executive. His model was Washington, the disinterested, moral, and patriotic leader who was above class, party, or section. He was, therefore, not a passive president. Within the executive branch, he controlled the cabinet and the power of appointing officials. His frequent cabinet meetings—about 180 sessions in eight years—provided him with information and ideas and also enabled him to develop a consensus on policy. Monroe realized that in the absence of party loyalty, the agreement of powerful cabinet members more readily assured support for measures in Congress and the countryside. He also used his annual presidential message to help set the nation's political agenda, and he often exerted a strong behind-the-scenes influence on Congress when controversial matters were before it. Considering the political obstacles confronting him, Monroe was quite successful in shaping the course of events.

The cabinet Monroe selected was, according to a leading authority, "one of the strongest that any President had assembled." He appointed Massachusetts' brilliant and dour John Quincy Adams as secretary of state. After failing to find a prominent Westerner to accept the War Department, he eventually settled on the young and talented South Carolinian John C. Calhoun. For Treasury secretary, Monroe maintained continuity with the past by reappointing William H. Crawford of Georgia, a "giant of a man," popular and exceedingly ambitious. Rounding out the cabinet were Benjamin Crowninshield of Massachusetts as secretary of the navy, a holdover from the Madison Administration, and William Wirt of Maryland, an accomplished lawyer and man of letters, as attorney general. The cabinet was unusually stable, the most notable turnover occurring in 1818, when Crowninshield resigned and was replaced by the New Yorker Smith Thompson.

Monroe paid a heavy price, however, for the excellence of his selections. Without the constraint of party discipline, its leading members ambitiously jockeyed for position in hopes of succeeding Monroe. Monroe remained in charge of his administration, but the harmony of the first years gradually evaporated and with it a portion of his effectiveness in dealing with Congress.

Domestic Initiatives

With his cabinet in place, the new president grappled with the substantive issues of politics. Buoyed by the country's prosperity, Monroe recommended in 1817 the repeal of internal taxes, and Congress enthusiastically responded. Prosperity also enabled Monroe to reduce the public debt. Despite problems caused by a drop in revenue during his first term, the debt was progressively lowered and Monroe could happily report by the end of his first term that nearly $67 million had been paid. By his last year in office, further reductions permitted Monroe to entertain a "well-founded hope" that the entire debt would be discharged within a decade. His wish was realized during Jackson's presidency.

Reducing government burdens was not undertaken at the expense of national needs. In keeping with his long-standing concern for national defense, Monroe forwarded with "zeal and activity" the system of coastal fortifications begun in Madison's administration. Congress appropriated substantial sums throughout his first term, and in December, 1819, Monroe announced the virtual completion of a survey of coastal defense as well as "considerable progress" in the construction of fortifications. By 1820, some $650,000 had been spent on various projects.

The panic of 1819 and consequent political maneuvering temporarily reduced expenditures, but once the economy rebounded, Monroe successfully urged larger annual appropriations. He could be satisfied when he left office that the nation's defense was considerably stronger than in the period before the War of 1812.

Much more problematic was the establishment of an acceptable policy toward internal improvements. This issue aroused competing sectional and constitutional claims. For Monroe himself, the desirability of such projects clashed with traditional Jeffersonian scruples about excessive federal power and violations of states's rights. In his first annual message Monroe seemed to rule out active federal participation by asserting that Congress "do not possess the right" to establish a system of internal improvements without a constitutional amendment. His sentiments provoked a House debate that provided much heat but little light on the subject. A combination of declining revenue, congressional opposition, and presidential caution effectively handcuffed internal improvements legislation during Monroe's first term.

During his second term, the issue again came to the fore in a way that gave Monroe an opportunity to present his full views on the subject. In April, 1822, Congress passed a bill authorizing the construction of tollgates and the collection of tolls to keep the Cumberland, or National, Road in repair. This impressive project had received the support of previous Republican presidents, and Monroe had approved bills for its extension westward toward the Mississippi River. He vetoed this bill on May 4, 1822, however, asserting that it unduly infringed on states' rights. Again denying Congress the power "to adopt and execute a system" of improvements, he now proclaimed that Congress had unlimited power to raise money and could *appropriate* it for "purposes of common defense and of general, not local, national, not State, benefit."

Monroe's compromise, which left the door open to federal assistance for national projects, satisfied neither extreme opponents nor proponents of internal improvements, but it managed to balance demands for better transportation with fears of excessive federal power and the dangers of opening the Treasury to competing sectional and local interests. In 1824, he signed both a bill subscribing to stock in the Chesapeake and Delaware Canal Company and a general survey bill authorizing a comprehensive survey of routes for roads and canals of national importance. The lasting impression made by Monroe's formula became evident in 1830, when President Jackson referred to it as a precedent for his famous Maysville Road veto.

The Panic of 1819 and the Missouri Crisis

The favorable circumstances attending the start of Monroe's presidency were shattered by two major upheavals during his first term, the panic of 1819 and the Missouri crisis. The economic and sectional unrest unleashed by these events acted like a corrosive to national harmony and the one-party political system. The issues raised at this time would help shape the course of national politics for a generation, but their full impact would become evident only after Monroe left office.

The postwar economic boom proved short-lived, and by early 1819, the country was immersed in a full-scale depression. The price of land and agricultural commodities plunged; laborers were discharged; factories, businesses, and banks failed; and farms came under the sheriff's gavel. The South and West were especially hard hit. By 1821, the economy was recovering, and a period of economic expansion that would last into the 1830's marked the remainder of Monroe's presidency.

Monroe was concerned about the nation's "pecuniary embarrassments," but he tended to discount the panic's severity and to adopt a traditional moral posture that such setbacks served as "mild and instructive admonitions" for Americans to return to their republican habits of "simplicity and purity." The solution for economic ills lay with the people and Providence, not government.

In fact, however, the government did undertake various measures to improve conditions. The Second Bank of the United States, which had irresponsibly aggravated the boom-bust cycle of 1815–1819 by its restrictive financial policies and had mismanaged its affairs, was being called the "Monster" by angry citizens. Monroe, who considered a national bank essential for the country's stability and growth, helped the bank weather the storm. He forced the resignation of the bank's incompetent president, William Jones, and approved the appointment of Jones's successors, first Langdon Cheves and then, in 1823, Nicholas Biddle. Under their management, the bank was placed on a sound footing and became an increasingly useful instrument in the government's monetary and fiscal transactions.

The panic also made imperative an adjustment of the nation's land policy. Fueled in part by liberal credit terms, a tremendous speculative boom had preceded the depression. When land prices tumbled, land purchasers owed the federal government $22 million and faced the prospect of losing their lands. Congress first responded in 1820 by abolishing credit purchases and selling land for cash only. This reform reduced speculation, but made land purchases more difficult. Monroe came under considerable Western attack for signing this Land Act of 1820.

The president consequently recouped some favor from critics by recommending "a reasonable indulgence" to relieve land debtors. Congress soon approved a relief bill that allowed buyers to apply their previous payments to portions of their claims, relinquishing those portions for which they could not pay. The Relief Act of 1821 slashed the land debt in half and eliminated this issue as a national concern. Westerners, however, continued to agitate for cheaper land for the next decade.

Hard times also set off a wave of sentiment in favor of reducing expenditures. This movement gained momentum in 1821, then peaked and evaporated the following year. It was particularly unwelcome to Monroe because it severely undercut his efforts to strengthen the nation's defense. Congress reduced the army from ten thousand to fewer than six thousand men, cut naval appropriations, and slowed the fortifications program. Efforts to reduce civil salaries, however, ground to a halt when cuts were proposed in the salaries of members of Congress.

The economy drive had political overtones as the supporters of Henry Clay, Crawford, and Calhoun sought to turn the movement against their rivals, sometimes embarrassing Monroe as well. More than politics, however, was involved. Many people, especially in the South, encouraged retrenchment as part of a larger campaign to reassert limited government principles. These "Old Republicans" warned that Monroe's moderate nationalism dangerously swelled federal powers and jeopardized liberty and states' rights.

The panic of 1819 stimulated sectional and political disaffection with the course of national affairs. So, too, did the famous Missouri crisis that erupted suddenly in February, 1819, when representative James Tallmadge, Jr., of New York, introduced an amendment to a bill permitting Missouri to form a state government that would have gradually abolished slavery in the future state of Missouri.

Once raised, the slavery question flared into heated controversy that brought the possibility of violence and civil war. The House, where the North predominated, passed the restriction amendment in a sectional vote, but the Senate, where slave and free states were balanced, rejected it. Congress adjourned in March, 1819, without resolving Missouri's fate.

When the Sixteenth Congress convened the following December, Maine was applying for statehood and opponents of slavery restriction promptly announced that they would block Maine's admission until antislavery forces agreed to Missouri's admission with slavery. After considerable debate, a sufficient number of Northern representatives (called doughfaces) retreated and a compromise was adopted that, in effect, admitted Maine and Missouri, without restriction, to the Union. In addition, slavery was prohibited in all of the Louisiana Purchase territory north of 36° 30', the Southern boundary of Missouri. By early March, 1820, the Missouri crisis was over.

Blinded to the genuine antislavery convictions involved in the restriction movement, Monroe believed that its leaders merely sought increased political power by rallying the nonslaveholding states against the South. Like many Jeffersonians, Monroe disliked slavery, but he was determined not to sign any bill that incorporated the principle that Congress could impose slavery restriction on a state, as distinct from a territory. He therefore drafted a veto message in case the restriction measure passed both houses of Congress.

Since Monroe "never doubted" Congress' power to regulate the territories, he supported the compromise. When the House approved the bill, he called his cabinet together to develop a consensus in support. The entire cabinet agreed that Congress could prohibit slavery in the territories, but there was considerable wrangling about whether that prohibition extended into statehood. Adams, who had strong antislavery convictions, ardently maintained against the rest of the cabinet that the restriction applied to future states. The impasse was finally resolved when the cabinet agreed to a vague and modest statement that the compromise was not unconstitutional. Monroe "readily assented" to this formulation, and on March 6, 1820, he signed the Missouri enabling bill.

Monroe was heartened by the "auspicious" resolution of the sectional contest, and he applauded the "patriotic devotion" of those who had put the nation's welfare above local interests. He considered the slavery issue as "laid asleep" but the Missouri crisis, in reality, boded ill for the future. Many Northerners were disappointed at the setback to the cause of freedom, whereas the Old Republicans in the South condemned the acknowledgment of Congress' power over slavery in the territories and grew more vocal in their complaints against federal aggrandizement. In Monroe's own state of Virginia, there was powerful opposition to his renomination because he signed the compromise, a telling sign of the resurgence of sectionalism and the erosion of Republican Party unity in the wake of the Missouri dispute.

Foreign Affairs: Relations with Spain

Although domestic issues had dramatic consequences for the nation, Monroe's most striking achievements as president were in foreign affairs. His objectives were to preserve amicable relations with other nations, to protect and encourage American commercial operations, and to expand American boundaries. Perhaps most conspicuously, he wanted to make the United States a respected and recognized power in world affairs. "National honor is national property of the highest value," he lectured his countrymen.

Ironically, Anglo-American relations proved to be considerably smoother than before the War of 1812. Great Britain was now eager to cultivate American goodwill and the American marketplace. Monroe and Adams were therefore able to resolve some thorny issues.

In July, 1818, negotiations began to resolve fishing and boundary differences, which resulted in the Convention of 1818, Monroe's first treaty. The agreement compromised the complex fisheries issue by restoring American fishing liberties "for ever" to limited areas of British North America. The treaty extended the boundary line of forty-nine degrees between Canada and the United States westward from the Lake of the Woods to the Rocky Mountains, securing to the United States an area of the Midwest rich in farmland and natural resources. The Oregon Country was left open to both sides for ten years, neither side renouncing its claim. Finally, it left to arbitration the issue of compensation for slaves taken by British troops during the War of 1812, and renewed the commercial convention of 1815 for trade between the two countries. The Convention of 1818, Monroe declared, gave "great satisfaction" and firmed the *rapprochement* between Britain and the United States.

Relations with Spain were probably the most engrossing problem of Monroe's presidency. The disintegration of Spain's empire not only posed problems for the United States in dealing with the struggling Latin American independence movement but also gave opportunities for expanding American boundaries at Spain's expense. Astutely combining patience and boldness, Monroe capitalized on this situation to gain Florida, further establish American claims as a continental nation, and announce a special American role in the Western Hemisphere.

Americans were naturally sympathetic to the cause of Latin American independence, and this sentiment was seized on by Henry Clay, who eloquently demanded American recognition of the newly independent states. Monroe's position was delicate. He, too, favored the revolutionaries, but he warned that premature recognition might provoke the European powers to intervene against them. Instead, he adopted a policy of neutrality, but a neutrality that gave the rebels belligerent status. To Monroe, this gave them "all the advantages of a recognition, without any of its evils."

Withholding recognition also gave Monroe a lever to loosen Spain's hold on East Florida, an area he had long coveted, and to define the western boundary between Spain and the United States. Spain contended that the dividing line was the Mississippi River and that the Louisiana Purchase was invalid. Negotiations between the Spanish minister, Don Luis de Onís, and Adams initially proceeded slowly, but in December, 1817, they were given a new impetus when Monroe ordered General Andrew Jackson to put down Seminole Indian border disturbances and authorized him to pursue the Indians into Florida if necessary.

Jackson responded with his customary energy, and by June, 1818, he had routed the Seminoles, overwhelmed the Spanish posts of St. Marks and Pensacola, executed two British subjects for allegedly aiding the Indians, and engaged in a dispute with the governor of Georgia over the killing of some of his Indian allies. He was also ready, he informed the president, to take Cuba, if that were desired.

Whether Jackson had Monroe's permission to seize Florida is still in dispute. Jackson contended that Monroe had signaled his approval; Monroe categorically denied it. Although Monroe was probably right, it is also evident that the administration took no action to caution or restrain a general whose expansionary appetite was well-known.

When word reached Washington of Jackson's exploits, the whole cabinet, with the exception of Adams, favored disavowing him. Adams thought the general entirely justified and even argued at first against restoring the posts to Spain. Monroe, employing "candor and good humor" in these exciting deliberations, skillfully built a consensus around his own views. Out of respect for Congress' war power and to deny Spain an excuse for war, he would return Spanish posts and acknowledge that Jackson had exceeded his instructions. Yet in justice to Jackson and to turn the incident "to the best account of our country," he refused to repudiate or censure Jackson. Instead, he alleged that the misconduct of Spanish officials justified Jackson's actions.

Monroe's refusal to repudiate Jackson supplied the "pressure" for Spain to conclude a treaty. The Transcontinental Treaty of 1819 ceded Florida to the United States and defined the western and northern boundary between the countries by drawing a line to the Pacific at forty-two degrees north latitude from the source of the Arkansas River, thereby granting to the United States Spain's claim to the Oregon Country. The United States agreed to assume up to $5 million of American claims against Spain and to yield its pretensions to Texas. Although ratification was delayed until February, 1821, the treaty was a major triumph for the administration. It not only acquired Florida, Monroe's primary objective, but also gained international recognition of the United States as a continental nation.

(Courtesy of the Library of Congress, Washington, D.C.)

Map of the United States, 1820

Final approval of the treaty, coupled with significant military victories by the revolutionary armies in Latin America in 1821, tipped Monroe toward the side of recognition. In March, 1822, he informed Congress that La Plata (Argentina), Colombia, Chile, Peru, and Mexico ought to be recognized as independent. Congress agreed, and the United States became the first nation outside Latin America to recognize the new Latin American states.

A Second Term: The Monroe Doctrine

In March, 1821, Monroe was inaugurated for a second term. He humbly accepted his overwhelming reelection—only one electoral vote was cast against him—as a sign of national unity, not as a personal victory. He hoped that similar accord could be reached on all national questions. Like other presidents, however, he would find that his second term would present less cause for satisfaction than his first.

The course of affairs in Europe seemed to pose an increasingly serious threat of foreign intervention to restore Spain's former colonies. The autocratic rulers of Europe, organized as the Holy Alliance, helped oversee Europe's post-Napoleonic arrangements. Increasingly, they interpreted their charge as the suppression of revolutionary challenges to established regimes. In late 1822, after a revolution broke out in Spain, France was authorized by the Holy Alliance to restore the deposed Spanish monarch to the thorne, and in April, 1823, French troops marched into Spain. That the Holy Allies, using the French navy, would next intervene in Latin America seemed a distinct possibility to Americans in the summer of 1823.

In reality, the chance of military intervention was remote, largely because Britain, with George Canning as foreign secretary, utterly opposed the use of force in Latin America. In August, 1823, Canning sought to bolster his anti-intervention stance by proposing to America's minister, Richard Rush, that the United States "go hand in hand with England" and issue a joint declaration on Latin American policy. This overture was forwarded to Washington in early October.

Although initially inclined to meet the British proposal, by the time Monroe convened his cabinet in early November, 1823, to deal with the European crisis, he favored rejecting Canning's offer. Adams vigorously supported this course. It was better for the United States to avow its principles independently, he argued, rather than "come in as a cock-boat in the wake of the British man-of-war." Adams recommended a systematic formulation of policy that would apply not only to the Holy Alliance but also to British pretensions in the Northwest and possibly Cuba, and to Russian claims on the Pacific Coast.

Adams advised the use of private diplomatic letters to Britain and Russia as the appropriate medium to convey American views. Monroe, however, desired to broadcast American ideals and principles to the world. Thus while the cabinet deliberated on the wording of the diplomatic correspondence, it also considered Monroe's draft on foreign policy for his annual message.

The Monroe Doctrine—the term itself was first applied in the 1850's—was announced in Monroe's message of December 2, 1823. Its crystallization of basic foreign policy tenets owed much to Adams, but its rhetoric and inspiration were indeed Monroe's. The document asserted the principle of noncolonization (the concept was Adams') that the American continents "are henceforth not to be considered as subjects for future colonization by any European powers." It also affirmed the principle of nonintervention, whereby the United States disclaimed any intent to interfere in the internal concerns of Europe and declared that any attempt by the European powers to extend their systems to this hemisphere was "dangerous to our peace and safety."

Although somewhat toned down from Monroe's original draft, which had seemed to Adams like a summons to arms against the Holy Alliance, the message was a high-minded expression of American nationalism. Issued before word reached Washington that an agreement between Britain and France had entirely removed any threat of European intervention in Latin America, it courageously and independently avowed American aspirations in both North and South America.

An attempt at a display of America's diplomatic muscle on the long-standing West Indies trade issue backfired, however. During Monroe's first term, Congress had passed retaliatory legislation against British restrictions on American trade in the West Indies. These Navigation Acts of 1818 and 1820 had indeed struck hard at West Indies prosperity, and Parliament, in 1822, yielded significant concessions by opening certain West Indies ports to American ships. Preference was still given, however, to British colonial trade. Monroe and Adams insisted that Britain do away with its system of imperial advantage and abandon intercolonial preferences. In March, 1823, Congress passed legislation granting the president authority to levy new discriminatory tariffs until Britain eliminated imperial preferences. Monroe quickly imposed the duties, the British retaliated, and by the close of his presidency, the West Indies trade remained restricted, a token of the administration's overzealous assertion of the principle of equal commercial opportunity.

Failure to Abolish the Slave Trade: The End of Republican Unity

Equally unsuccessful, though for different reasons, were efforts to reach an agreement to abolish the odious international slave trade. Great Britain, the foremost agent in the campaign against the trade, urged adoption of a proposal that would have granted a reciprocal right to search vessels and established tribunals to judge cases. Monroe and Adams both wanted to end the trade, Monroe calling it "an abominable practice," but they vividly recollected previous British violations of American shipping. They therefore rejected the proposal as "repugnant to the feelings of the nation and of dangerous tendency."

Instead, the United States acted unilaterally. In 1819, Congress provided for the use of armed vessels to patrol the African coast, sometimes in cooperation with British patrols, and the following year legislation declared the participation of American citizens in the trade piracy was punishable by death.

(Courtesy of the Library of Congress, Washington, D.C.)
Scene in the Hold of the "Blood-Stained Gloria"

These measures proved ineffective, and continued British pressure and growing public outrage at the trade brought stronger demands for international cooperation. The administration therefore modified its previous stand. The United States would in effect permit the right of search by declaring the slave trade piracy—pirates were not protected by a flag—without conceding the general principle of freedom of the seas.

In March, 1824, a slave trade convention was concluded with Britain, which declared the African slave trade piracy, and authorized the search, seizure, and punishment of offenders. In the Senate, however, Crawford supporters and Southerners anxious about cooperating with British antislavery forces rallied in opposition. An "astonished" Monroe urged ratification, but its foes were sufficiently strong to add crippling amendments that led Britain to reject the convention. Not until 1862, after the South seceded, did the United States sign a treaty suppressing the slave trade.

The trouble over the slave trade treaty was indicative of the problems posed during Monroe's second term by the political scuffling associated with the breakup of the Republican Party into personal factions. Three of the five major presidential contenders were in Monroe's cabinet—Adams, Crawford, and Calhoun. The other two leading candidates were Clay and Jackson. Personal relations among cabinet members cooled, and an "embittered violent spirit" was often evident among their congressional followers. Monroe expressed "embarrassment and mortification" at the maneuvering of the candidates. He adopted a strict neutrality among them, but this only allowed the flames of factionalism to spread unchecked.

The end of Republican unity brought the demise of the congressional caucus. It met for the last time in February, 1824, when a small group of congressmen nominated Crawford. The other candidates disregarded the decision and condemned the caucus as undemocratic. The ensuing contest among Jackson, Adams, Crawford, and Clay—Calhoun dropped out to seek the vice presidency—ended without a majority selection. The decision went to the House of Representatives in February, 1825, where Adams received the votes of a majority of states. When he chose Clay as his secretary of state and likely successor, the Jackson men cried "corrupt bargain" and organized an opposition that would, four years later, bring Old Hickory to the White House. The one-party system was dead, and the second American party system was emerging.

In the midst of this feverish presidential activity, Monroe gained a modest triumph when, in May, 1824, he signed a tariff bill providing for increased protection for manufactures. He had continually recommended that Congress encourage manufacturing, which he considered essential to national security, unity, and prosperity. Congress at first agreed, and in 1818 raised duties on iron and textiles, but the panic of 1819 and the Missouri controversy sparked hostility to protection, particularly in the South. In the spring of 1820, a new bill failed in the Senate by one vote, as the South and Southwest showed stiff opposition.

Despite this setback Monroe persisted. In early 1824, with the ardent protectionist Clay once again in the speaker's chair, Congress passed legislation providing additional support for iron, wool, hemp, cotton bagging, and textiles. Although the new rates were moderate, they were distinctly protective, and a howl of protests arose from the South. Southern spokesmen denounced the tariff as unjust and, even more ominously, as unconstitutional. The vote on passage resembled the sectional alignment over Missouri, an omen of the bitter tariff battles that lay ahead.

Expansion and Other Euphemisms: Indian Removal

Monroe's second term also marked an important turning point in Indian relations. Previous Indian policy included a number of different and sometimes conflicting programs: Efforts to encourage the Indians to adopt white ways, inducements to remove tribes to Western lands, and efforts to cede only portions of the Indian domain to land-hungry white frontiersmen. Under Monroe the confusion of multiple programs continued, but his administration brought a new vigor in all areas, particularly to Indian removal.

Monroe's interest in expansion and concern for national security led to the conclusion of a number of cession treaties, sometimes moving all or a portion of tribes westward. Treaties virtually cleared the old Northwest of Indians and opened millions of acres of fertile land in the South. At the same time, Monroe urged a continuation of efforts to extend the "advantages of civilization" by encouraging education, religious training, and the individual ownership of land. Beginning in 1819, Congress appropriated $10,000 annually to this program, and by December, 1824, Monroe claimed that the Indians were making "steady" progress.

Despite Monroe's humanitarian intentions, it was increasingly evident that Indian relations were reaching a crucial juncture. The problem was brought to a head by the state of Georgia, which stridently complained that the federal government had failed to live up to an 1802 agreement to extinguish the Indian title in the state. Both the Creek and Cherokee tribes stood fast against ceding any more land or moving westward, and when Monroe informed Georgia officials of this situation, the state's congressional delegation delivered a protest in March, 1824, demanding the eviction of the Indians and reproaching the government for encouraging them to stay. Monroe considered the protest an "insult," defended his efforts to gain cession treaties, but refused to consider the forcible removal of tribes as "unjust" and "revolting."

Nevertheless, the controversy with Georgia resulted in a new emphasis on removal as a means of saving the tribes and furthering their acculturation to white ways. In the last year of his presidency, Monroe called for the adoption of some "well-digested plan" of removal whereby civilization efforts could proceed "by degrees." He again rejected force, relying instead on such inducements as secure land and financial compensation to secure Indian approval. Congress, however, failed to implement Monroe's recommendation before his term expired. Monroe's struggle with the Indian problem ended on a sour note when, on the day before he left office, he submitted a treaty with the Georgia Creeks so fraudulently negotiated that President Adams was compelled to withdraw it and negotiate another.

Despite the discord evident at the close of Monroe's administration, he, as well as the nation, regained a sense of the nationalistic euphoria that marked its beginning when the marquis de Lafayette returned to the United States in August, 1824, and undertook a nationwide tour that extended through and beyond the remainder of his term. The outpouring of affection for the "Guest of the Nation" recalled the great revolutionary cause of liberty and the "blessings" derived from it. With Monroe's active promotion,

Congress granted Lafayette $200,000 and a township of land to alleviate his financial embarrassments.

Monroe's Presidency: Steadiness in a Period of Change

Monroe left office on March 4, 1825, in a period of rapid social change and of political and sectional conflict. Yet throughout his presidency, his personal character and presidential style conveyed a sense of dignity, unity, and national purpose that eased the country's transition into the more dynamic and complex world of the nineteenth century. As Adams later wrote in a fitting tribute, "By his mild and conciliatory policy . . . a large and valuable acquisition of territory was made; the foundations for national prosperity and greatness were laid; and . . . the American Union was advancing, with the vigor and stride of a giant, on its path to true glory and fame."

Monroe retired to his Oak Hill plantation, where he busied himself largely with farming and personal matters. He avoided partisan activity but did not entirely neglect politics. During the late 1820's, he condemned disunionist proceedings in the South and reiterated his support of internal improvements and protective tariffs. He also defended his record from misrepresentation, particularly on the issue of his ordering Jackson's invasion of Florida. Retirement did not erase a lifetime habit of public service, either. He was an active member of the Board of Visitors of the University of Virginia, and until ill health forced him to resign, he served as president of the Virginia constitutional convention of 1829–1830, characteristically working to effect a compromise between conservative planters and Western demands for a greater voice in government.

Monroe left the White House in serious financial distress, having accumulated over his public career a debt of about $75,000. Selling his Albemarle estate provided some relief, but he concentrated his efforts on gaining congressional reimbursement for his past public expenses. A portion of this bill was paid to him in 1826, but not until five years later did Congress, in response to public sympathy, appropriate another substantial sum, enabling Monroe to pay off most of his debt.

In the fall of 1830, after his wife's death, a distressed and enfeebled Monroe moved from Virginia to New York to live with his younger daughter and family. There, on July 4, 1831, he died. Throughout the country, Americans commemorated the passing of a leading figure of their revolutionary past.

Richard B. Latner

Bibliographical References

Anyone wanting to find out more about the life of James Monroe should consult the authoritative biography by Harry Ammon, *James Monroe: The*

Quest for National Identity, 1971. Monroe's style of presidential leadership is explained deftly by Ralph Ketcham, *Presidents Above Party: The First American Presidency, 1789–1829*, 1984; see also James Sterling Young, *The Washington Community: 1800–1828*, 1966. For Monroe's administrative contribution, see Leonard D. White, *The Jeffersonians: A Study in Administrative History, 1801–1829*, 1951. A provocative view of Republican Party doctrine is given in Drew R. McCoy, *The Elusive Republic*, 1980. The period of Monroe's presidency is wonderfully captured in two books by George Dangerfield, *The Era of Good Feelings*, 1952, and *The Awakening of American Nationalism: 1815–1828*, 1965; see also Frederick Jackson Turner, *Rise of the New West*, 1906, 1962. The sectional battle over Missouri is chronicled in Glover Moore, *The Missouri Controversy: 1819–1821*, 1953, whereas the revival of states' rights sentiment in the South is discussed by Norman K. Risjord, *The Old Republicans: Southern Conservatism in the Age of Jefferson*, 1965. Ernest R. May provides the domestic and diplomatic context for the Monroe Doctrine in *The Making of the Monroe Doctrine*, 1975, and Dexter Perkins, *A History of the Monroe Doctrine*, rev. ed., 1963, traces its origins and history. A fascinating account of diplomacy during Monroe's presidency is found in Samuel Flagg Bemis, *John Quincy Adams and the Foundations of American Foreign Policy*, 1949. Biographies of leading figures are an excellent means of understanding the era. Among the best are Robert V. Remini, *Andrew Jackson and the Course of American Empire: 1767–1821*, 1977, and *Andrew Jackson and the Course of American Freedom: 1822–1832*, 1981, and Charles M. Wiltse, *John C. Calhoun: Nationalist, 1782–1828*, 1944. Two first-rate studies of Indian policy are Francis Paul Prucha, *American Indian Policy in the Formative Years: The Indian Trade and Intercourse Acts, 1790–1834*, 1962, and Bernard W. Sheehan, *Seeds of Extinction: Jeffersonian Philanthropy and the American Indian*, 1973. Finally, one can become immersed in the day-to-day richness of politics and personalities in the appropriate volumes of the readily available *Memoirs of John Quincy Adams, Comprising Portions of His Diary from 1795 to 1848*, 1874–1877, edited by Charles Francis Adams.

John Quincy Adams.

JOHN QUINCY ADAMS

1825-1829

No American, it can safely be said, ever entered the presidency better prepared to fill that office than John Quincy Adams. Born in 1767 in Braintree, Massachusetts, he was the son of two fervent revolutionary patriots, John and Abigail Smith Adams, whose ancestors had lived in New England for five generations or more. When John Quincy was seven years old, his father wrote Abigail of their duty to "Mould the Minds and Manners of our children. Let us teach them not only to do virtuously but to excel. To excel they must be taught to be steady, active, and industrious." Already drilled in these traits, John Quincy wrote at this time, in his earliest surviving letter, that he was working hard on his studies (emphasizing ancient history) and that he hoped to "grow a better boy." A year later, in an event he often recalled, he held his mother's hand as they stood on a hill near their farm and saw the fires of Charleston and heard the cannon of the Battle of Bunker Hill. Experiencing the battles of the Revolutionary War around Boston in 1775–1776, and reading his father's letters from Philadelphia about the tense struggle to declare independence, John Quincy Adams was literally a child of the Revolution. He absorbed in his earliest memories the sense of destiny his parents shared about the new nation born when he was a precocious nine-year-old.

At age ten he entered public service, in a way, by accompanying his father on a dangerous winter voyage to France. On the crossing the ship was struck by lightning (killing four of the crew), survived a hurricane, and fought off British vessels. Returning a few months later, John Quincy perfected his own French by teaching English to the new French minister to the United States and to his aide, Barbé Marbois, who, twenty-five years later as Napoleon's foreign minister, would negotiate the sale of Louisiana to the United States. When his father was appointed a commissioner to negotiate peace with Great Britain, he again took John Quincy to Europe, this time as his private secretary. When their ship sprang a serious leak, John Quincy, with the other passengers, manned the pumps as the unseaworthy vessel barely reached the Spanish coast. A fascinating but grueling journey of two months across Spain and France finally returned them to Paris in February, 1780. After a year at school in Holland, at age fourteen he was appointed secretary to Francis Dana, American commissioner to the Russian court. John Quincy thus took two more long, eye-opening, and hazardous journeys across Europe, in between which he wrote and translated for Dana and pursued his own studies of history, science, and the ancient languages. He spent three more years in Paris and London as his father helped negotiate the peace treaty of 1783 with Great Britain and then served as first American minister to the former mother country.

When, in 1785, at age eighteen, he returned to America to enter Harvard College, he had already been five years in public employment, knew four or five modern languages, as well as Greek and Latin, and had shared in the most important diplomacy of the American Revolution. A bright, handsome, and serious youth, he never failed to impress the renowned American, French, Dutch, Russian, and British statesmen whom he met during his seven years abroad. His proud father declared him "a Son who is the greatest Traveller of his age, and without partiality, I think, as promising and manly a youth as in the whole world." Though the office was not yet created, he had also served an ideal apprenticeship for being president of the United States.

After graduation from Harvard and a few years as law student and young barrister, John Quincy resumed his preoccupation with public affairs by engaging with his father in strenuous newspaper polemics over the French Revolution. President Washington returned him to the public service in 1794 by appointing him minister to Holland. His skill in negotiations there and in London and his brilliant reports to the American government on the wars and revolutions convulsing Europe earned for him Washington's praise as "the most valuable public character we have abroad." Before he returned to the United States in 1801, he served four years as American minister to Prussia, translated a long German poem into English, wrote letters warning of the ambitions of Napoleon Bonaparte (Adams called him "the Corsican ruffian"), and married Louisa Catherine Johnson, the daughter of a Maryland merchant then acting as American consul in London.

In eight years at home John Quincy served briefly in the Massachusetts Senate and then for five years in the United States Senate where he was an increasingly unorthodox Federalist. He approved of the Louisiana Purchase (1803), refused to take a pro-British stance as the Napoleonic Wars reached their climax, and increasingly aligned himself with the policies and views of Secretary of State James Madison. Adams' adherence to his own principles in supporting the Embargo Act (1807) at once earned for him the gratitude of the Jeffersonian Republican Administration, the bitter hostility of the Federalists (who forced his resignation from the Senate), and—150 years later—a place in John F. Kennedy's *Profiles in Courage*. In 1806, he was made professor of rhetoric and oratory at Harvard (his lectures were soon published in two volumes), and three years later he argued the landmark

Fletcher v. Peck case before the Supreme Court. These distinctions were enough to earn for him in 1810 an appointment from President Madison to the Supreme Court, which the pressure of other tasks forced him to decline. The proffered appointment reached him in St. Petersburg, where he was American minister to Russia in the final years of the Napoleonic era. He represented critical American interests there for four years as he and his young family endured the rigors of Russian winter and marveled, half in horror, at the dazzling court of the czar. From 1813 to 1815, he traveled about Northern Europe seeking a negotiated end of the War of 1812, an effort capped by Adams and other American commissioners when they signed the Treaty of Ghent, ending the war respectably if not triumphantly, on Christmas Eve, 1814. Adams concluded his long and brilliant career as a diplomat in Europe (he had lived there for more than twenty years between 1778 and 1817) by serving for two years as American minister to Great Britain, a post his father had held at the end of an earlier war with Britain and in which both Adamses stood staunchly for a dignified equality between mother country and former colony that would assure lasting peace between them.

John Quincy Adams was President James Monroe's widely approved choice to be secretary of state in the new administration. His service there, 1817–1825, has rightfully earned for him standing as the premier secretary of state in American history. He guided negotiations with Great Britain that resolved the remaining disputes between the two countries and began an "era" of friendly relations between the two nations which still continues. Included in the settlement was a prohibition on armaments along the border with Canada that has made it the longest and longest-lasting unfortified national boundary in the world. He also arranged for the purchase of Florida from Spain and negotiated a transcontinental treaty with that nation which established the boundary between Spanish and American possessions from the Gulf of Mexico to the Pacific Ocean. He adopted a posture of benevolent neutrality toward the independence movements in Spain's New World possessions and guided the joint British-American resistance to European efforts to thwart independence that resulted in the Monroe Doctrine in 1823. Adams was proud of these signal accomplishments in the State Department, regarding them as fulfilling the goals of the new nation he had seen form in the battles around Boston a half century earlier: equal standing in the family of nations, security within transcontinental boundaries, and sympathy for the national independence and republican aspirations of all the countries of the New World.

The Election of 1824: The Era of Sectionalism
 Though Adams devoted his energies mainly to the large tasks of the State Department, he also was heavily engaged in the politics of the misnamed

"Era of Good Feelings." The Federalist Party had disappeared and Monroe's elections as president were virtually unanimous, but factions seethed within his National Republican Party. The able members of his cabinet jockeyed for position to succeed Monroe. Secretaries W. H. Crawford and John C. Calhoun had respectable aspirations for the presidency, as did House Speaker Henry Clay and the hero of New Orleans, General Andrew Jackson. Adams nevertheless regarded himself as the legitimate heir apparent: The patriotic history of his family, his own long, brilliant public service, and his success in the usual stepping-stone position as secretary of state made him the obvious choice—or at least so he thought. During Monroe's second term the politics of his succession increasingly dominated conversation and alignments in Washington. Adams still accepted the ideal of the antiparty presidency held by Monroe and his predecessors, yet he was intensely ambitious and did all he could "backstage" to further his interests. His detailed diary, kept faithfully during these years, is by far the fullest account available of the intense, increasingly bitter politicking.

The jockeying in Washington among potential candidates mirrored in many ways the changes and traumas of the years following the War of 1812. Though a burst of national pride and enthusiasm followed immediately on the conclusion of the war, during the Monroe Administrations rancorous disputes accumulated. New manufacturing interests grew in New England and the mid-Atlantic states. Settlement of the West accelerated. Canals, turnpikes, and, soon, railroads increasingly connected the country and provided myriad sources of conflict. The Missouri Compromise controversy polarized slave and nonslave states. The power of the reenfranchised National Bank heightened animosities in the nation's financial system. Perhaps most aggravating of all, a severe depression afflicted the nation as it sought to adjust to the post-Napoleonic era. Farm prices fell sharply as war-fueled demand for grains in Europe subsided; the price of flour, which was $15 per barrel in Baltimore in 1817, had fallen to less than $4 by 1821. Low-priced manufactured goods from Great Britain threatened to overwhelm fledgling American producers. As hardship spread, competition intensified, and bankruptcies threatened, the rancor within the political system grew apace.

As these animosities burgeoned, the old political parties, which might have contained and modulated them, largely ceased to function as effective national organizations. The Federalist Party had disappeared by 1824, and the National Republican Party was so incoherent that only 68 of its 261 members in Congress participated in its presidential nominating caucus in February of 1824. The effect was to give free rein to the always-potent sectional divisions within the country, divisions reflected in the regional strengths of the leading presidential aspirants. Jackson and Clay had strength mainly in the West, Crawford and Calhoun principally in the South, and Adams' support was confined largely to New England and some of the mid-Atlantic states. This properly named "Era of Sectionalism" was especially unwelcome to Adams because his own earlier career and strong sense of national purpose led him to denigrate regional biases—although his opponents, and, indeed, much of the country, saw him as very much the Northeastern sectional candidate.

After this failure of the National Republican caucus to nominate a majority candidate, the aspirants set out to gain as much support in the states as possible. Calhoun soon dropped out to assure his election as vice president. It appeared, too, that Clay and Crawford would lag well behind Jackson and Adams in both popular and electoral votes. When the returns were in, Adams was clearly behind Jackson in both tallies: He had 84 electoral votes to Jackson's 99 and only 114,000 popular votes to Jackson's 153,000 (in states where the electors were chosen by popular election). Nevertheless, the 41 electoral votes for Crawford and 37 for Clay threw the decision into the House of Representatives, where each state would have one vote for any of the three leading candidates. The final contest was between Jackson and Adams, and both maneuvered for support from Clayites and Crawfordites. The Jackson forces, with their clear pluralities in the popular and electoral votes, thought the contest was rightfully theirs. Adams' solid base of six New England states plus enough support elsewhere (much boosted by Clay's efforts to throw his strength to Adams), though, gave him the victory on the first ballot in the House of Representatives, thirteen states to seven for Jackson and four for Crawford.

Thus, despite his splendid preparation for the office and earnestly nationalistic outlook, John Quincy Adams entered the presidency on March 4, 1825, with distinctly minority backing, which was decidedly sectional as well. Furthermore, even before his inauguration, Jackson's backers charged that Adams and Clay had entered a "corrupt bargain" in which Clay supported Adams' election in the House of Representatives in exchange for a promise that he become secretary of state in the new administration. There probably was an agreement of sorts between the two men, but not one either regarded as corrupt. They were generally aligned in their more nationalistic views, as opposed to the more states' rights stand of the other candidates, and each regarded the other as an able and distinguished public servant. Clay thought Adams infinitely more qualified to be president than Jackson, and Adams believed Clay would be an excellent secretary of state. Nevertheless, the charges of corrupt bargain persisted, and Jackson's supporters began immediately to oppose and thwart Adams in every way they could, looking ahead to the 1828 election. Adams entered the White House, then, with severe and debilitating political liabilities.

A National President, Above Party

Adams announced his energetic, nationalist, nonpartisan outlook and program in his inaugural address and in a remarkable first annual message to Congress. As he assumed office, Adams acknowledged to the American people that he was "less possessed of your confidence in advance than any of my predecessors," but he promised to make up for this with "intentions upright and pure, a heart devoted to the welfare of our country, and the unceasing application of all faculties allotted to me to her service." Then, on a note of self-delusion or wishful thinking, he assured his audience that ten years of good feelings had "assuaged the animosities of political contention and blended into harmony the discordant elements of public opinion." He condemned party rancor and regional biases in appealing to all Americans to unite behind a common program for the public good. He hinted at his approach to promoting it by endorsing federal support for internal improvements and other energetic uses of national power. The address approached pure fantasy as the president doggedly asserted his active, above-party idea of leadership and public purpose in a political landscape where sectional disputes, contentions over states' rights, and party factionalism blossomed on all sides.

Adams returned, in detail and lofty rhetoric, to his theme of broad national purposes in his first annual message in December, 1825. "Were we to slumber in indolence or fold up our arms and proclaim to the world that we are palsied by the will of our constituents," the earnest and Puritan-descended president intoned, "would it not be to cast away the bounties of Providence and doom ourselves to perpetual inferiority? . . . The great object of the institution of civil government," Adams asserted, echoing a theme he had found in Aristotle, Cicero, and other advocates of good government through the ages, "is the improvement of the condition of those who are parties to the social contract. . . . No government . . . can accomplish [its] lawful ends . . . but in proportion as it improves the condition of those over whom it is established." Within this conception Adams had little use for strict constructionist, states' rights, special interest dicta that denied deliberate, effective pursuit of the common national good.

In particular, the president recommended establishment of a national university and national naval academy to help train the wise and patriotic leadership he thought the country needed. He also advocated an extensive system of internal improvements (mostly canals and turnpikes, but railroads were also clearly in the offing) to be paid for out of increasing revenues from Western land sales and a continuing tariff on imports. He called, too, for the establishment of a uniform system of weights and measures and the improvement of the patent system, both to promote science and to encourage a spirit of enterprise and invention in the land. In a further effort to support science and spread its benefits to the nation and to the world, Adams advocated not only an extensive survey of the nation's own coasts, land, and resources but also American participation in worldwide efforts for "the common improvement of the species." "[Are] we not bound," the presi-

(Courtesy of the Library of Congress, Washington, D.C.)

Lockport, Erie Canal
Engraving by W. Tombleson after W. H. Bartlett

dent asked, "to contribute our portion of energy and exertion to the common stock?" He urged American initiatives to explore the South Seas (partisan bickering largely thwarted attempts to launch an American expedition) and erection of an astronomical observatory, "light-houses of the skies," so the United States could make at least one such contribution to the advancement of knowledge to supplement the 130 observatories that had already been erected in Europe.

In general, Adams proved himself completely out of step with Congress, and perhaps the nation as well. His proposals were greeted with scorn and derision, regarded as so many efforts to enlarge the national power under his control and to create a national elite that would neglect the common people and destroy the vitality of state and local governments. Senator Martin Van Buren complained of the "most ultra-latitudinarian doctrines" in Adams' message, and former President Thomas Jefferson condemned some of the proposals as unconstitutional (echoing disputes he had had with John Adams a quarter century or more earlier). With Congress dominated by an unruly collection of his political enemies and the mood of the country preoccupied with the release of its diverse sectional and individual energies,

Adams had virtually no legislative success with his programs and found himself increasingly isolated, apparently living in a bygone age.

Adams sought to further his nationalistic, nonpartisan outlook through the design of his cabinet and in other appointments to office. He intended to retain as much as possible Monroe's cabinet, he said, to sustain a sense of continuity and national unity and to avoid implications that he would fill offices with his own friends and supporters. Samuel Southard agreed to remain as secretary of the navy, John McLean as postmaster general (not yet a full cabinet office), and William Wirt as attorney general. When the ailing W. H. Crawford declined to stay as secretary of the treasury, Adams appointed an able and politically sympathetic Pennsylvanian, Richard Rush, to the office. This opened up the post of minister to Great Britain for a New Yorker, first offered to De Witt Clinton, who declined, and then accepted by the aged Federalist Rufus King. Adams intended the War Department, vacated by Calhoun's election as vice president, for Andrew Jackson, but the general's contempt for the Adams Administration precluded a formal nomination. Adams then gave the office to James Barbour, a Virginian and supporter of Crawford. The appointment of Clay to the State Department completed an able cabinet with a reasonable balance of men from the various sections of the country, which was, however, with the exception of Rush, filled with people friendly to other presidential aspirants. Nevertheless, owing to Adams' obvious intention to act in the national interest and his effectiveness as an administrator, and also to Clay's great personal affability, the cabinet functioned with harmony and good humor for most of its four-year existence.

Adams professed indifference to this political disarray because he was determined to exclude partisanship from the presidency. He was well aware, though, as his diary attests, that he was to face debilitating political quarrels in the years to come. In other appointments he renominated, as his predecessors had, "all against whom there was no complaint." He refused, he said, to make "government a perpetual and intermitting scramble for office." Throughout his term of office he removed only twelve incumbents from federal jobs, and those for gross incompetence. While his enemies intrigued around him and used appointments for blatantly political purposes, Adams adhered strictly to his above-party ideology. He presented a paradoxical picture of a president intent on ignoring, even to the point of apparent naïveté, party politics, while surrounded by some of the most avid, factious political warfare in American history. Thus unenviably positioned, he turned his attention to the day-to-day problems of his presidency. Bald, of average height, erect in bearing, somewhat stern visaged, with a rather long, sharp nose and tending toward the stoutness that characterized his family, Adams gave the impression of a man determined to do his duty as he saw it.

Foreign Affairs: Trade Agreements and the Collapse
of Spain's New World Empire

Adams sought in his conduct of foreign relations (which he expected to be the dominant concern of his administration) to further the Jeffersonian goals of competitive world trade and access to foreign markets under terms favorable to American trading interests. This meant reciprocal trade agreements, giving the United States "most favored nation" status in peacetime and protection of neutral's rights on the high seas in time of war, all objectives of critical concern to the nation since its founding and which had been the substance of Adams' long diplomatic career. With Secretary of State Clay, he negotiated general commercial treaties that improved American relations with Britain, France, the Netherlands, Sweden, Austria, Portugal, Turkey, and Mexico. Though Adams and Clay accepted less than ideal terms in some of these treaties, in each case American interests were furthered and a precedent set for amicable trade relations likely in the future to be beneficial to each nation. Meanwhile, trade with the growing number of newly independent nations of Latin America, released at last from the constrictions of Spanish regulation, remained unsettled and often chaotic.

More troublesome were the administration's efforts to remove the long-standing burdens imposed on American trade with European colonies in the Western Hemisphere, especially with British possessions in the West Indies. Continued efforts by Britain to monopolize trade with its North American possessions and, it seemed as well, to sustain a century-long preference for its West Indian merchants and planters at the expense of mainland producers of food and lumber resulted in irritating and sometimes insulting strictures on United States trade. Patient efforts by Adams and Clay to protect American interests and at the same time open up profitable trade, however, became entangled in domestic politics. Pro-Jacksonians, based in the South and West, alleged that the rigidity of the New England-biased administration in defending American merchants led to neglect of the needs of staple exporters. Britain sought to take advantage of the dissension by framing its regulations to favor first one side and then the other, and then ridiculing American negotiators caught in the political cross fire. As a result, there was no satisfactory agreement, and the Adams Administration was blamed for inaction. The problem found its long-range solution in the diminishing importance of United States trade with the British West Indies.

Looming beyond the diplomacy of commerce were the ideological and geopolitical implications of the near demise of Spain's New World empire. Using rhetoric echoing Thomas Paine and Jefferson, John Quincy Adams welcomed the end of Spanish tyranny in Latin America and hoped the newly independent nations would become both kindred republics and partners in the economic growth of the New World. "The natural rights of mankind, and the sovereignty of the people were . . . fundamental maxims which we from our cradle first proclaimed," Adams averred, should become the foundation of all the nations of the Americas, as "the will of kings" was expelled from the hemisphere. He shared as well, though, his father's reservations about whether the former Spanish colonies, untutored in any of the habits of self-government, would be able to establish stable republican institutions. Disputes among factions in the former colonies, incessant efforts by European powers to interfere for their advantage, and the difficulty of exercising any United States influence without also seeming to interfere or dominate complicated the fluid and volatile situation. The prospect that Spain might retain control of Cuba and Puerto Rico, the possessions of most strategic interest to the United States, added further complications. American efforts to encourage republican independence in Mexico, Central America, Colombia, and La Plata (Argentina) were inconclusive and left the Adams Administration with more problems than resolutions. Yet, circumstances seemed to call for United States leadership.

The issue came to a head when, shortly after Adams became president, the United States received an invitation from Colombia and Mexico to attend an "assembly of Plenipotentiaries" of the newly independent Latin American states to be held in Panama. Britain and the Netherlands, who along with the United States had opposed the reactionary designs of the Holy Alliance to reestablish Spanish power in her former colonies, were also invited. Adams, with Clay's enthusiastic support, favored American attendance, though both were aware of many difficulties. Would the United States be drawn into the wars still going on between Spain and her former colonies or drawn into wars with European powers? Would American commercial interests be better protected by bilateral negotiations with the new nations than by an international congress with an unpredictable agenda? Most complicated of all, what about Cuba and Puerto Rico? The United States preferred continued (weak) Spanish control to British or French domination of the islands, to conquest of them by Colombia or Mexico, and most of all to a slave revolt that would plunge Cuba and Puerto Rico into the Haitian nightmare of bloodshed and black domination. Yet, strong sentiment existed in the United States for both independence (under white settler control) and annexation of the strategic islands.

All of these possibilities were aired in Congress and the press when Adams appointed American commissioners to the Panama congress and requested funds for their mission. Political opponents denied the president's authority to respond to the invitation without consulting Congress, pictured the whole enterprise as another federal-presidential power grab, and insisted that it betrayed the already hallowed injunctions of Washington and Jefferson against "entangling alliances." Southerners feared the congress would act against slavery and encourage black revolt and tumult in the Caribbean. As a result the approval of the American commissioners was so delayed that they missed the congress (one of them died en route of tropical fever), and all the world could see that political discord within the United States would prevent her from taking any leadership role. The congress, in any case, failed to reconvene for its second session, so the whole idea of a Pan-American Union died. Adams had a certain sympathy for the idea and wanted the United States to encourage republican self-government in Latin America, but his political weakness and the continuing volatility there prevented significant results. Altogether, Adams and Clay were unable to respond constructively to the opportunity opened by the demise of Spanish power in Latin American.

Domestic Policies: The "American System" and the "Tariff of Abominations"

Even more than in foreign affairs, political liabilities and ineptitude vitiated the domestic policies of the Adams Administration. Both the president and his secretary of state sought to translate their belief in active guidance of national development by the federal government into what Clay called the "American System." Essentially, it entailed protective tariffs to encourage American industry, land and Indian policies designed to hasten settlement of the West and provide revenue for internal improvements, the enlargement of markets for Western grains and Southern cotton, federal support of internal improvements to bind the nation together for the benefit of all, and the strengthening of the National Bank as a device for guiding the economy of the country. Adams liked especially the grand design of the American System: its encouragement of growth in all sections of the country, its planned use of the resources of the nation, and the important role it gave to the federal government in organizing and fostering the common welfare. To him, such a design fulfilled, in a deliberate and coherent way, the purposes of the American Revolution and what he often saw as "the hand of Providence" in American history and his own ideas of the active, above-party role of the nation's leader.

During Adams' administration, he, Clay, and Secretary of the Treasury Richard Rush spoke eloquently about the American System and managed to push many measures for federal subsidy of canals, harbors, and roads through Congress. Support for them, though, arose more from local enthusiasm for particular projects than from any sense of national purpose. The administration also broadened the effectiveness of the National Bank, but again criticism of administration policies by various sectional interests foreshadowed crippling controversies to come. Adams continued policies of removal of Eastern Indians to new reservations in the West (more humanely than would be characteristic of later Jacksonian administrations) and of a carefully controlled, revenue-producing sale of frontier lands. In both areas, however, Southerners and Westerners saw prejudice against their interests in favor of those of the Northeast and the middle states extending westward from Pennsylvania to Ohio and Kentucky.

Most troublesome of all was the question of protective tariffs. Adams repudiated the argument "that the Congress of the Union are impotent to restore the balance in favor of native industry destroyed by the statutes of another realm" and saw the advantages of fostering domestic manufactures, but he misjudged the degree of Western and Southern hostility. Jacksonians in Congress, moreover, saw an opportunity to manipulate the tariff issue in a way most damaging to the administration. In 1828, they maneuvered through Congress a tariff bill that gathered together various objectionable and contradictory features advocated by special interests—and then blamed the legislation on the administration, which had backed a revision of the tariff. The "Tariff of Abominations," as the act was called, became a rallying point of opposition to the administration and played a significant part in the campaign of 1828.

The Growing Strength of the Party System

The Adams presidency in its last years became increasingly engulfed in administrative tangles, quarrels within and between the armed forces, and, worst of all, the swirling political forces gathering around the popular but combative figure of Andrew Jackson that were determined to push Adams and all he stood for out of office. As the tariff legislation illustrated, proposals and alliances in Congress were calculated according to their likely effect on the next presidential election. Appointments to office were blocked or shifted in Congress according to their political colorations. Everywhere the burgeoning energies of the nation created new and often centrifugal forces and political alignments that thwarted or bypassed Adams' earnest, systematic efforts at orderly national development.

Adams was caught, as he perceived but could do nothing about, in one of the key transformations in American political history. He still sought, as the first five American presidents had done, to be a leader in the style of "civic republicanism" that harked back to the standards of good government, nonpartisan citizenship, and active pursuit of the public welfare he had learned from his study of Aristotle, Cicero, Plutarch, and other classical writers. Thus he regarded political parties as inherently corrupt because they were parts, or factions, of the whole. A president who celebrated, led, or even condoned parties was, *ipso facto*, not what a good national leader should be. Adams sought to sustain the apparent demise of the rival parties during Monroe's presidency and instead to include all political energy within a national republicanism that sought an inclusive public good.

Sectional and economic interests became more diverse, vociferous, and effective as access to politics broadened under the democratizing reforms (particularly within the states) of the 1820's, transforming the public life of the country into the vigorous, bewildering arena of "factions" that Madison had predicted, in *Federalist No. 10*, would be the fruit of freedom. Adams understood and accepted this in a way and did not oppose the enlargement of political participation, but he was deeply disturbed by the decline of active pursuit of the common good.

Jacksonian partisans, particularly Martin Van Buren, articulated and brought into existence a new, positive idea of political party. They saw political parties as manifestations of the needs and interests of the people of a free society. The job of the party and its leaders was to accept, enlarge, and fulfill the aspirations of the multitude of factions in the country and mold them into a political instrument (that is, party) that could gain national power. Instead of this goal being corrupt or partisan as Adams and his predecessors thought, to Van Buren it represented the triumph of democracy. The party would stand for certain principles and coordinate diverse interests, defining the public good in the only way suited to a free and pluralistic nation. The continuing competition between the parties would be "the life blood of democracy," providing policy alternatives to the citizens and a ceaseless criticism and honing of public needs.

Within this framework the president had the responsibility of leading and sustaining his political party as a necessary part of the machinery of a democratic society. It would be proper for a president to welcome the support of various interest groups, to campaign for office, to build party organization, to encourage party discipline in Congress, and even to use appointments to office to strengthen the party, all on the grounds that strong political parties were good for democracies. Van Buren declared that party disputes would "rouse the sluggish to exertion, give increased energy to the most active intellect, excite a salutary vigilance over public functionaries, and prevent that apathy which has proved the ruin of Republics."

The Election of 1828: Triumph of the Jacksonians

Under this new ideology of party, Van Buren and others organized the Jacksonian party, beginning before Adams' inauguration in 1825. Resting on solid Western and Southern opposition to Adams' alleged Northeastern bias, responsive to a wide diversity of interests, and gathering the forces of Calhoun, Crawford, Van Buren, and all the other anti-Adams politicians, the Democratic Party came into being around the objective of electing Andrew Jackson president in 1828. At the same time, it rejected not only John Quincy Adams but also all the older conceptions of good government and national purpose for which he stood. Calhoun and other pro-Jacksonians held "opposition" meetings even before Adams entered the White House. The Tennessee legislature nominated Jackson for the presidency in October, 1825, and Van Buren traveled about the country putting the party machinery together. Proadministration forces were active as well, especially Clay and his supporters, in seeking local support and fostering newspaper advocacy of Adams' programs. The president himself, however, held stiffly aloof from what he regarded as "politicking," which was beneath the dignity of his office, though he earnestly wanted to be reelected and did what he thought permissible behind the scenes to further his cause.

By mid-1828, the campaign became increasingly rancorous, and it was clear that the tide was running strongly for the Jacksonians. The pro-Adams press (operating without Adams' support, encouragement, or often even his approval—played up scandalous charges about Jackson's marriage, whereas the pro-Jackson press dredged up stories about Adams' alleged aristocratic airs and misuse of public funds on his missions abroad. One newspaper even charged that Adams had acted as "a pimp" in arranging for one of his servants, while he was in Russia, to be the czar's mistress. New England and some of the mid-Atlantic states remained faithful to Adams, but the Jacksonians successfully enlisted the burgeoning sectional and democratic energies of the country and benefited from the skillful party-building efforts of Van Buren and others. When the returns were in, Jackson had gained a 178 to 83 victory in the electoral college and had a 647,276–508,064 margin in the popular vote. The heroic general swept every state in the South and West (both he and his running mate, John C. Calhoun, were slave-owning planters) and even managed to win Pennsylvania and more than half the electoral votes of New York. The gloom and illness in the Adams Administration as it prepared to leave office during the winter of 1828–1829 and the joyous, tumultuous celebrations of the Jacksonians as they inaugurated their leader in the White House on March 4, 1829, measured the decisive change that had taken place in the nation's political life.

Adams and the Presidency: An Uncompromising Vision of Good Government

To Adams his defeat marked nothing less than the end of the noble aspirations of his first annual message that an active, above-party president and government might lead the nation in deliberate, coordinated pursuit of the public good. Five days after Jackson's inauguration Adams wrote bitterly that the new administration would "be the day of small things. There will be neither lofty meditations, nor comprehensive foresight, nor magnanimous purpose." Henceforth, Adams complained a few years later, national development would depend on "the limping gait of State legislatures and private adventure, and the American Union is to live from hand to mouth, and to cast away, instead of using for the improvement of its own condition, the bounties of Providence." Grand purposes and rational ideals, such as the planned development of national resources or the gradual abolition of slavery (a cause Adams fostered courageously during a unique and remarkable eighteen-year, postpresidential career in the House of Representatives), were to give way to what he regarded as the often shortsighted, selfish interests and designs of the increasingly diverse peoples and sections of the nation.

The John Quincy Adams presidency, then, somewhat like that of his father, ended in frustration and a sense of having lost a vital battle to new and, to the Adamses, unwelcome political forces. Though sometimes regarded as antidemocratic (so the Jeffersonians in 1800 and the Jacksonians in 1828 charged), the Adamses are more properly seen as upholding a different model, or style, of republican leadership. John Quincy Adams accepted earnestly the idea of government by consent. He hoped as well that inspired national leadership in the public interest, eschewing the divisive forces of faction and party, might enlist support among the people. This would sustain what Adams regarded as the vital principle of good (wise, virtuous) government even in a democratic era. He despised his Jacksonian opponents, not because they were democrats, but because they assumed that partisanship and the clash of sectional and economic interests would by themselves result in the common good. Yet, this new ideology of liberal, private enterprise, suited to the energies that would develop the frontier and absorb million of immigrants, seemed the wave of the future, and it did in fact characterize American growth and public life in the century to come. In the years before his fatal stroke on the floor of the House of Representatives on February 23, 1848, Adams refused to approve the "new politics" of the nation. He continued to believe that his own presidency had been a worthy, though perhaps futile, effort in sustaining a more purposeful and virtuous public life in the nation he had seen born in the revolutionary battles and diplomacy of his youth.

Ralph Ketcham

Bibliographical References

The basic source for the life and presidency of John Quincy Adams is the *Memoirs of John Quincy Adams . . . 1795 to 1848*, edited by C. F. Adams, 12 vols., 1874–1877. New editions of *The Papers of Henry Clay*, 8 vols. 1959, and *The Papers of John C. Calhoun*, 15 vols., 1959, also furnish abundant source material. Three biographies are essential. Samuel F. Bemis, *John Quincy Adams and the Foundations of American Foreign Policy*, 1949, and *John Quincy Adams and the Union*, 1956, are excellent on Adams' pre- and postpresidential careers. Marie B. Hecht, *John Quincy Adams: A Personal History of an Independent Man*, 1972, gives a full account of his family life and is also very good on his career in the House of Representatives, 1821–1848. Mary Hargreaves, *The Presidency of John Quincy Adams*, 1985, is a detailed, scholarly account of his presidency, especially thorough in its recording of the economic and political context of Adams' presidency. Ralph Ketcham, *Presidents Above Party: The First American Presidency, 1789–1829*, 1984, explains the place of Adams' Administration in the history of the American presidency, and Daniel W. Howe, *The Political Culture of the American Whigs*, 1979, surveys the ideas and practices of the party closest to Adams.

Andrew Jackson

ANDREW JACKSON

1829–1837

Andrew Jackson, seventh president of the United States, is one of the great mythic characters of American history. Acclaimed a hero for his military prowess, he became the dominant political figure of the half century between Thomas Jefferson and Abraham Lincoln. He was the first president elected from west of the Appalachians and the first to rise from humble origins to the White House. He became a symbol of the new opportunities open to the common man in nineteenth-century society and of the triumph of the democratic principle in American politics. While serving as president, he fashioned his personal following into the Democratic Party, the longest surviving of all American political organizations. Jackson lent his name first to a movement, then to a party, and finally to an era in American history.

A Leader Formed on the Frontier

Jackson was born on March 15, 1767, in the Waxhaw settlement, a community of Scotch-Irish immigrants located along the North Carolina–South Carolina border. His father died just before his birth, and Andrew's mother and her three small boys moved in with her nearby relatives, the Crawfords. Growing up in the Crawford household, Andrew received a satisfactory elementary education and perhaps a smattering of higher learning. According to later remembrances, he was a tall, lanky, and high-spirited youth.

The revolutionary war shattered Jackson's placid childhood and wiped out his remaining family. Fighting in the Carolina backcountry was particularly savage, a nightmare conflict of ambushes, massacres, and sudden skirmishes. The Jacksons devoted themselves wholeheartedly to the Revolution. Andrew's oldest brother, Hugh, enlisted in a patriot regiment and died, apparently of heatstroke, on the battlefield. Too young for formal soldiering, Andrew and his brother Robert fought with American irregulars. In 1781, they were captured and contracted smallpox, of which Robert died soon after their release. Shortly afterward, Jackson's mother also succumbed to disease contracted while trying to retrieve two nephews from a British prison ship.

Alone in the world at the war's end, a combat veteran at the age of fifteen, Jackson drifted for a time, taught school, then read law in North Carolina. Completing his studies in 1787, he soon accepted a friend's offer to serve as public prosecutor in the newly organized Mero District west of the mountains. The seat of the district was Nashville on the Cumberland River. Founded in 1780, it had a population of only five hundred but excellent prospects for growth, and it offered fine opportunities for an aspiring young lawyer of small education but already much experience of the world. In Nashville, Jackson rose rapidly. He was ambitious, energetic, shrewd, and an agreeable companion. He did not know much law, but neither did anybody else, and a frontier town that was awash in bad debts and disputed land titles provided plenty of business. Jackson built a large private practice to supplement his public duties, entered into trading ventures, and began to acquire slaves. He also ingratiated himself with the leaders of Nashville society and with Tennessee's leading politician, William Blount, who became governor when the district was set off as a federal territory in 1790.

Jackson solidified his rising status in Nashville by marrying Rachel Donelson Robards, daughter of the late John Donelson, one of the city's founders. The circumstances of the marriage caused much controversy during Jackson's presidential campaign many years later, for at the time of their union, Rachel's estranged first husband, Lewis Robards, had initiated but not yet completed his divorce proceedings against her. Frontier Nashville, however, saw nothing wrong in the marriage. To ensure its legality, Andrew and Rachel reperformed the ceremony after Robards finalized his divorce.

Despite its haste, Andrew's marriage to Rachel was perhaps the happiest event of his life, for the union proved an enduring success. It brought Jackson into an extensive and influential Tennessee clan and provided countless in-laws to replace his own lost family. The couple's youthful ardor matured into a devotion that deepened as they grew older. Lengthy periods of separation, the loss of Rachel's girlish beauty, and her increasingly religious, sometimes hysterical temperament could not shake Jackson's affection for her. Not surprisingly, in view of his violently attenuated childhood, Jackson was a man of fierce and, at times, uncontrollable emotions. He carried a reputation as a hellion from some youthful escapades, and explosive quarrels surrounded him well into middle age, but his passions and inexhaustible energies never swayed him from his attachment to Rachel. Their mutual affection and utterly conventional domestic life furnished a needed emotional anchor throughout his turbulent military and political career.

Only one misfortune marred their marriage. Though Jackson loved children and desperately desired some of his own, the couple remained childless. Rachel's brothers and sisters obligingly provided a corps of nieces and nephews for the Jacksons to stand godparent to, and one, Andrew Jackson, Jr., son of Rachel's brother Severn, for them to adopt.

Jackson's adherence to Governor William Blount brought him rapid political preferment in the 1790's. Chosen a delegate in 1795 to Tennessee's state constitutional convention, he was then elected the state's first congressman and shortly promoted to senator. After a year, he resigned to take a job closer to home, as judge of Tennessee's superior court. Meanwhile, he was undertaking large-scale land speculations in partnership with John Overton. Still a very young man, Jackson seemed destined for greatness, but the next few years brought a series of setbacks that halted his meteoric rise and threatened to close out his political career.

The Blount faction fell from power at the turn of the century, and Jackson fell with it. Over his head in land speculations, Blount entered into a conspiracy to seize Spanish Florida and Louisiana for the British. The conspiracy came to light; Blount was expelled from the United States Senate in 1797 and died in 1800. Governor John Sevier, commanding a rival faction, replaced him as Tennessee's most powerful politician. Jackson and Sevier quarreled first in 1797, when Jackson was in Congress. The dispute was patched over, but it reopened in 1802 when Jackson challenged Sevier for election as major general in command of the Tennessee militia. Jackson won the post, but the aftermath brought the two men to a showdown in the streets of Knoxville, followed by preparations for a formal duel. No one was hurt, but his estrangement from the now-dominant Sevier faction shut Jackson off from further political advance in Tennessee. His subsequent angling for a federal appointment in Louisiana also came to nothing.

The Sevier feud inaugurated a series of quarrels, over matters both vital and trivial, between Jackson and a variety of Tennessee foes. The most notorious of these, in 1806, began with a minor misunderstanding over a horse race and ended with a duel in which Jackson shot young Charles Dickinson dead after taking Dickinson's own bullet in his chest. A coterie of close friends—most notably John Coffee, John Overton, and the Donelson clan—stood by Jackson (and sometimes fought in his behalf) through these troublous affairs, but they made for him many other enemies and earned for him a reputation as a bellicose and perhaps unstable man.

Financial reverses accompanied the collapse of Jackson's political prospects. In the course of his freewheeling speculations, Jackson had carelessly endorsed the notes of one David Allison of Philadelphia. The notes came due, Allison defaulted, and Jackson found himself hard pressed by creditors. He met his obligations, but only by unloading some of his holdings and exchanging his Hunter's Hill plantation for a less-developed property named the Hermitage. In subsequent years, Jackson recouped his losses by raising cotton at the Hermitage and breeding and racing horses. He also continued his ventures in trading and storekeeping, though without much success. The Allison episode, however, taught him prudence. Henceforth, he trusted no one in money matters and avoided debt at all hazards—lessons that he later labored in vain to impart to his spendthrift adopted son, Andrew, Jr.

(Courtesy of the Library of Congress, Washington, D.C.)

The Hermitage

In 1804, Jackson relinquished his judgeship, and for the rest of the decade he focused his ambition on military rather than political objects. Still holding his militia command, he yearned for the war that would bring honor, glory, and a vent for his relentless energy. He also had old scores to settle—with the British who had destroyed his family, with the Indians who had once terrorized Tennessee and still hovered over its Western and Southern borders, and with their aiders and abettors, the Spanish in Florida and Mexico. Jackson's thirst for action led him to befriend Aaron Burr when the latter came through Nashville in 1805, seeking recruits for his shadowy schemes of Southwestern conquest. Jackson cut loose from Burr in time to avoid implication in his alleged treason, but he was still eager for war against the Spanish. In the following years, Jackson busied himself with militia reorganization plans, and he volunteered himself and his troops for service at every hint of Indian trouble. He also watched with mounting indignation the government's inept efforts to win redress from Great Britain for violations of American neutral shipping privileges.

The War of 1812: The Making of a National Hero

In June of 1812, the United States at last declared war on Great Britain. Jackson immediately tendered his services, but the government had no use for him. In November, however, orders arrived for a Tennessee force to proceed to New Orleans, and Governor Willie Blount (William's half-brother) designated Jackson to command. Jackson gathered two thousand volunteers and led them as far as Natchez, where he received a curt War Department order dismissing him and his troops. Fuming and raging at the government's imbecility, Jackson marched his command back to Nashville, where it dispersed. Throughout the summer of 1813 he awaited orders. In the interlude, he fell into another quarrel about nothing, this time with the Benton brothers, Jesse and Thomas Hart, the latter of whom had recently completed services as a colonel under Jackson's command. The affair terminated in a street brawl; Jackson took a bullet that nearly cost him his left arm.

In September, 1813, Indian hostilities finally brought an end to Jackson's inactivity. Summoned to punish the Creek Indians for frontier massacres, he regathered his volunteer force and invaded the Creek homeland in northern Alabama. In a series of engagements culminating at Horseshoe Bend in March, 1814, Jackson annihilated the main hostile Creek force. In subsequent treaty negotiations, he exacted a huge cession of land—more than twenty million acres—from the vanquished tribe. The Creek Indians would never again be a formidable power.

Jackson's success in the Creek War made him a minor national hero; his defense of New Orleans was to make him an icon. In May, 1814, he was

(Courtesy of the National Portrait Gallery, Smithsonian Institution, Washington, D.C.)

A Correct View of the Battle Near the City of New Orleans
by Francisco Scacki

commissioned United States major general and given command of the Southern frontier. The British were planning an attack on New Orleans, strategic gateway to the American interior. Jackson beat off a preliminary assault at Mobile Bay, then raided eastward to destroy the British base at Pensacola before returning to New Orleans. In December, a British seaborne invasion force made landfall and reached the Mississippi ten miles below the city. Jackson blocked their advance upriver. For two weeks, the British probed his position astride the Mississippi. Failing to find an exploitable weakness, on January 8, 1815, British general Sir Edward Pakenham ordered a direct frontal assault on Jackson's lines. The attack was a complete failure. Pakenham's men advanced over exposed and difficult terrain toward Jackson's fortified position and were mowed down by American artillery and rifle fire. The British suffered more than two thousand casualties, including Pakenham, dead on the field; Jackson's losses were thirteen killed, fifty-eight wounded and missing.

Almost simultaneously with the word of Jackson's incredible victory came news that British and American commissioners in Europe had signed a peace treaty two weeks earlier. Though unconnected, the two events fused in the public mind to make Jackson appear as the agent of deliverance from a mismanaged and nearly disastrous war. After a series of defeats and disappointments that sorely tried their patriotism and their patience with the government, Americans hailed Jackson and his frontier soldiers with unrestrained adoration. For a generation of patriots, Jackson became the symbol not only of American military prowess but also of the superior republican virtue that produced it.

Jackson had begun the War of 1812 as major general of Tennessee militia, amateur commander of an amateur force. He ended it as a regular major general, second highest ranking officer in the United States Army. After failures at trading, storekeeping, and land speculation, and a promising but stunted political career, he had at last found an occupation that matched his talents. Though no master strategist, Jackson for that time and place was a very good general. He lacked formal military training, but he knew the prerequisites for successful frontier warfare. His judgments were always decisive and his movements energetic. Most important, he understood the role of supply in waging wilderness campaigns and the necessity for discipline in leading half-trained, often insubordinate soldiers. He commanded the full confidence of his troops and the absolute loyalty of his subordinate officers.

Jackson stayed in the army when the war ended. Its main peacetime job was to protect the frontier against Indians, a task that suited his tastes exactly. He had long believed that white settlers and savage Indian nations could not coexist in peace; and as the former represented a higher civilization, the Indians must abandon their nomadic habits and settle down as individuals in white society or remove westward beyond the advancing frontier. Jackson's dual position as army commander and treaty commissioner gave ample opportunity to implement those views, and in the years after the war, he extracted major cessions of land from the Chickasaw, Choctaw, and Cherokee.

In December, 1817, Jackson received orders to subdue the Seminoles, who were raiding across the border from Spanish Florida. Liberally interpreting his vague instructions, Jackson effected a lightning conquest of Florida itself, in the process capturing, trying, and summarily executing two British nationals whom he accused of encouraging the Seminoles. Jackson's invasion brought foreign protests and domestic calls for his court-martial or congressional censure, but he successfully rode out the storm. Spain soon ceded Florida to the United States, thereby accomplishing his ulterior object. Jackson defended himself by claiming that he had merely carried out the real but unstated desires of President James Monroe and Secretary of War John C. Calhoun. This was a defense of much merit but in later years, as the controversy continued to smolder, Jackson weakened it by fashioning (with the help of compliant friends) a chain of evidence to show that Monroe had expressly authorized the campaign. Monroe denied it on his deathbed; whether Jackson believed his own concoction is difficult to say.

On the conclusion of the Florida cession treaty in 1821, Monroe offered the governorship of the new territory to Jackson. He accepted, but after presiding in stormy and controversial fashion over the installation of American authority there, he resigned and came home to Tennessee. There, his friends were beginning to promote him as a candidate for the presidency in 1824.

Presidential Aspirations

James Monroe, heir to Thomas Jefferson and James Madison in the Virginia presidential dynasty, was now in his second term, and he had no obvious successor. Three seasoned statesmen vied for the post: Secretary of State John Quincy Adams of Massachusetts, Treasury Secretary William Harris Crawford of Georgia, and Henry Clay of Kentucky, speaker of the House of Representatives. Jackson's own candidacy was first floated to serve the local purposes of his friends in Tennessee, but it quickly caught on elsewhere. In the absence of party opposition from the moribund Federalists, the machinery for fixing on a single Republican candidate had broken down, leaving a vacuum to be filled at the polls by personal popularity. The returns made it plain that Jackson's military heroics had a far greater hold on the public imagination than the civil attainments of Adams, Crawford, or Clay. Jackson was the only candidate whose strength transcended a regional base. He gathered a plurality of popular votes, carrying eleven states out of twenty-four, including Pennsylvania, New Jersey, and the Carolinas, along with the entire Southwest. No one received a majority of electoral votes, however, so the contest among Jackson, Adams, and Crawford was thrown into the House of Representatives. There, speaker Clay announced his support for Adams, and his influence, together with a general suspicion of Jackson's unfitness for the presidency by both temperament and training, enabled Adams to win the requisite majority of states on the first ballot. He promptly appointed Clay secretary of state. Jackson cried that a "corrupt bargain" had swindled him out of the presidency and began planning for a rematch in 1828.

The four years of John Quincy Adams' presidency really constituted one long, increasingly acrimonious, and, in the end, one-sided presidential campaign. To Jackson's own tremendous popularity was added widespread outrage against the method of Adams' ascension to power. While Adams floundered in Washington, alienating key constituencies with indiscreet policy statements, Jackson drew around him a deft group of organizers and publicists to manage his campaign. They avoided discussion of issues and credentials and focused their propaganda on Jackson's mystique: his rise from humble origins, his heroism in war, his indomitable patriotism. As Jackson's candidacy gathered strength, powerful regional leaders swung to his side: Vice President John C. Calhoun of South Carolina, deserting the administration to accept the same post on Jackson's ticket; Martin Van Buren of New York, marshal of the former Crawford men; and Thomas Hart Benton, Jackson's former antagonist, now a senator from Missouri. In the end, the combination of a superior candidate and superior management produced a rout. In the 1828 election, Jackson carried the entire West and South, plus New York and Pennsylvania.

Hard on the news of this victory came personal sorrow. In its latter stages, the presidential campaign had turned ugly, as editors and pamphleteers mercilessly exposed the private lives of the candidates. Adams' publicists scrutinized the peculiar circumstances of Jackson's marriage, labeling him a wife stealer and Rachel a bigamist. As if in response to this torrent of abuse, Rachel withered and sickened. On December 22, she died at the Hermitage. For days Jackson was inconsolable.

An Outsider in the White House

Jackson's victory in 1828 represented a radical break from tradition in the young republic. He was a genuine outsider in Washington, the first such to be elected president, and this fact was to color his perceptions and actions throughout his presidency. His election inspired trepidation among veteran politicians and bureaucrats, for he was, as Henry Clay warned, a "military chieftain" rather than an accomplished statesman. Jackson's predecessors in office had undergone extensive apprenticeships in national politics and diplomacy. Jackson had less formal education than any of them; he had acquired a little experience in Congress and almost none in public administration. Further, he had on occasion in his military career displayed an apparent contempt for civil authority. Though prominent men had attached themselves to his candidacy, his real political strength came from the mass of voters, who seemed not to care about his lack of traditional qualifications. Some established politicians admired Jackson; many feared him; few knew him well. They could only guess at what he might do in office.

Many doubted whether he could even survive his term. He was sixty-two, the oldest president to take office up to that time. Despite age and infirmity, Jackson's appearance was still striking: He carried his lean body erect, and his firm countenance and direct gaze won immediate respect, while his frank but dignified manners inspired admiration. He had, however, recently sustained a devastating blow in the death of his wife of thirty-seven years. He still carried bullets from Charles Dickinson and Jesse Benton in his chest and arm and he suffered from persistent cough, wracking headaches, and debilitating digestive troubles.

His first task was to choose a cabinet. The chief place, the State Department, went to Martin Van Buren of New York, who had contributed vitally to Jackson's election and commanded the reigning political machine in the nation's largest state. The rest of Jackson's choices were weak and, to many of his supporters, alarming. Treasury Secretary Samuel Ingham of Pennsylvania, Navy Secretary John Branch of North Carolina, and Attorney General George M. Berrien of Georgia were politicians of modest reputation who brought no great strength to the administration. As all these men were practically strangers to Jackson, he saved the last post, the War Department, for a trusted confidential friend. The nod went to John Henry Eaton, a senator from Tennessee and Jackson's campaign biographer. Ironically, it was the appointment of Eaton—the safest one, in Jackson's mind—that eventually brought the whole cabinet down.

Reforming the Federal Bureaucracy: Jackson and the Spoils System

Having selected his cabinet, Jackson began a housecleaning at the second level of federal officeholders—the Washington bureau chiefs, land and customs officers, and federal marshals and attorneys. During the campaign, he had cried loudly for "reform," charging the Adams bureaucracy with fraud and with working to thwart his election. Now as president, Jackson implemented a policy of removals designed to eliminate the corruption, laxity, and arrogance that he associated with long individual tenure in office. Haste and naïveté in naming replacements did much to confuse Jackson's purpose. Under the guise of reform, many offices were doled out as reward for political services. Newspaper editors who had championed Jackson's cause came in for special favor. Jackson denied that he was injecting political criteria into the appointment process; yet he accepted an officeholder's support for

Adams as evidence of unfitness, and in choosing replacements he relied exclusively on recommendations from his own partisans, few of whom shared his own concern for honest and efficient administration.

Some of Jackson's early appointments were truly appalling. He made John Randolph of Virginia, the most undiplomatic man in the United States, minister to Russia, and he placed an alcoholic editor at the head of the General Land Office. He raised the postmaster generalship to cabinet rank and filled it with William Taylor Barry of Kentucky, a genial bungler who reduced the postal system to chaos. Several of Jackson's land-office appointees defaulted for large sums. Most damaging to his administration's reputation—he ignored warnings from Van Buren and Ingham—was the appointment of an old comrade, Samuel Swartwout, as collector of the New York Customhouse, through which passed nearly half of the federal government's revenue. Swartwout absconded with more than $1 million in 1838.

Jackson is usually charged with bringing the "spoils system" into American politics. That was the result, though not his intent. He always claimed, and evidently believed, that he had introduced greater efficiency and economy into government. He had, indeed, broken the hold of a bureaucratic clique on federal offices and thrown them open to all comers. The result was a democratization of public service at a temporary sacrifice in efficiency and honesty, though Jackson later found capable subordinates who instituted important administrative reforms. Jackson claimed the credit for returning the opportunity for office to the people at large, but he also deserved the responsibility for opening the way to manipulation of the federal bureaucracy for purely partisan purposes.

Indian Affairs: An Aggressive Policy

With his purge of the officeholders under way, Jackson bent his energies toward removing the Indians, particularly the powerful Southern tribes, beyond the frontier of white settlement. In its Indian relations, the federal government had hitherto continued the early practice of treating with the tribes as though they were foreign nations, while reserving to itself the abstract right of ultimate sovereignty. As a frontier negotiator, Jackson had protested this anomaly, claiming that the treaty form clothed the tribes with the trappings of an independent sovereignty that they did not really possess. Nevertheless, the practice continued. Jurisdictional conflict between the tribes and the government was avoided simply by inducing them to remove whenever white advances created a demand for their land and threatened their tribal integrity. Just as Jackson took office, the underlying issue was finally joined. The Cherokee tribe, having acquired many of the attainments of white civilization, asserted sovereignty over its territory in Georgia and adjacent states and called on the federal government to defend it under treaty obligations. Georgia countered by formally extending its laws over all the state's Cherokee domain. Alabama and Mississippi followed by extending state jurisdiction over their Choctaw, Chickasaw, and Creek lands.

Faced with a direct contradiction between federal treaty stipulations and state sovereignty, Jackson came down unhesitatingly on the side of the latter. The government had no right to intercede on the Cherokee's behalf against Georgia, he announced; if the Indians wished to retain their tribal government and landownership, they must remove outside the state. To facilitate the removal, Jackson induced Congress in May, 1830, to pass a bill empowering him to lay off new Indian homelands west of the Mississippi, exchange them for current tribal holdings, purchase the Indians' capital improvements, and pay the costs of their westward transportation. With this authority, Jackson departed for Tennessee in June to conduct the initial negotiations in person.

To the Indians, Jackson presented a simple alternative: Submit to state authority or remove beyond the Mississippi. The Chickasaw met Jackson near Nashville and agreed to emigrate. The Choctaw followed in September, treating with Jackson's intimates John Henry Eaton and John Coffee. The Creek and Cherokee refused to come in, preferring to seek judicial support for their treaty rights, but after holding out two more years, the Creek capitulated in March, 1832.

Only the Cherokee resisted to the bitter end. In *Cherokee Nation v. Georgia* (1831) and *Worcester v. Georgia* (1832), the Supreme Court upheld the Cherokee's independence from state authority, but the decisions pointed out no practical course of resistance to Georgia's encroachments. Tacitly encouraged by Jackson, Georgia ignored the rulings. Still, the Cherokee, led by Chief John Ross, refused to remove. Jackson cultivated a minority faction within the tribe, and with this rump he negotiated a removal treaty in 1835. Under its authority, the resisting Cherokee were rounded up and removed by force after Jackson left office.

Meanwhile, dozens of similar treaties closed out the remaining pockets of Indian settlement in other states and territories east of the Mississippi. A short military campaign on the upper Mississippi quelled resistance by Black Hawk's band of Sacs and Foxes in 1832, and in 1835, a long and bloody war to subdue the Seminoles in Florida began. Most of the tribes went without resistance.

Granted the coercion and sometimes trickery that produced them, most of the removal treaties were fair, even generous. Their execution was miserable. The treaties included elaborate provisions to ensure fair payment for the Indians' lands and goods, safe transportation to the West and sustenance on arrival, and protection for the property of those individuals who chose to remain behind under state jurisdiction. These safeguards collapsed under pressure from corrupt contractors, unscrupulous traders, and white trespassers backed by state authorities. Federal officials' efforts to protect the tribes were further hamstrung by the Jackson Administration's drive for economy and its desire to avoid confrontation with state governments. For this abysmal record Jackson bore ultimate responsibility. Even under the best of circumstances, the logistics of the gigantic removal operation would have taxed the federal government's limited resources. Jackson did not countenance its inadequacies, but he did little to prevent or correct them. Though usually a stickler for the precise performance of formal obligations, he allowed his administration to enter into engagements with the Indians that it was manifestly unprepared to fulfill.

The precepts of Jackson's Indian policy differed little from those of his predecessors. Like previous presidents, he regarded Indians as children and believed that only through an extended tutelage in quarantine from white society could they absorb civilization and thus escape ultimate extinction. Yet while his predecessors undertook to uproot the tribes only in response to pressing white demand for their land, Jackson anticipated that demand, and by his posture he did much to encourage it. He made removal of the Indians, a peripheral concern in previous administrations, a central priority of his own. Inevitably, his impatience to remove the tribes encouraged other men who desired the same end and were not scrupulous as to means.

Petticoat Politics and the Nullification Controversy

Meanwhile, Jackson's Cabinet was embroiling him in difficulties. Shortly before the inauguration, John Henry Eaton, his secretary of war, had married Peggy O'Neale, the daughter of a Washington boardinghouse keeper. Peggy's previous husband, a naval purser, had committed suicide under suspicious circumstances only shortly before her marriage to Eaton. Scandalous rumors circulated about Peggy's sexual promiscuity, and Washington's formal society refused to accept her. Among those who collaborated in snubbing her were the wives of cabinet secretaries Ingham, Branch, and Berrien.

Jackson came charging to Peggy's defense. Believing her innocent, he divined a deeper plot to drive Eaton from his Cabinet, isolate himself among strangers, and control his administration. At first he blamed Henry Clay's partisans, but his suspicions soon fixed on his vice president, John C. Calhoun, whose wife, Floride, was among Peggy's persecutors. To cement Jackson's convictions, the old controversy over his Seminole campaign of 1818 suddenly flared up again. In the spring of 1830, Jackson learned that Calhoun, as secretary of war, had privately advocated disciplining Jackson for exceeding his orders while publicly posturing as his defender. Jackson now accused Calhoun of treachery, initiating an angry correspondence that ended in the severance of social relations between the two chief officers of the government.

Secretary of State Van Buren, who had no wife to contend with, also sided with Peggy Eaton's defenders, and the controversy over her morals became the vehicle for a struggle for supremacy in the administration between him and Calhoun. Both men were aspirants to the presidential succession; further, they represented competing, though loosely defined, branches of the Jackson electoral coalition. Both opposed the nationalizing "American System" policy of a protective tariff and federal subsidies for

(Courtesy of the National Portrait Gallery, Smithsonian Institution, Washington, D.C.)

John C. Calhoun
by Charles Bird King

road and canal construction (known as internal improvements) espoused by Henry Clay and embraced by the previous Adams Administration, but their opposition rested on very different grounds.

Calhoun represented a group of politicians, in his home state of South Carolina and throughout the plantation South, whose opposition to the American System rested on essentially sectional motives. The central burden of their complaint was the protective tariff. They saw it as the culprit for all the South's economic ills, especially the stagnation in cotton prices, and as a humiliating reminder of their inferior and threatened position in the Union. An unheeding Congress had raised the tariff in 1824 and again in 1828 despite their anguished protests. As they saw it, the affront was not only to their pride and pocketbooks but also to their very way of life, for the emergence of a small but vocal Northern antislavery movement had raised the specter of a strong central government controlled by a sectional antislavery majority. Though the Calhounites sought refuge in states' rights, they were not doctrinaire strict constructionists. They opposed internal improvement expenditures mainly because these created a demand for tariff revenues, and some of them defended the constitutionality of the federally chartered Bank of the United States.

Against the tariff menace, Calhoun had conceived of a procedural remedy. He and his radical cohorts considered the current tariff unconstitutional; although federal taxation of imports was clearly authorized by the Constitution, the underlying purpose—to foster American manufactures—in their opinion was not. Building on the Jeffersonian notion of a state's right to protect its own citizens from federal tyranny, Calhoun elucidated a process by which a state could formally nullify an unconstitutional federal law and prevent its enforcement. Though he had not yet publicly avowed his nullification doctrine, Calhoun was known as its author by 1830.

Van Buren's opposition to the American System came from a different quarter. He was not against a protective tariff; indeed, he had helped engineer the tariff of 1828 that so outraged the plantation South. Van Buren's political musings lay in the direction of resurrecting the old transsectional Jeffersonian Republican Party. To do so would require conciliation on the tariff, but the key in Van Buren's mind would be to return to Jeffersonian strict constructionism—in particular, to the party's traditional antagonism to federal internal improvements and a national bank.

Where Jackson stood on these questions no one yet knew. His electoral coalition had embraced not only all the American System's opponents but also many of its staunch advocates in Pennsylvania and the Northwest. Jackson himself had ducked the tariff and internal improvement issues in the 1828 campaign, and his previous record was hard to read. He claimed allegiance to the old Republican Party and its strict constructionist doctrines. As a Westerner, a strident nationalist, and a military man, however, he had also in the past supported a protective tariff to make the United States industrially self-sufficient in wartime, along with internal improvements to strengthen the frontier and facilitate military movements.

Actually, Jackson's private views were quite close to Van Buren's. Like Van Buren, he accepted the constitutionality and, within limits, the wisdom of protective tariffs. He also nursed a deep animus against the Bank of the United States. Though in other areas he had once inclined toward constitutional latitudinarianism, the transgressions of the Monroe and Adams Administrations convinced him of the urgent need to return the government to its original simplicity and purity. That meant clamping the lid on mushrooming internal improvement expenditures and returning to strict economy in government. Jackson craved the honor of presiding over the extinction of the national debt, already much reduced by previous administrations from its War of 1812 high.

Hence, as petticoat politics threw Jackson and Van Buren together, they found grounds of agreement that extended far beyond their common faith in Peggy Eaton's moral character. Though a cotton planter and slaveholder himself, Jackson decried Calhoun's brand of narrow sectionalist politics. Nullification he regarded as incipient treason, a prelude to disunion and civil war. At a political dinner in April, 1830, he pronounced his ban on it by staring at Calhoun and toasting, "Our federal Union: *It must be preserved.*"

Jackson's first move to clarify his policy came in May, 1830. When Congress convened the previous December, he had urged moderation on both the tariff and internal improvements, and on sectional conciliation in general. Ignoring his plea for restraint, the majority in Congress pushed through several major internal improvement subsidies, including three in the form of purchases in the stock of private road and canal companies. Jackson vetoed all three, singling out for an explanatory message the most politically vulnerable, a bill to subscribe $50,000 for construction of the Maysville Road in Henry Clay's home state of Kentucky. Van Buren helped write the veto message, which questioned the constitutionality of internal improvement subsidies and complained that they would exacerbate sectional tensions and postpone payment of the national debt. Southern antitariffites greeted the veto with apprehensive applause. They approved its tendency but suspected quite correctly that Jackson was not entirely in their camp. Indeed, his compromise proposal to distribute some federal funds directly to the states for their own use struck Calhoun and many Southerners as even more objectionable than direct federal internal improvement spending.

Calhoun's estrangement from Jackson deepened with the establishment of the *Washington Globe* in December, 1830, as the administration's newspaper office. A different paper, the *United States Telegraph*, had done excellent service as Jackson's campaign organ and had hitherto served as his official mouthpiece, but the *United States Telegraph*'s editor, Duff Green, was wholly devoted to Calhoun, and Jackson thought that his columns displayed too much sympathy with nullification and the Bank of the United States. To supplant him, Jackson brought in Francis Preston Blair of Kentucky. Closely associated with Blair in founding the *Washington Globe* was another Kentuckian, treasury auditor Amos Kendall. Blair and Kendall were not Van Buren's men, but like Van Buren, and unlike Green or Calhoun, they gave Jackson their complete loyalty and won his confidence in return. Together with a few other intimates—most notably Jackson's nephew and private secretary, Andrew Jackson Donelson, and his political manager, William B. Lewis—they formed a ring of confidential advisers who gave Jackson invaluable assistance in formulating his policies and presenting them to the public. Jackson's foes derisively dubbed them the Kitchen Cabinet.

A New Cabinet and a New Conception of the Cabinet's Role

While Jackson drew closer to Van Buren, the Eaton controversy smoldered on. Jackson's own household split over Peggy's acceptability, and his niece, White House hostess Emily Donelson, was banished to Tennessee for refusing to call on her. Her husband, private secretary Donelson, was at one point reduced to communicating by letter with Jackson even while living with him at the White House. Finally, to avoid utter paralysis of the administration, Van Buren and Eaton offered to resign in the spring of 1831. Jackson seized the occasion to demand the resignations of the opposing secretaries, Ingham, Branch, and Berrien. In their place, he appointed an entirely new Cabinet.

The consequences of this move were momentous. Van Buren remained in Jackson's confidence as chief counselor and expected running mate in 1832. Calhoun and his faction were formally cast out. After two years of distraction and division, the administration was now prepared to steer a direct and unimpeded course. No less important, Jackson had liberated himself from the cabinet intrigues that had ensnared his own and previous administrations. Henceforth, his official advisers would be men he chose to implement his own ideas, not factional emissaries planted there to influence him. The most successful of Jackson's later cabinet secretaries—Roger Taney, Lewis Cass, Levi Woodbury, and Amos Kendall—were workhorses who administered their departments efficiently, offered advice when asked, accepted direction when given, and stood clear of political intrigue. Those who could not harmonize with administration policy were expected to keep quiet, invited to resign, or, if necessary, simply dismissed. For the remainder of his tenure, Jackson dominated his administration as no president had before, and he pioneered for future generations the conception of the cabinet as a subordinate agent of the presidential will.

Jackson vs. The Bank of the United States

The Cabinet reconstruction of 1831 cleared the way for Jackson's next major policy move—his assault on the Bank of the United States. The bank had received a twenty-year charter from Congress in 1816. It was a private corporation, created for public purposes. The government held one-fifth of its stock and one-fifth of the seats on its board of directors. The bank's notes were legal tender for debts due the United States, and its branches served as exclusive federal depositories in their respective cities. The charter obliged the bank to perform various services, including transferring and disbursing federal funds without charge; in return, the charter guaranteed that Congress would create no competing institution.

Since its creation, the bank had provided a national currency through its notes, and in other ways had made itself useful to the Treasury. Jackson, however, was one of many who had never become reconciled either to the bank's constitutionality or to its financial power. Over his cabinet's objections, Jackson announced his opposition to a recharter of the bank in his very first message to Congress, and he had since recommended replacing the existing bank with a wholly governmental agency.

The bank's charter was due to expire in 1836. In January, 1832, its president, Nicholas Biddle, determined to apply for a recharter under the urging of Senators Daniel Webster of Massachusetts and Henry Clay of Kentucky, who were looking for an issue against Jackson in the pending presidential race. The recharter bill duly passed Congress, and on July 10, Jackson vetoed it.

The veto message, one of the most significant state papers in American history, was less an argument directed at Congress than a political manifesto to the American people. Jackson recited his constitutional objections to the bank and introduced some peculiar economic arguments against it, chiefly criticizing foreign ownership of some of its stock. (On any rational grounds, foreign investment in the underdeveloped American economy was to be welcomed, not scorned.) The crux of the message, however, was its attack on the special privileges that accrued to the bank's stockholders from their official connection to the government. Jackson did not attack wealth as such—he issued no call for class warfare or redistrubition of private assets—but he condemned the addition of public privilege to private advantages. He also set forth an alternative vision of the government as a neutral arbiter in the economy, neither assisting nor obstructing the accumulation of private fortune, intervening only where necessary to protect basic rights. Jackson's earlier congressional messages and the Maysville Road veto had intimated this fundamental theme; the bank veto stated it powerfully and definitively.

Historians have debated whether Jackson attuned his blast against the bank to the ears of Western farmers, Northeastern mechanics and laborers, or rising entrepreneurs. In fact, it was aimed at no particular class or section. Rather, it was an appeal to all of society's outsiders—to anyone who had to make his way without benefit of inherited fortune; to those who worked with their hands, owned no stock in corporations, and to whom no congressman hearkened; to those outside the commercial community that connected every city and town and that in Jackson's mind had controlled the country before his election. It was a convincing appeal because it was heartfelt. Though Jackson's own success qualified him for admission to the existing centers of political and economic power, he had never felt at home there. He had run for president in 1824 against the regular political establishment, and even in 1828, his candidacy had secured only the grudging approval of some of its members. Not a member of the bankers' circle himself, he felt the outsider's resentment against its manipulation of public power for private purposes. Hence it was with no sense of incongruity that Jackson, a well-to-do planter and slaveholder, cast himself as the tribune of the people against the aristocracy of wealth and power.

Jackson and his opponents alike seized on the bank veto as the central issue of the 1832 presidential campaign. The American System men, under the name of National Republicans, nominated Henry Clay and savaged the veto for its display of economic ignorance, its demagogic appeal to the masses, and its obstruction of the people's will as expressed through their elected representatives in Congress. The campaign was complicated by the participation of two splinter groups: the anti-Masons in the Northeast, whom the National Republicans vainly tried to absorb, and the Southern antitariffites. After failing to substitute Philip Barbour of Virginia for Van Buren as vice presidential candidate, most of the latter supported the Jackson ticket, but South Carolina ominously refused its vote to any of the national candidates.

The election returns spelled a virtual repeat of 1828. Jackson again carried New York, Pennsylvania, and all the West and South, except South Carolina and Henry Clay's home state of Kentucky. Whether the Bank veto—or any other specific issue—cost or gained Jackson votes is uncertain. His foes traced their defeat solely to his untouchable personal popularity; Jackson himself read it as a popular ratification of his policies.

A Challenge from South Carolina: Resolving the Nullification Crisis

Jackson planned a further attack on the Bank, but before he could pursue it he faced a crisis in South Carolina. There, within days after the election, a state constitutional convention formally declared the tariff laws null and void and initiated steps to prevent the collection of customs duties within the state.

Nullification was a desperate move. A series of congressional ploys against the tariff in Jackson's first term had all failed, and South Carolinians no longer saw hope for relief from Washington. Congress had indeed reduced some duties earlier in the year, and with the national debt approaching extinction, Jackson now called for still further reduction. Even as it lowered some rates, however, the tariff of 1832 enshrined the protective principle, and a majority in Congress apparently regarded the issue as settled. South Carolinians felt themselves thrown back on their own resources.

To Jackson and to most Americans, including a majority of antitariffites outside South Carolina, nullification was an inadmissible recourse. Inclined by nature to personalize every dispute, Jackson traced South Carolina's action to Calhoun's corrupt ambition to rule at home if he could not rule in Washington. Still, Jackson also saw clearly the fundamental principle at stake. Calhoun claimed that nullification would actually save the Union, by providing a method short of state secession for resisting the federal government's unconstitutional excesses. To Jackson, this was nonsense. He was a strict constructionist, an advocate of limited government, and, to that extent, a states' rights man. The reserved rights of the states, however, did not in his opinion extend to defying legitimate federal authority. The tariff was an act of Congress duly and lawfully passed, and its constitutionality, though denied by South Carolina, had never been doubted by Congresses, presidents, or the Supreme Court. If a state could unilaterally repudiate federal laws and ban the collection of federal taxes, then the Union was no Union at all. To Jackson, nullification was tantamount to secession, and secession was treason.

Jackson was prepared to uphold federal authority in South Carolina at the point of a gun, but he preferred peaceful remedies or, if there were to be violence, that the state should strike the first blow. He quietly prepared for military action yet also pointed the way to accommodation. He again urged Congress to reduce the tariff, then followed with a proclamation warning South Carolinians to abjure their folly. In ringing phrases, the proclamation enunciated Jackson's conception of the United States as an indissoluble nation, not a mere league of sovereign states. Jackson followed up the proclamation by asking Congress for legislation to enforce the collection of customs duties over South Carolina's legal obstructions.

With Jackson applying pressure from all sides, the issue was successfully compromised. Congress passed a "force bill," giving Jackson the coercive powers he requested, but it simultaneously adopted a new tariff, which reduced duties to a uniform low rate over the next nine years. South Carolina accepted the new tariff and rescinded its ordinance of nullification. The adroit solution allowed all sides to claim victory, while Jackson basked in public acclaim throughout the North for his firmness in preserving the Union. What popularity he gained in the North, however, he lost in the South. The proclamation and the force bill angered Southern states' rights

men. They gave credit for resolving the crisis, not to Jackson, but to Henry
Clay, who had introduced the compromise tariff bill, and to John Calhoun,
who had supported it.

Jackson's Second Term: The Bank War

The resolution of the nullification crisis in March, 1833, brought Jackson's
first term to an end. His record thus far was one of signal success. He had
survived the incapacitating Eaton affair and established control over his
administration, set the removal of the Indians in train, won a resounding
reelection over the opposition's best candidate, and maneuvered his man
Van Buren into position to succeed him. More important, by circumscribing
internal improvements and orchestrating the tariff settlement, he had finally
got clear of the sectional wrangling that had paralyzed the Adams Administration and threatened to rip apart the Union. He had presided over the
extinction of the national debt and revitalized the old Jeffersonian doctrine
of strict construction and limited government.

Yet, in Jackson's mind, his task was only half finished. His victories thus
far were merely personal and incomplete. He had yet to convert his own
electoral mandate into an effective instrument of policy. Congress was
uncooperative. Politicians of varying creeds were all too willing to attach
themselves to his name, and Jackson had repeatedly endured the frustration
of seeing men elected under his banner defy his most cherished recommendations. The Senate had rejected a string of important appointments,
including even Van Buren himself for minister to Great Britain after the
cabinet breakup of 1831. Congress' eagerness to spend and susceptibility to
lobbying pressure had forced Jackson to employ vetoes as his chief instruments of policy.

Jackson never doubted that the American people were on his side. He
expected popular vindication for everything that he did, and thus far his
confidence had been justified. In the face of his own resounding public support, Congress' ungovernability demanded explanation. By early 1833, Jackson had identified the culprit and had begun to see all of his myriad political
antagonists as instruments of one central foe. The reconciliation of Clay and
Calhoun, which he had anticipated long before, confirmed his suspicions;
though directly opposed to each other on the sectional issues of Jackson's
first term (with Jackson himself in the middle), they were both in his mind
instruments of the concentrated economic and political power directed by
that "hydra of corruption," the Bank of the United States.

News of the bank's activities since his veto of its recharter in 1832
outraged Jackson. The bank had been created and endowed with monopo-
listic privileges to serve the government's own needs, not those of its
stockholders or directorate. As a creature of the government, the bank,
therefore, in Jackson's eyes, had no right to an independent political char-

acter, no right to attempt to influence public policy even in defense of its own existence. Yet the bank had lavishly pamphleteered in its own defense (and implicitly against Jackson's reelection) in the 1832 campaign and had lent freely to congressmen and newspaper editors. Despite the election verdict of 1832, informants warned Jackson that Bank president Nicholas Biddle still aimed to procure a recharter.

Jackson determined to draw the bank's fangs. The bank's enormous economic and political leverage stemmed largely from its role as the depository of federal funds. The government deposits augmented the bank's own capital and enabled it to restrain the lending of state banks by gathering and presenting their notes for redemption in specie. Jackson therefore fixed on withdrawing the deposits as the surest way to disarm the bank for the three years remaining under its original charter.

Removing the deposits was a maneuver that required some delicacy. Legal authority to do it lay with the treasury secretary, not the president, and the House of Representatives had only recently voted by 109 to 46 that the deposits were safe where they were. In the spring of 1833, Jackson carefully canvassed his cabinet and confidential advisers on removal; most of them opposed it, but he got the support and arguments that he needed from Attorney General Roger Taney. Jackson next dispatched Amos Kendall on a mission to recruit state banks to accept the federal deposits. On Kendall's return, Jackson announced to the cabinet his decision to begin depositing federal revenues with selected state banks, simultaneously drawing down the government's balances in the Bank of the United States.

Here, a sticking point appeared. Treasury Secretary William John Duane, who alone possessed legal authority to order the change, refused to do it. He also refused to resign, so Jackson dismissed him and put Taney in his place. Taney duly issued the necessary order, and the drawdown, or removal, commenced on October 1. It was largely complete by the time Congress convened in early December.

The obstreperousness Jackson had met from previous Congresses was nothing to the fury he encountered in this one. A majority in Congress had supported the bank's recharter, but even many of its enemies there could not countenance Jackson's method of proceeding against it. Under the law, the secretary of the Treasury, though an appointee of the president and member of his Cabinet, was a distinct agent who, unlike other department heads, reported directly to Congress. Jackson's dismissal of Duane therefore looked like a bold stroke to draw all power over the federal purse into his own hands, and his hasty removal of the deposits seemed calculated to preempt action by Congress on a matter rightfully under its own authority. Moreover, Jackson appeared to be recklessly tampering with the nation's finances, removing control over the money supply from the responsible and lawfully sanctioned hands of the Bank of the United States to an untried, unregulated, and perhaps thoroughly irresponsible collection of state bankers. Jackson himself spoke of the arrangement with the state banks as an "experiment." Naturally, the removal forced the bank to curtail its widespread loans, and whereas Jackson and his allies accused it of exaggerating the contraction for political effect, the commercial community blamed the resulting distress on the president himself.

In the 1833–1834 congressional session, known as the "panic session," the deposit issue finally prompted Jackson's enemies to coalesce into a coherent political grouping. They called themselves Whigs, the name of British opponents of royal prerogative, to denote their opposition to Jackson's executive sway. Although political expediency obviously influenced the cooperation of men so different in principle as Clay and Calhoun, a genuine unity of outlook underlay the anti-Jackson coalition. The Whigs saw in Jackson the same danger that he saw in the bank—the threat of an unbridled centralized power, wielding sufficient money and influence to overawe or corrupt the opposition and ultimately to destroy the substance, if not the form, of republican government. It was true that Jackson claimed both a popular mandate and constitutional sanction for his actions—but tyrants have ever spoken in the name of the people. Also, Jackson's assertions of presidential authority, though made familiar to the modern ear by later experience, sounded positively dangerous to men accustomed to legislative supremacy in government.

Fortunately for Jackson, his adversaries overplayed their hand. While denunciations raged in Congress, Biddle carried the bank's financial contraction beyond what was necessary, in an undisguised effort to force a recharter on Congress and the president. The maneuver served only to confirm Jackson's strictures against the bank's unwarranted power over the national economy. The House of Representatives refused to support either recharter or the restoration of the deposits, forcing the Whig majority in the Senate to wage battle on peripheral ground. The Senate rejected Jackson's nominations for the government seats on the bank's board of directors, rejected Taney as secretary of the Treasury, and on March 28, 1834, adopted Henry Clay's resolution that "the President, in the late Executive proceedings in relation to the public revenue, has assumed upon himself authority and power not conferred by the Constitution and laws, but in derogation of both."

To this unprecedented censure, Jackson returned a formal protest, complaining that the Senate had neither specified the grounds of his offense nor followed the constitutional process of impeachment. The Senate rejected the protest as an abridgment of its own freedom of expression. The Whigs, however, could do no more. The panic eased as the congressional session closed, and the bank, defeated, began preparations to wind up its affairs.

(Courtesy of the Library of Congress, Washington, D.C.)

The Downfall of Mother Bank

The Bank War aroused violent political passions on both sides. The future not only of the bank but also of the American system of government seemed to ride on the outcome. For Jackson, his struggle took on even religious significance; he saw himself serving "the Lord" against "the worshippers of the golden Calf." Partisans on both sides attributed the vilest motives to their adversaries. Biddle privately referred to the president and his advisers as "these miserable people," whereas Jackson raged against "reckless and corrupt" United States senators.

The right and wrong of the Bank War are difficult to sort out even today. The verdict depends more on one's point of view than on any dispute over facts. The bank's defenders, then and later, argued that its management had been prudent and responsible. The bank had regulated credit and the currency precisely as Congress had chartered it to do, and did it far more efficiently than any substitute Jackson was prepared to offer. To the Whigs, the president's wanton destruction of the one great stabilizing influence in the economy was thus unpardonably ignorant at best, criminally vicious at worst.

To Jackson, such arguments were essentially irrelevant. Useful or not, the bank was illegitimate: a private institution, unsanctioned by the Constitution, employing public funds and public power to serve the ends not of the government or the people but of its own wealthy, privileged stockholders. Jackson believed that the country could do without the bank, but his fundamental grievance against it was political, not economic.

Between these opposing views no real accommodation was possible. The bank's dual public and private functions provided endless ground for misunderstanding. If it expanded its loans, Jackson accused it of political bribery; if it contracted, of blackmail. The bank's dealings with congressmen and editors, damning evidence of corruption in Jackson's eyes, were from a less malign viewpoint simple and sound business transactions. Jackson demanded reports of the bank's transactions from the government directors, in fulfillment of their public office; to the rest of the directorate, the reports were violations of bankers' confidence that justified excluding the government directors from participation in the bank's deliberations and access to its books. In these circumstances, a true noninvolvement in politics, to which Biddle had originally adhered, proved impossible to maintain, and if the bank were not the partisan agency that Jackson claimed it to be at the beginning of the Bank War, it had certainly become so by its end.

Solidifying the Democratic Party

The Bank War furnished the opportunity Jackson and his advisers had long been seeking to shape his adherents into a unitary political organization. Opposition to the Bank of the United States became the first test for membership in the new Democratic Party, and as Jackson's own thinking on monetary policy progressed, that test was expanded to include opposition to any central bank, then to banking in general. Jackson himself by mid-1834 had come to advocate stripping banks of their monetary function entirely, and replacing their notes of small denomination with gold and silver coin as the medium of everyday exchange. Banks, said Jackson, were essentially swindling machines, whose obscure transactions and erratic currency fluctuations bilked the common man of the rightful fruit of his labor.

On the banking issue thus broadly defined, the Democrats went to the people. Theirs was, again, an appeal to the outsiders in society, to the simple producers—farmers, laborers, mechanics—who did not comprehend the mysteries of banking and finance and resented the commercial community's use of them to control the economy. It was a powerful appeal, for improvements in transportation were transforming the American economy, making it more stratified and specialized, more dependent on regional and national markets. Some American heralded the new complexity and the opportunities it created, but to others, it foretold the loss of control over their lives, the end of their economic independence and political freedom. To these men, Andrew Jackson stood forth as the champion of their liberties and of the old, simple, republican virtues. As Democrats carried his message to the state and local level, they broadened it to appeal to other outsiders as well, especially to ethnic and religious groups (most notably Irish Catholics) outside the native Protestant mainstream.

Simultaneously, Jackson's men conducted a purge of the party apparatus in the states. The chief instrument of the purge was a campaign to compel the Senate to expunge the censure of Jackson from its journal of proceedings. Thomas Hart Benton of Missouri made an expunging motion in the Senate, and resolutions supporting it were promptly introduced in state legislatures. Legislators and senators who opposed expunging were thrust out of the party. With this weapon, Jackson's lieutenants forced several senators from their seats and finally brought the rebellious Senate to heel. On January 16, 1837, Benton's motion passed the Senate, and the censure was formally expunged.

Foreign Policy

While the expunging campaign progressed, the administration suddenly found its attention diverted to foreign affairs. In dealing with overseas nations, Jackson had contented himself with negotiating trade openings and settling commercial damage claims, mostly left over from the Napoleonic Wars. In these routine endeavors, he had succeeded well. His agents had secured recognition of American claims against Denmark, Spain, France, and Naples, and they had concluded commercial treaties with Turkey, Austria, Russia, Siam, Muscat, Venezuela, and Chile. Jackson's repudiation of the Adams Administration's negotiating position in order to win an agreement with Great Britain on the West Indian colonial trade in 1830 provoked partisan attack, but otherwise his overseas diplomacy was not controversial.

His attempt to collect American claims against France, however, brought the country to the brink of war. In an 1831 treaty, France had agreed to pay Fr 25 million for Napoleonic depredations on American shipping. The first installment was due in February, 1833, but the French Chamber of Deputies refused to appropriate the funds. When another year went by without payment, Jackson lost patience and asked Congress to authorize reprisals should France stall any further. The insulted French then demanded explanation of this threat as a condition of payment. Jackson responded in effect that what he said to Congress was none of a foreign power's business. The impasse deepened throughout 1835; ministers were recalled and military preparations begun. Finally, under British urgings, the French decided to construe a conciliatory passage in a later message to Congress as sufficient explanation. France paid the debt, and the crisis, once resolved, left no repercussions.

The same could not be said of Jackson's dealings with Mexico. Jackson had craved Texas for the United States ever since his days as a Tennessee militia general, and he made its purchase from Mexico the first priority of his presidential diplomacy. Given the instability of Mexico's government and its suspicion of American designs, a Texas negotiation required extreme patience and discretion to have any hope of success. The agent Jackson chose,

Anthony Butler of Kentucky, possessed neither of those qualities, and Jackson's own careless instructions encouraged Butler's clumsy dabbling in the diplomatic underworld of bribery and personal influence. Butler's machinations, combined with the flow of American settlers into Texas, served only to arouse Mexican apprehensions that the United States was bent on fomenting a revolution there. In 1835, American emigrants in Texas did revolt successfully against Mexican authority. Jackson prudently declined to back the annexation of the new Texas republic to the United States, or even to recognize its independence from Mexico without prior congressional approval, but his earlier inept efforts to purchase the province had helped to sow the seeds of mutual distrust that erupted into war between the two countries a decade later.

The Rise of the Whigs

Jackson's primary concern as his administration drew toward its close was to ensure that his policies, and particularly his hard-money and antibanking campaign, would continue beyond his own retirement to the Hermitage. He had long before settled on Martin Van Buren as the man best qualified to carry on his work, and he now bent every effort to secure Van Buren's nomination and election to the presidency. It was a difficult battle, for Van Buren was as roundly distrusted as Jackson was loved and revered. Rivals resented Van Buren's closeness to the president, and Democrats and Whigs alike considered him an artful schemer and flatterer. Further, Jackson's own forthright stance on every prominent issue of his long administration, and his vigorous and unprecedented conduct of the executive office itself, had aroused opposition at one time or another in many quarters. Men who could not bear—or did not dare—to disagree directly with Jackson himself were quick to assign responsibility for their grievances to Van Buren. He had become, unwittingly, the universal scapegoat of the Jackson Administration.

Given his initial unpopularity and the weight of accumulated complaints against him, Van Buren needed the full weight of Jackson's influence behind his candidacy. Jackson wrote letters, attended political functions (which he had shunned during his own campaign), threatened reprisals on dissenters, and oversaw the Democratic convention that nominated Van Buren in May, 1835. The Whigs, who lacked a central directing head and hence lagged behind the Democrats in party organization, capitalized on the diversity of disgruntlement with Van Buren by encouraging the candidacies of regional favorites. William Henry Harrison of Ohio emerged as their main candidate, but Daniel Webster of Massachusetts and Hugh Lawson White of Tennessee also received Whig backing. Tennessee deserted the Democrats for White, a former Jackson intimate who had gradually fallen out of his confidence. The defection mortified Jackson, and he poured out his bitterest denunciations against White and the Democratic apostates who backed his candidacy.

Van Buren won the election. Even without a national candidate against him, however, he garnered a bare majority of the popular vote, and the real message of the campaign was the rise of the Whigs and Jackson's failure to pass on his own personal popularity to his Democratic successors. The party Van Buren inherited was better disciplined and more clearly focused than the diffuse coalition that had swept Jackson into office eight years before, but it was also smaller. Henceforth, Whigs and Democrats would do battle on nearly equal terms.

A Debased Currency

While working to ensure the succession, Jackson also refined and extended his campaign for hard money. His destruction of the Bank of the United States had inadvertently encouraged the spread of bank currency, as state governments proceeded to fill the void by chartering new banks that issued notes without any central restraint. There was an eager demand for this capital, for a decade of general growth and prosperity had begun to culminate in a speculative land boom. Federal revenue from Western land sales, which had previously hung at $2 to $3 million annually, leaped to $11 million in 1835 and to $24 million in 1836. Unwanted banknotes of dubious convertibility poured in, producing an embarrassing treasury surplus.

Jackson was appalled at this debasement of the currency, so contrary to his own intentions. He viewed the problem as essentially moral, tracing the profusion of banknotes not to impersonal economic forces but to the unrestrained spirit of speculation and avarice. He called again for the stricter regulation of banking and for the elimination of notes of small denomination, and in July, 1836, he directed the issuance of a specie circular, which required payment in coin for federal lands. In June, Congress did provide statutory regulation of the federal deposit banks and limited their issuance of notes, but, by the same act, disbursed the deposits among a much larger number of banks, then unloaded the treasury surplus by returning it to the state governments as a "deposit"—in form, a loan; in effect, a gift. These measures merely forced a shifting of balances among the banks. Even had they understood it to be necessary, neither Jackson nor Congress possessed the tools for the delicate and perhaps impossible task of easing down an overheated economy. As Jackson prepared to leave office, the nation's financial structure teetered on the edge of a deflationary collapse.

The Impact of Jackson's Presidency

Jackson's quiet departure from the White House in March, 1837, stood in sharp contrast to his tumultuous entrance eight years earlier. The administration's final weeks were calm, almost spiritless. Age and an accumulation of bodily ailments had finally caught up with Jackson; during his last congressional session, he was practically an invalid. Before retiring, however, he roused his strength for one more veto—of a bill overriding the specie circular—and for a farewell address, issued on the day of Martin Van Buren's inauguration as president.

The very act of delivering such an address bespoke Jackson's understanding of the extraordinary importance of his presidency. No chief executive since George Washington had departed office with a formal valedictory. Jackson began humbly, thanking the people for their confidence. In fatherly phrases, he admonished them to cherish the Union, avoid sectional divisions, and preserve the Constitution in its original purity.

Jackson's mood shifted sharply as he went on to discuss banking and currency. He condemned paper money as an engine of oppression in the hands of the bankers. In dark tones, he warned of a conspiracy of "the money power" to control the state and federal governments and subvert the liberties of the people.

In eight years, Jackson had fundamentally reordered the American political landscape. He entered the presidency at the end of a decade when the stresses and hardships of economic development had given rise to sectional conflict over the issues of the tariff and internal improvements. More than any politician of his day, Jackson stood above sectional feelings. Seeing that sectional antagonisms jeopardized the permanence of the Union, he sought with remarkable success to quiet the issues that prompted them. Though the ultimate sectional issue—slavery—began to intrude into politics during his term, the economic questions of the previous decade lost most of their divisive force under his conciliatory influence.

Jackson, however, substituted a new set of demons for the old. In the place of sectional opponents, he identified a new threat to the republic in the commercial oligarchy of bankers, speculators, and chartered corporations. Like many Americans, he was alarmed by the growing complexity and interdependency of the national economy. Interpreting it as a corrupt conspiracy rather than an economic process, he appealed in vivid language for the American people to redeem their traditional liberties and virtues from this alien power.

Jackson's attack on the money power set the tone for a generation of Democratic politicians. At the same time, his conduct of the presidency reshaped the structure of American politics. Elected president on a wave of popular enthusiasm, he had interposed his will against Congress, vetoing more bills than all of his predecessors put together. For justification, he appealed over the head of Congress directly to the mass of people, in the unshakable conviction that they would support him. Reversing a tradition in American politics, he claimed that he as president represented the people directly, whereas Congress represented only special interests. To make this claim effective, to transform his personal popularity into a workable instrument of policy, he and his advisers labored to shape his following into a political party. In thus forging a link between the highest and lowest levels of government, between the people and the president, Jackson elevated the importance of the presidential office and reduced the importance of Congress—especially the Senate—by bringing its members within reach of the party apparatus. At the same time, Jackson's bold measures and political innovations prompted his foes to coalesce into an opposing partisan organization. The Democratic Party was Jackson's child; the antebellum two-party system was his legacy.

Yet with all of his importance to the development of the American political system, Jackson's dominance of an era rested as much on his forceful personality as on his particular achievements. His character, which combined tremendous strengths with appalling weaknesses, inspired devotion from his friends, loathing from his enemies. Contemporaries disagreed violently in their assessment of Jackson, and historians have followed in their paths.

Concluding Perspectives: Jackson the Man

Jackson cut such a titanic figure that both admirers and detractors reckoned him an elemental force rather than a human being. Henry Clay likened him to a tropical tornado. Jackson's determination and willpower impressed friends and enemies alike. Intimates marveled at his fortitude. He suffered constant pain, and he often appeared so feeble that friends feared for his life; yet he met the demands of a brutal work and social schedule. He seemed to keep himself alive by sheer determination, an awesome domination of the will over the flesh. His moods, like the weather, were unpredictable. His violent rages were legendary, yet he could be perfectly cool when the occasion required. White House visitors who were expecting to see a growling monster were charmed by his courtly demeanor and pleasant conversation.

Jackson radiated a magnificent self-assurance. Both as a general and as a president, he never admitted the possibility of defeat and never suffered it. His faith in his own ability to master the task at hand, no matter how formidable, mesmerized his associates. He seemed to be without weakness and without fear. Jackson's confidence in himself was an important political asset. It enabled him to overawe his enemies, for few men could face him without blinking; and it drew to his side weaker men, less sure of themselves, who found their strength in him.

Yet Jackson upheld this tremendous strength of character only at great cost in flexibility. He was indeed indomitable, but not infallible; yet, like many of his admirers, he tended to confuse the two. Though he condemned flattery, he was an easy mark for it. He could not take criticism, and he was extraordinarily sensitive to imagined personal slights. He viewed himself entirely too seriously to enjoy or even permit a joke at his own expense; indeed, he seemed to find little humor in anything. Though he made many errors in his long career, he could not acknowledge them, even to himself. He never apologized and rarely explained. His self-righteousness, combined with a wholly unwarranted confidence in the accuracy of his own memory, trapped him in one pointless personal controversy after another, and when he was in the wrong he sometimes stooped to substitute bluster for truth.

Throughout his life, Jackson wore a pair of moral blinders. He saw his own path of duty marked clearly ahead and followed it rigorously, but no alternative perspectives or courses of action ever entered his field of vision. He simply believed that whatever he did was right. Hence, he never learned to accept political disagreement with the equanimity of a Henry Clay or Martin Van Buren. He took all opposition as a personal affront. Trusting as much in the people's virtue as in his own, he ascribed every victory of an opposition candidate to fraud or deception. Jackson was neither gracious in adversity nor magnanimous in triumph. He railed bitterly after his own defeat in 1824 and Van Buren's in 1840, and he exulted at Whig president William Henry Harrison's sudden death after only one month in office.

Trapped inside his own clear but narrow view of the world, Jackson failed to see the contradictions in his own career, which critics wrongly attributed to conscious hypocrisy. He thought himself modest and humble, though he was neither. He repeated so often the myth that he had never sought public office that he apparently came to believe it, even though his whole career bespoke otherwise. Although outraged at violations of his own confidence, he willingly read others' private mail when it was shown to him. He excoriated the Adams Administration for corruption and partisan manipulation of the patronage, failings that were much more evident in his own. Opposed to a strong central government, he greatly strengthened the presidency, its most concentrated locus of power.

The depth of Jackson's emotional engagement in his political career, his unremitting search for personal vindication and for victory over his foes, suggest a character controlled by some deeply seated animus. His enemies—and some later historians—appraised him as a driven, vengeful, self-obsessed man. Yet the traits they condemned were fused with others that inspired reverence and devotion from those who knew him well.

Jackson was a faithful husband and a loving and indulgent father. He lavished affection on the wife and children of his adopted son, Andrew, Jr., and he exhibited endless patience with Andrew's own serious failings. Curiously, Jackson found it much easier to forgive personal shortcomings than political transgressions, and from those who gave him their loyalty he could tolerate almost any fault. He had many wards—relatives and children of deceased comrades—and he gave freely of money for their education and advice to guide their careers. Examples of his private generosity and kindness are legion. Widows and orphans found him an easy touch. He demanded good treatment for his slaves and dismissed overseers who handled them too roughly.

Though he did not join the Presbyterian church until very late in life, Jackson was a religious man. He cared little for doctrine, but he enjoyed hearing sermons and found consolation in the Bible and devotional literature. He coupled an unquestioning faith in his own destiny with a humble, almost fatalistic submission to the workings of Providence. A simple Christian charity was the centerpiece of his religious practice.

Jackson's mind was quick and forceful, but not subtle. His associates marveled at his ability to cut through to the heart of a difficult subject—which indeed he could do if the argument were reducible to a simple principle of direct action. More complex and sophisticated expositions eluded his comprehension; he dismissed them as trickery. Firm in his political convictions, he saw no need to explore them through systematic thought. With the great moral and intellectual dilemma of his era—the problem of slavery—he never concerned himself; he simply accepted the institution. Characteristically, he interpreted the rising abolitionist agitation as a political ploy to disrupt the Union and the Democratic Party, and on that ground he condemned it.

Jackson had few intellectual or cultural pursuits, though he liked to attend the theater, and few diversions other than horse racing, to which he was passionately devoted. He read mainly newspapers. He had acquired the gentleman planter's expensive tastes in food and wine, along with a sufficient veneer of higher learning to scatter classical allusions (sometimes misplaced) throughout his letters. Contemporaries attested his extraordinary abilities as a conversationalist, but they left little hint of what he talked about besides politics.

Jackson's writing lacked polish, but he had a gift for vigorous expression. He was best with maxims: "Our federal Union: it must be preserved" and "Ask nothing that is not right; submit to nothing that is wrong" were classics, and he repeated them often. With the help of Andrew Jackson Donelson, Jackson kept up a voluminous private correspondence. For aid in formal composition, he relied on Donelson, Van Buren, Kendall, and Blair, plus other advisers of the moment. The nullification proclamation was largely Edward Livingston's work; the farewell address, Roger Taney's. Most of Jackson's major presidential papers were group productions. They were always intended for the public eye, even when addressed to Congress. Measured against the florid standards of that era, Jackson's state papers were masterpieces of clarity and lucidity.

Throughout Jackson's presidency, he yearned for a quiet retirement at the Hermitage, but when the time for it came, he found that he could not let go of politics. Indeed, he was as unprepared as ever to lead the withdrawn life of a country gentleman. He yearned to see his policies carried through and what he called "my fame" upheld. In the financial panic that broke as Jackson left office, President Van Buren required guidance and fortitude. Jackson willingly supplied both. He demanded a complete divorce of the government from the banks and badgered Van Buren and Francis Preston Blair with advice, exhortations, and warnings. He summoned all of his failing energies in behalf of Van Buren's independent treasury plan and his reelection bid in 1840.

William Henry Harrison's defeat of Van Buren staggered Jackson, but he soon found cause for rejoicing in Harrison's death and his successor John Tyler's reversion to Democratic principles on banking and the tariff. To his great satisfaction, Jackson's influence was again required from Washington, this time in behalf of the annexation of Texas. Ever eager for Texas, Jackson enlisted avidly in the annexation cause and when Van Buren declared against it, he helped set in train the movement to jettison Van Buren in favor of Tennessean James K. Polk for the 1844 Democratic nomination. Before Jackson died, he reaped the final vindication of seeing his loyal disciple Polk installed in the presidency to carry on his work.

Honors and tributes enriched Jackson's retirement. He was the living apostle of democracy, and an endless parade of well-wishers journeyed to the Hermitage to do him homage. Jackson welcomed them all. Though he accepted public tributes with an air of diffident humility, he never tired of them, and in 1840, he dragged himself to New Orleans for an exhausting celebration of the twenty-fifth anniversary of his great military triumph. Conscious of his historical importance and jealous of his reputation, Jackson occupied much of his spare time in arranging his papers and overseeing preparations for Amos Kendall's projected biography.

Financial worries darkened Jackson's final years. The luckless Andrew, Jr., conjured up debts without end and meeting them gradually drained away Jackson's assets. In the end, despite his horror of indebtedness, the old chief was driven to borrowing large sums from the faithful Francis Preston Blair. Jackson died in comfort but with his once ample estate heavily encumbered by debt.

Gradually, the weight of age, illness, and worry bore down on Jackson. For years, his health had been precarious, yet he had recovered from the brink so many times that friends half seriously questioned his mortality. Jackson knew better. He had long anticipated death, and he faced it without fear. In the spring of 1845, his condition worsened, and on June 8 he died, surrounded by family and friends. He was buried at the Hermitage, next to Rachel.

Daniel Feller

Bibliographical References

Andrew Jackson has had several biographers. The newest biography, Robert V. Remini's three-volume *Andrew Jackson*, 1977–1984, is an adoring portrait. Marquis James, *Andrew Jackson*, 1933–1937, makes lively reading, as does Remini's one-volume *Andrew Jackson*, 1966. Arthur Schlesinger, Jr., *The Age of Jackson*, 1945, presents the most provocative and influential view of Jackson's historical significance. For critical psychological assessments, see Michael Paul Rogin, *Fathers and Children*, 1975, and James C. Curtis, *Andrew Jackson and the Search for Vindication*, 1976. The earliest and biggest scholarly biography, by James Parton, *Life of Andrew Jackson*, 1860, is still in many ways the best. There is extensive recent literature on some of the chief topics of Jackson's administration—Indian removal, nullification, and the Bank War.

The Papers of Andrew Jackson, a comprehensive edition of fifteen volumes, is now in publication. John Spencer Bassett's *Correspondence of Andrew Jackson*, 1926–1935, though less thorough, presents an excellent selection. No one interested in Jackson's presidency should fail to consult his state papers, collected in James D. Richardson, *Messages and Papers of the Presidents*, 1896–1899.

MARTIN VAN BUREN

1837–1841

On March 4, 1837, Martin Van Buren became the eighth president of the United States. It was a beautiful early spring day, and great numbers turned out for the occasion. Some lined the route from the White House to the Capitol to see Van Buren and the outgoing president ride by in an open carriage; many others gathered at the East Portico to witness the inaugural ceremonies. Yet a dramatic happening at the end of the ceremonies showed that the crowds belonged to the old president and not the new one: As the inaugural party returned to the carriage, Andrew Jackson was greeted with thunderous cheering and applause. "For once," Thomas Hart Benton later recalled, "the rising was eclipsed by the setting sun." Three days later President Van Buren escorted Jackson to the rail station where the old hero began the first leg of his journey back to the Hermitage. Only then, many felt, did the new presidency begin.

Or was it the "third term" of Jackson? Most observers supposed that Van Buren had become president through Jackson's influence and had bound himself to defend the heritage. His preelection pledge "to tread generally in the footsteps of President Jackson" was thus welcomed by Democrats and understood by Whigs in the same light, even though they would at times indulge the temptation to taunt Van Buren for a "footsteps administration." The central domestic measure of his presidency, the independent Treasury, followed logically from the policy of his predecessor: Jackson's Bank War had separated the Treasury from the national bank; in response to the panic of 1837, Van Buren divorced Treasury operations from the state banks as well. To him also fell much of the burden for carrying out Jackson's policy of Indian removal. In other ways, however, Van Buren pursued a distinctly different course. More cautious than Jackson, he kept the peace at a time when problems with Mexico and Great Britain might have drawn a bolder spirit into war. With a keen awareness of the sectional tensions generated by abolitionism, he worked, in like manner, for sectional peace. After the stormy events of Jackson's administration, moreover, the new president sought to give the nation a period of repose. Finally, a brief review of Van Buren's earlier career will show that he had helped to shape the heritage he vowed as president to defend.

(Courtesy of the New York Historical Society, New York City)
The Rejected Minister
We never can make him President, without first making him Vice-President

The Fox of Kinderhook

The long road Van Buren followed from Kinderhook, New York, to the White House also dramatized the remarkable achievements of a self-made man. He was born on December 5, 1782, into the household of Abraham and Hannah Van Buren, both of respectable if undistinguished Dutch stock. From his father, a somewhat improvident farmer and tavern keeper, the son received an amiable temper, robust health, and Republican politics, but not the means for a good education. Ending his formal schooling at fourteen, the young Van Buren read law for the next seven years and then began his own practice in Kinderhook. Once established in the law, he married a childhood playmate, Hannah Hoes, and began a family amounting to four sons before her untimely death in 1819. (Though there were later flirtations and the rumor of a union with Thomas Jefferson's granddaughter, he never remarried.) Meanwhile, a move to Hudson and then to Albany marked growing success in his profession, earning for him a comfortable estate, the respect of his fellow lawyers, and consideration in the 1820's for appointment to the Supreme Court. In default of higher education, the law provided the basic discipline for his mind and served to deepen a conservative instinct to accept the existing arrangements of society. As a public official he was ever disposed, as in his law practice, to react to specific events rather than to shape them.

Politics, along with the law, engaged Van Buren from an early day and opened the pathway to power. Political talk in his father's tavern, revolving around the dramatic struggles in the 1790's between Federalists and Republicans, fired a lifelong passion. During the next two decades, he exhibited a sure instinct for the winning side among the warring factions in New York and reaped, as a reward, appointment as a county judge, election to the state senate, and the commission of attorney general. Attributing his success to the shady arts of management and intrigue, foes condemned him as a "politician by trade," a low-class upstart presuming to enter the political sphere once reserved for gentlemen. Close associates of Van Buren, by contrast, pointed to a keen knowledge of human nature which enabled him to penetrate the motives and foil the designs of his enemies. He possessed as well a remarkable capacity for self-control, a suavity of manners, and a smoothness of style that helped him conciliate friends and relate with good sportsmanship to opponents.

Personal appearance added to the force of his style and lent some measure of support to the image foes cast of him as a "red fox" or "little magician." Fashionably dressed, meticulously groomed, and endowed with grace of movement, he struck most observers as shorter than five foot six, and this impression remained as obesity overtook him later on. Even more striking was his large round head, bald by the middle years and framed by thick sideburns of sandy red and gray hair. Giving further feature to his countenance were big blue penetrating eyes and the ever-present trace of a smile, suggesting benign contentment to some and calculating guile to others. It was the face of a man who might be expected, as one contemporary observed, "to row to his object with muffled oars." Others found in it an explanation for his "noncommittalism," that is, his knack of drawing out the views of others without revealing his own. Van Buren often chuckled at this charge and included one outrageous example of it in his autobiography. When asked if he thought the sun rose in the east, he replied, "I presumed the fact was according to the common impression, but, as I invariably slept until after sun-rise, I could not speak from my own knowledge."

Political success for Van Buren ultimately depended on the power of party. By the first quarter of the nineteenth century, two developments— the triumph of egalitarian ideals and the extension of suffrage to all adult white males—rendered increasingly obsolete older patterns of deference and rule by patrician elites. Permanent party organization and techniques of mass appeal were a response to the new democratic realities, providing a means for mobilizing voters, defining issues, and choosing officials. Politics became a profession and "new men" of politics embraced the opportunity to participate in the governing process. As one of the new men, Van Buren played a central role in party organization. During the decade after the War of 1812, he and close associates forged a disciplined party based on spoils, the secret caucus, and an ethos of absolute loyalty to majority rule. With this organization, soon to be known as the Albany Regency, they were able to challenge their patrician adversary, De Witt Clinton, and lay a solid base for controlling the state. Claiming lineal descent from Jefferson, they also embraced the old republican ideology.

Elected to the United States Senate in 1821, Van Buren went to Washington with the aim of reviving party competition at the national level. The demise of the Federalist Party after the War of 1812 ushered in the so-called era of good feelings, hailed by many as a return to the normal state of affairs. Van Buren, however, saw it as an era of bad feelings: The breakdown of party competition across state and sectional lines fragmented political conflict, led to the Missouri controversy, and assured the election of neo-Federalist, John Quincy Adams, in the disputed presidential contest of 1824. He thus sought to resuscitate the old party alliance of Southern planters and the plain republicans of the North on which Jefferson had built the old Republican Party. As a spokesman for states' rights and strict construction, Van Buren warned of the consolidationist tendencies in the policies Adams proposed. Meanwhile, he took a leading role in the coalition behind Andrew Jackson to foil the bid of Adams for reelection. He was especially anxious to harness Jackson's enormous popularity for party purposes and to make the election of 1828 a rerun of earlier contests between Federalists and Republicans. Van Buren also ran for governor of New York in 1828 to help the national ticket, and the favorable returns confirmed the wisdom of this move.

After a tenure of three months as governor, Van Buren resigned the post in Albany and returned to Washington in early 1829 to join the Jackson Administration. There he served in turn as secretary of state, minister to England, and vice president in the second term. As a diplomat he succeeded in opening trade with the British West Indies and in initiating the negotiations that led to French payment of past claims. In domestic affairs Van Buren exerted little influence over specific policies other than Jackson's opposition to internal improvements. His greatest influence came in the role as confidant to the president, as political interpreter of events, and, most of all, through his efforts to shape Jackson's perception of the presidency in party terms. All earlier presidents, however political and partisan, had clung to the old ideal of the president above party, but starting with Jackson the president began to see himself as the leader of a party as well as the leader of the nation. In the midst of the tumultuous Bank War, out of which the Whig opposition finally formed, Van Buren summarized for Jackson the statesmanship of a politics of conflict. "Their hatred is the best evidence of your orthodoxy," he assured the president, "and the highest compliment that can be paid to your patriotism." Van Buren saw that party competition was both the inescapable product of a free society and the best means to keep it free.

The great influence Van Buren enjoyed in Jackson's administration predictably inspired opponents to charge that the little magician was at it again. How else, they asked, could a suave New York "politician" gain favor with the "border captain" except by management and intrigue? It was true, of course, that Van Buren was not unversed in the arts of flattery; solicitude for Jackson in their private correspondence was matched in public statements with praise for the old hero's virtues. Yet there was something in the relationship that did credit to both men. For all his prudence and caution, Van Buren at times expressed genuine admiration for Jackson's boldness and unflinching courage, his intuitive sense of public opinion, and his ability to command the trust of the people. Jackson also derived great benefit from the relationship. With sensitivity and good taste, Van Buren served as friend and comforter to an often ill and lonely old man. Jackson also depended on his counsel in assessing political situations. While Van Buren was in England, Jackson complained that one adviser could never say no and another "knows nothing of mankind." Most of all, Van Buren was loyal, supporting Jackson's decisions once made with "immovable constancy." Though he initially opposed the Bank War, he assured Jackson in the midst of the battle that "I go with you agt. the world." If this sounded like shameless sycophancy, it expressed even more clearly a political ethic of subordinating private judgment to the will of the party. Even before the political fireworks in Washington brought about the fall of John C. Calhoun, whom many took to be the heir apparent, Jackson had privately confided to a friend that Van Buren was worthy of the succession.

The Jackson Succession

With Jackson's support Van Buren was chosen by the Democratic Party convention in 1832 to be the vice presidential running mate, and four years later he was nominated to succeed Jackson as president. While thus treading in Jackson's steps, he was also following some of his own, for he had done much to shape the party that chose him. A number of political circumstances in 1836 also indicated that he would need to take other steps on his own. Many elements contributed to a pervasive sense of restlessness in the nation. The arising incidence of mob action was directly linked by the Whigs to the Caesarian personality of Jackson and his stormy policies. At the same time a new and strident voice of abolitionism arose in the North. Among other things its petitions to Congress and the distribution of "inflammatory" propaganda through the mails brought tensions in the South to a new level. One response was the storming of the Charleston post office by a mob; another and more fateful one was the emergence of the argument for slavery as a positive good.

The movement of economic forces enhanced the sense of restlessness and lent new urgency to political debate. A cycle of economic expansion after 1830 mounted to a speculative boom by 1835 and then by the middle of the following year, began to give way to the opposing forces of contraction. Whigs pointed a finger at Jackson's war on the national bank which, in their view, had exerted a stabilizing influence over the state banks and the currency. More serious for Van Buren was a division within his own party over banking and currency. Senator Thomas Hart Benton spoke for the "hard-money" Democrats who blamed the economic fluctuations on the state banks, a number of which were being used by the Treasury as depositories. He believed that a greatly enlarged circulation of specie would serve to keep bank paper in check and stabilize the economy. Other Democrats, soon to be called Conservatives, defended the state banks, believing that if properly managed by the Treasury they could at once stabilize the currency and sustain a desirable level of economic growth. Personal ambition gave an added dimension to these intraparty differences. Senator William C. Rives of Virginia, one of the leading Conservatives, felt bitter because he had been passed over for the vice presidential nomination, which went instead to a Western hero of sorts, Colonel Richard M. Johnson of Kentucky, the reputed slayer of the Indian chief Tecumseh.

Whig strategy in 1836 exploited Van Buren's problems. Instead of uniting behind one candidate, Whigs supported three in the hope that the sectional appeal of each—Senator Hugh L. White of Tennessee, General William Henry Harrison of Ohio, and Senator Daniel Webster of Massachusetts—might keep Van Buren from winning an electoral majority and thereby throw the choice of president into the House of Representatives. Making a virtue of their diversity, moreover, Whigs invoked old antiparty ideals for the purpose of condemning Van Buren as a spoilsman politician and the handpicked puppet of Caesar. Finally, they spoke a various language in different parts of the country. In the South, they pictured Van Buren as a covert abolitionist; in the West, as a foppish sycophant in contrast to Harrison, who had defeated the Indians at Tippecanoe; and in the Northeast, as a proslavery champion and a "Loco Foco," that is, a hard-money man scheming to wreck banking and commerce. Happily for Van Buren, his 170 electoral votes, compared with 124 votes for all of his foes, foiled the Whig strategy.

Van Buren as President: A Call for National Repose

Van Buren entered the White House in 1837 determined to give the nation a breathing spell or, as one adviser put it, to "let the troubled waters subside." To the surprise of many, who considered him the prince of spoilsmen, he made no outright removals from office. If sensitive to the spoilsman charge, he also feared that the competition for jobs might deepen intraparty divisions. He likewise decided to retain Jackson's cabinet which, in any case, he had played a large role in selecting. For the one vacancy, secretary of the War Department, he turned first to Senator Rives, hoping by the appointment to reassure the South and mollify the senator's disappointment. When Rives refused the appointment, Van Buren gave it to Joel R. Poinsett, a Unionist leader in South Carolina during the nullification crisis.

Van Buren's inaugural address can also be read as a call for national repose. Fifty years after the Constitution was written, he observed, the "great experiment" had proved a success. Most of the dangers that the Founding Fathers feared might wreck the Union had been overcome; now it remained only for the sons to "perpetuate a condition of things so singularly happy." The heroic Fathers had won freedom on the battlefield, ordered it by "inestimable institutions," and left to later generations the task of preservation. To dramatize the unheroic role of preservation remaining to the sons, Van Buren pictured himself as a lesser figure of a later age and invited others to share his reverence for the illustrious predecessors "whose superiors it is our happiness to believe are not found on the executive calendar of any country." If seen as a bow to the conventional pieties of the day, his self-deprecating position must also be taken as a statesmanlike effort to assess the point at which the nation had arrived.

In this light he saw only one great danger that remained, namely, the disorganizing effect of abolitionist agitation. Addressing the danger, he reaffirmed a campaign pledge to veto any measure of Congress touching slavery in the District of Columbia. John Quincy Adams, back in the House after his term as president, called Van Buren a "northern man with southern feelings." Van Buren, however, saw himself as a Northern man with national feelings, driven by the conviction that the federative Union fashioned in a spirit of concession and that compromise was the highest good.

Maintaining sectional harmony was one of the important achievements of Van Buren's presidency. As the leader of a party, he worked for an accommodation between its Northern and Southern members, and the course he charted while vice president continued after he entered the White House. On the one side, he enlisted the support of Northern Democrats against abolitionism. In concert with leaders in New York, he orchestrated protest meetings condemning the new wave of antislavery agitation. While presiding over the Senate, he cast the deciding vote for Calhoun's bill giving postmasters discretionary power in handling "inflammatory" materials. Behind the scenes in the Capitol, he also supported the so-called gag rule, a procedural rule in the House by which abolitionist petitions would be admitted into the chamber but then tabled.

On the other side, Van Buren persuaded party spokesmen from the South to yield for the time their desire for the annexation of slaveholding Texas. Poinsett, a former minister to Mexico, and Secretary of State John Forsyth of Georgia were among those strongly in favor of Texas, but as good party men they recognized the volatility of the issue in the North and the need to harmonize party councils. When the Texas minister formally requested annexation in August of 1837, Secretary Forsyth served as Van Buren's polite but firm voice against it.

Foreign Affairs

Van Buren's efforts for sectional harmony were matched by his efforts for peace with foreign countries. The bad state of relations with Mexico at the end of Jackson's term required immediate attention. Bent on the annexation of Texas, Jackson had mounted pressures on Mexico to pay old claims, threatening reprisals and delivering a final ultimatum from a naval vessel. Van Buren reversed these priorities, dropped the idea of annexation, and sought peace with Mexico. The response of Mexico to his first effort at negotiation in 1837 was not acceptable, but he quickly agreed to a counter-proposal made in April, 1838, for submitting the claims issue to an arbitration commission. The president went an extra mile with Mexico, moreover, patiently indulging delays that held up the formation of a commission until August, 1840. The final award of $2 million to the United States came after he left the White House, but peace was for him of greater value.

Two crises with Britain posed a greater threat to peace. One rose out of the rebellion in Canada, which began in the lower provinces and spread by the end of 1837 to the upper part. Sympathy for the rebels among Americans along the border led many to send aid and others to enlist for action. In this context the *Caroline* affair in late December seemed to make war imminent. The *Caroline*, a small craft supplying rebels out of Buffalo, was seized by British forces on the American side of the Niagara River and sunk with the loss of one life. Yet the drums of war in western New York sounded much fainter in Washington, where two quick decisions by President Van Buren signaled a peaceful intent. He filed a formal demand for explanations from the British minister, Henry Fox, but indicated a willingness to wait for the response from the home government. He then issued a proclamation, warning Americans that any violations of neutrality would forfeit their right to protection by the government.

A second flare-up came in October, 1838, when Americans joined the rebel invasion of Canada in the Detroit area and at Prescott on Lake Ontario. Strong British forces easily repelled the attacks, in the process of which more than two score of Americans were killed and a larger number captured. News of the defeat cooled enthusiasm for the rebels, as did a second and more strongly worded proclamation from the president in November. By the following year, the promise to Canada of more self-government contained in Lord Durham's report substantially ended the rebellion. Van Buren never received an apology for the *Caroline* incident from the British, but the blessings of peace disposed him, as one close acquaintance observed, to "let sleeping dogs lie."

A second and more serious crisis arose in early 1839 over the disputed Maine-New Brunswick boundary. Possessing little geographical knowledge of the area, the treaty makers at Paris in 1783 probably expected the boundary to be fixed by later negotiation. From the 1790's through the Jackson Administration, however, a number of efforts brought agreement on only one thing—that the lower part of the St. John, a river that flowed in a southeast direction from the St. Lawrence highlands to the Bay of Fundy, belonged to New Brunswick. With regard to the upper St. John, profound differences emerged. Americans claimed it all—the main Aroostook tributary on the south side closest to the Maine settlements and the Madawaska tributary farther up the St. John on the north side. For diplomatic reasons Britain also claimed it all, but her primary concern was the Madawaska, the control of which was vital for an overland military road from the Bay of Fundy to Quebec during the winter when the St. Lawrence was frozen. Complicating the prospects of compromise was the political situation in Maine, where each party sought to outmatch the other in opposition to any concessions to the British. By the time Van Buren became president, incidents on both sides had raised tensions to a new level. The presence of Maine census takers in the Madawaska alarmed New Brunswick, and timber poachers from New Brunswick in the Aroostook area threatened one of Maine's vital interests.

The crisis came to a head in February, 1839. Without prior consultation with the president, Governor John Fairfield ordered the Maine militia northward to the Aroostook; in response, British forces at the Madawaska went on the alert. Van Buren moved quickly and evenhandedly to regain control of the nation's relations with Britain. While calling on Congress for added means to defend the nation, he sternly warned Maine that the central government would assume no responsibility for the aggressive actions of the state militia. He then worked out the essentials of a truce with the British minister in Washington to keep the peace until the home governments reached a final settlement of the boundary. By its terms, the Madawaska would be considered in the New Brunswick "sphere of influence," while Maine retained control over the Aroostook. To secure the truce Van Buren then sent General Winfield Scott to the troubled area and by the end of March, Scott was able to announce that the governors of Maine and New Brunswick had agreed to the truce. Van Buren thus achieved his goal of "peace with honor." He also paved the way for a final settlement three years later: The terms of his truce defined the basic boundary provisions of the

Webster-Ashburton Treaty.

The Indian Question

The question of peace or war was also involved in another matter of concern—the removal of the Southern Indian tribes to Oklahoma. In 1830 Jackson had pushed enabling legislation through Congress for that purpose, and by the end of his term all the tribes had moved or were in motion, except the Cherokee and the Seminoles. The Cherokee were the larger tribe, numbering from fifteen to twenty thousand and scattered over the states of North Carolina, Georgia, Alabama, and Tennessee. Under the Treaty of New Echota, made in December, 1835, they were to move the following year, but the repudiation of the treaty by many of the chiefs was among the reasons for delay. With a new deadline fixed for May, 1838, Van Buren called on General Scott to supervise the removal. Using some regular army units and a larger number of state militia, he began the process of rounding up the Indians from their scattered villages and directing them to three staging areas on the upper Tennessee River. Low water caused by a summer dry spell held up the process until fall, at which time the Cherokee began the long and painful journey over the "Trail of Tears." Van Buren had more personal doubts about removal than Jackson, yet he accepted it as a commitment that had to be honored. Given the anguish and suffering involved, the removal was a relatively peaceful and orderly process for which Scott won Van Buren's praise.

(Courtesy of the Woolaroc Museum, Bartlesville, Oklahoma)

Trail of Tears by Robert Lindreux

The Seminoles of Florida posed a far different problem. Along with other reasons for resisting removal was the presence of hundreds of blacks, many of them runaways from Georgia and Alabama plantations. Their language skills and knowledge of farming gave them added influence with their hosts, and they used this influence in opposing the government's policy, fearing that the removal of the Indians would leave them behind for reenslavement. Tensions, mounting as the December, 1835, deadline neared, finally erupted in violence with the ambush of more than one hundred United States troops in the Tampa area. With an occasional truce the war dragged on for seven years. Difficult terrain, a wretched climate, and the scattering of the Indians made it a "dirty war," marked by search-and-destroy missions, treachery, and truce violations on both sides. One of the most publicized instances was the capture of the Indian chief Osceola under a flag of truce. George Catlin's sympathetic portrait of him languishing in prison surely expressed the ambivalent feelings of many at the time.

The back of the war was broken under General Philip Jesup during the first two years of Van Buren's term. His strategy was to detach the blacks and to stage the Indians at Tampa Bay for removal by way of New Orleans. An undetermined number of blacks did fall into the hands of slaveholders, but as many as four hundred accompanied the Seminoles to Oklahoma. Key statistics summarize what Van Buren's last annual message regarded as a sad and distressing affair: In removing 3,500 to 4,000 Indians, the United States suffered 1,500 casualties and expended upward of $30 million in treasure.

The Panic of 1837

Meanwhile, the livelihood of all Americans was being affected by two basic economic events in the Van Buren presidency—the panic of 1837 and, after a brief recovery, the severer downturn two years later. Several forces contributed to a cycle of expansion after 1830 and then a countermovement of contraction. One was the rapid growth of banks—from 330 to 788—and the loose practices many of them followed. In earlier days, banks had extended credit mainly in the form of discounts on short-term commercial paper, and this fairly liquid asset, along with adequate specie held in their vaults, had secured the notes they put in circulation. The spirit of enterprise, however, and a growing hunger for capital began to pressure even sounder banks to make long-term loans and keep less specie in their vaults. A second force at work after 1830 was an inflow of English credit, much of it used for bank capital in the Southwest and elsewhere for state projects of internal improvement. Although supporting new economic growth, this credit also exerted a specifically inflationary effect on the currency. By paying for the excess of imports over exports, it kept specie from flowing abroad and thus removed a powerful check on the banks. Another inflationary force was a surplus in the Treasury, which began to mount rapidly with the retirement of the national debt. Placed on deposit in selected state banks after Jackson cut the Treasury's ties with the national bank, these funds provided the basis for further loans. In a circular fashion, finally, a mania of speculation greatly increased government land sales and added to the surplus.

The power of English credit to stimulate economic expansion was also the power to take away. In the third quarter of 1836, the Bank of England raised the interest rate to strengthen its own specie reserves. The resulting curtailment of credit to Americans ended the pattern of the preceding years and caused specie to start flowing out of the country. Eastern banks were affected first, and two actions by the government increased the pressures on them. One was the specie circular, an order from the Treasury requiring that after December, 1836, only specie would be received in payment for government lands. It had the effect of keeping specie in the West against the otherwise natural tendency of specie to flow eastward into the channels of trade. At the same time, an act of Congress ordered the Treasury to distribute its mounting surplus among the state governments. This meant that considerable sums would have to be withdrawn from the big Eastern deposit banks, particularly those in the New York area where about two-thirds of the nation's import duties were collected. Under this pressure the Eastern banks greatly curtailed their loans and thereby created severe money pressures in the mercantile community.

Political foes placed all the blame on the specie circular and called on the new president to rescind Jackson's order. Politically, however, Van Buren did not feel free to undo the pet measure of his predecessor. He believed, moreover, that specie in the West helped to shore up the deposit banks there. It was probably too late, in any case, to check the forces of contraction that led New York banks on May 10, 1837, to suspend, that is, to cease paying specie on demand to their depositors and the holders of their notes. Within a week almost all other banks across the country followed the New York example.

Suspension put the federal government in a difficult position. By law the Treasury could pay and receive only in specie or the notes of specie-paying banks, and it could deposit its funds only in such banks. Except for a small amount of specie at the Mint, however, the only funds available to the Treasury were the notes of the suspended deposit banks. Nor was much specie likely to flow into the Treasury very soon, for many import merchants were already behind in paying their duty bonds. Faced with these problems, President Van Buren called for the new Twenty-fifth Congress to meet in special session on September 4, 1837. When it assembled, Congress quickly passed a number of relief measures proposed by the president. The banks and import merchants were given additional time to make good on their obligations; the further distribution of the surplus revenue was postponed;

and an issue of $10 million in Treasury notes was authorized. Used to pay creditors of the government and made receivable at par for import duties, these notes entered quickly into circulation.

Beyond the measures for immediate relief, Van Buren set before the special session, as his basic response to suspension, the proposal to divorce the Treasury from the state banks. He therefore asked Congress to provide permanent facilities for the Treasury to keep and disburse its own funds, and to make the divorce a total one, he further proposed that the Treasury receive and pay only in specie and not in bank notes. The idea of divorce was considered at the time Jackson withdrew government funds from the national bank, but it was rejected as too radical a departure from previous practice. The panic of 1837 created a new political situation, however, and made divorce the next logical step for Van Buren and his party to take. Only by divorce, Democrats now argued, could the funds of the government be made safe and secure. Whigs answered this part of the new debate with their old cry of Caesarism, warning that an independent Treasury would in fact become a giant government bank which, by uniting purse and sword, would give tyrannical power to the executive.

NEW EDITION OF MACBETH.   BANK-OH'S! GHOST.

(Courtesy of the Library of Congress, Washington, D.C.)

Of far greater importance in the debate over the divorce proposal, however, was the impact it was expected to have on the currency. All agreed that divorce would be deflationary, but differences arose over the extent and desirability of this effect. Clearly, the funds held by the Treasury would not be available to banks for new loans and discounts. The steady demand for specie to pay government dues would be another constraint. The added specie put in circulation by Treasury disbursements also meant less specie in bank vaults to serve, by some multiple, as the basis for further note issues. In a less tangible way as well, the refusal of the Treasury to receive bank notes took away the credit the government could bestow on them. In sanguine moments radical hard-money Democrats professed to believe that the withdrawal of government credit from the credit system of banking would wreck it and create at last an exclusively metallic currency. Moderates such as Van Buren hoped that a larger amount of specie in circulation could stabilize the currency.

Opponents of the divorce proposal in the special session invoked the spirit of enterprise and put themselves forward as the champions of the credit system. Exaggerating the deflationary effect of divorce, they damned the president for making war on the banks and leading the nation backward, as one put it, to a primitive economy of "Dorian purity, iron money, and black broth." Unique circumstances and not any basic flaw, according to Senator Rives, had temporarily thrown the state banks "out of gear." Although most Whigs privately favored a national bank, they publicly lent support to Rives and other Conservative Democrats on behalf of renewing the connection of the Treasury with the state banks. In mock fashion Webster exclaimed that Van Buren's proposal made him feel as if he were on another planet. For him the power and the interests of the government should be mingled in a benign and nurturing way with the interests of its citizens, particularly on behalf of a well-regulated paper currency. In like fashion Henry Clay saw Americans as a "paper money people" and a mildly inflationary currency under government patronage as the basic need for economic recovery and growth.

Politically, the divorce issue served to give greater coherence to party lines and to mature what has come to be called the "second party system." During the Bank War in 1834, Jackson's assorted foes—including Calhoun's Nullifiers and Clay's Nationals—came together under the new Whig banner on a platform condemning Jackson as a Caesar. Three years later an important realignment took place as Calhoun left his Whig allies to support the divorce proposal and many Conservatives, led by Rives and Senator Nathaniel P. Tallmadge of New York, broke with Van Buren and moved toward the Whigs. The combined vote of Conservatives and Whigs defeated the divorce proposal at the special session and held firm against his renewed efforts in the two regular sessions of the Twenty-fifth Congress.

Van Buren nevertheless persisted in his course. The trait of "Dutch stubbornness" some saw in him was rather, a close associate felt, his "firmness of principle." It reflected, in any case, his concept of the presidency as based on party. He took the divorce proposal to be an irreversible commitment of his party, one that was consistent with its past experience and contributed to its evolving creed. If a politician by trade, he was also an ideologue of party, keenly aware that adherence to basic principles gave direction and corporate identity to his party which, he profoundly believed, spoke the voice of the nation. Having helped to place Jackson's presidency on a party basis, he was resolved to govern the same way. Private convictions about banking and currency also reinforced this sense of party need. Actions taken during his earlier career had consistently come down on the side of restraint: As a state senator for eight years, he voted for only one new bank charter; as governor he signed into law a measure setting up a safety fund for New York banks and creating a state regulatory commission. The resumption of the state banks by summer, 1838, also strengthened Van Buren's will to persevere. Encouragement from Washington and pledges of financial backing in New York contributed to resumption, but the basic cause was recovery in England and a new flow of credit to the United States.

The Independent Treasury: A Second Declaration of Independence

Paradoxically, however, a new round of bank suspensions by the last quarter of 1839 paved the way for passage of Van Buren's central domestic measure, the independent Treasury. With a second and far more austere policy of retrenchment in England, the flow of credit to the United States virtually ceased. On October 9, the old national bank, under a Pennsylvania charter since 1836, suspended specie payment, and before long almost all other banks to the west and south of Philadelphia took the same action. The new suspension, unlike that in 1837, was followed not by a quick recovery but by a profound economic downturn that lasted for four years.

In his message to the new Twenty-sixth Congress in December, 1839, the president renewed his proposal for divorce and skillfully linked it to recent events. The second suspension clearly strengthened his claim that the funds of the government could only be safe if held as specie in the Treasury's own vaults. On the currency side of divorce, he argued that the inherent fluctuations of bank note issues were greatly aggravated by the ebb and flow of English credit. Indeed, the "chain of dependence" forged by that credit ultimately tended to place the freedom and fortunes of the nation in the power of its ancient enemy. With "Spartan firmness," as one admirer noted, Van Buren advised the nation to pay off its old debts and incur no new ones. Freed from the artificial way in which English credit maintained an imbalance of imports over exports, the nation would be compelled to buy no more than it sold and to make up any yearly imbalance by the export or import of specie. As a complement to the policy of divorce, foreign trade in real goods for real money would exert a salutary and steady check on banks in the United States. These views clearly embodied Van Buren's more general belief that a laissez-faire posture for the government would allow the natural forces of economic equilibrium to work for enterprise at a sound and sober pace. Beyond present distress he looked to a future relatively free of violent fluctuations.

Democrats in Congress applauded Van Buren's message and supplemented its force with debate over two related matters. The first was a proposal for a federal bankruptcy act that would set up machinery for closing any state bank that suspended specie payments. Strong opposition never allowed the measure to come to a vote, but it did reveal the desire to secure a sound bank currency. Democrats succeeded in a second matter, that of defeating the call of the Whigs for the federal government to assume the debts that the states owed to England. Communications from London bankers suggested that a pledge of the federal revenues to pay old debts might soon induce the flow of new English credits to the United States. This, however, was precisely what Democrats did not want, namely, to be linked in the chain of dependence once more. Although Whigs were reconciled to the passage of the independent Treasury bill, their delay tactics in the House held up the final vote until the end of June, 1840. Because of the timing, President Van Buren waited until July 4 to sign the bill, and the party paper in Washington hailed it as the "Second Declaration of Independence."

Unhappily for Van Buren, the second declaration of independence did not assure him a second term in the White House. Deepening depression by summer, 1840, made even more appealing Whig praises for the credit system and the Whigs' promise of increasing the currency. Support in Congress for an insolvency law, in place of the Democrats' bankruptcy bill, also identified Whigs with the spirit of enterprise. By this means a debtor would be able to initiate action with his creditor and gain freedom to start over again. Clearly, the Whig view of government as a benign means for bringing recovery and economic growth contrasted with what they called the Spartan counsels of Van Buren. With cries of "Van, Van, a used up man" and "Martin Van Ruin," they pointed to a central issue in the presidential campaign of 1840.

The Campaign of 1840: "Tippecanoe and Tyler, Too"
Enhancing the force of Whig economic views were a new sense of party unity, a popular candidate, and effective appeals to the voters by a "log cabin" campaign. Whig antiparty ideals and three separate candidates in 1836 gave way to a united convention that passed over Clay and Webster in favor of General William Henry Harrison, the hero of Tippecanoe, and John Tyler of Virginia. Although Tyler was not chosen as running mate for euphonious reasons, his name did lend itself nicely to the slogan "Tippecanoe and Tyler, too." Taking shameless liberties with the truth, Whig campaigners pictured Harrison, scion of an old Virginia family, as a simple farmer at North Bend living in a log cabin with the latchstring always out. Van Buren, by contrast, was presented as a foppish dandy luxuriating in the aristocratic trappings of the White House, sipping French wine, eating from

golden spoons, and preening like a peacock before mirrors larger than barn doors. Van Buren became so enraged by the exposure of his life-style, one editor mischievously observed, that he "actually burst his corset!"

Harrison struck another democratic note by becoming the first candidate ever to campaign openly for the presidency. His presence often sparked a final element of frenzy generated at mass rallies by torchlight parades, the raising of a log cabin, and group singing in the mode of Methodist revivals. Democrats unctuously deplored the humbuggery of it all, forgetting the hickory poles and other devices used earlier on Jackson's behalf. The second party system had clearly come of age. In a moment of exasperated candor, one Democratic editor exclaimed, "We have taught them how to conquer us!"

From An Old Print Reproduced by Bloomer
The Cabin on Wheels often was the storehouse for refreshments

"Rolling the Ball"

This particular ball was rolled from Cleveland, O. to Lexington, Ky.

(Courtesty of the Smithsonian Institution, Washington, D.C.)

Conforming to the practice of past presidents, Van Buren took no active role in the campaign. Occasional letters in response to inquiries indicated his willingness to stand on his record and party principles, but by September, he later wrote, he had resigned himself to defeat when he realized that the Whigs would leave no expedient untried in their determination to win. On the face of the returns, he suffered an overwhelming defeat: He won 60 electoral votes from seven states, while Harrison received 234 electoral votes from the remaining nineteen states. Some consolation doubtless came with the knowledge that he received 400,000 more popular votes than in 1836 and that a shift of about 8,000 votes in four large states would have brought him a majority in the electoral college. At last, however, he suffered the fate of most incumbents in time of economic downturn, and the pattern of the vote points to the crucial issue of currency in the campaign. The seven states that supported Van Buren—Missouri, Illinois, New Hampshire, Virginia, South Carolina, Alabama, and Arkansas—were less integrated into the market economy, and they were less imbued with the spirit of enterprise than the other states.

Van Buren accepted defeat in a spirit of good sportsmanship that had always characterized his political career. Visitors at the White House found nothing in his cheerful demeanor to suggest that he was about to relinquish the highest office in the land. When Harrison came to Washington in early 1841, Van Buren paid a social call at his hotel, invited him to the White House as guest of honor, and even offered to vacate the executive mansion so Harrison could move in early. Had he been invited, he would also have attended Harrison's inaugural ceremonies; only later did it become the custom for the outgoing president of a different party to attend the inauguration of his successor. In any event Van Buren did not see defeat as fatal either to himself or to his party. Profoundly convinced that there could be only one genuinely popular party, he expected the "sober second thought" of the people to see through the delusions of the log cabin campaign and restore Democrats to their rightful place.

The Achievements of Van Buren's Presidency

Informed with this belief, Van Buren's last message to Congress proudly summarized the achievements of his presidency and reaffirmed its principles. The nation remained at peace and enjoyed relatively secure frontiers. Here, it might be added, Van Buren had resisted the Machiavellian advice of some who would have him divert attention from ills at home by precipitating war abroad. The past obligations of the government had also been met, including the difficult and costly task of Indian removal. In spite of a "formidable" political opposition and "pecuniary embarrassments," moreover, he had met these obligations without incurring a new debt or raising taxes. Silence on slavery, the only specific issue raised in his inaugural, likewise spoke of success in maintaining sectional harmony. Although recognizing that individuals had experienced derangement in their economic pursuits, he believed that the independent Treasury would contribute to a sound recovery and to stable enterprise. In larger perspective his policy of divorce completed the work of Jackson's presidency in bringing government back to its simple republican tack. As if looking to future elections, finally, he warned that vigilance would be required to preserve these principles: "The choice is an important one, and I sincerely hope that it will be made wisely."

The sequel of events provides a final perspective for assessing Van Buren's presidency. Opposition to the annexation of Texas in 1844 denied Van Buren a third nomination for president by his party. It went instead to James K. Polk on a platform of territorial expansion to the Pacific. War with Mexico in the wake of Texas annexation realized this "manifest destiny," but it also opened in fateful form the sectional controversy over slavery expansion. By the mid-1850's the deepening debate sundered the second party system Van Buren had helped to shape and had used so well to contain sectional tensions, and by the time of his death on July 24, 1862, the sectional conflict had become a civil war that was to transform the federative Union he wanted to save into a consolidated nation. His independent Treasury lasted longer, remaining in operation until the Federal Reserve System was established. Recurring booms and panics in the last half of the nineteenth century belied his hopes that it would bring stability to enterprise. There is no reason to believe, however, that a national bank would have served much better at taming the spirit of enterprise in a rapidly expanding economy. Van Buren began his presidency with the hope of bringing repose to the nation; relative success in achieving this goal constituted a modest but real act of statesmanship.

Major L. Wilson

Bibliographical References

Three older biographies are still useful for examining Van Buren's earlier career: Edward M. Shepard, *Martin Van Buren*, 1889; Denis Tilden Lynch, *An Epoch and a Man: Martin Van Buren and His Times*, 1929; Holmes Alexander, *The American Talleyrand*, 1935. Two later biographies—John Niven, *Martin Van Buren: The Romantic Age of American Politics*, 1983, and Donald B. Coles, *Martin Van Buren and the American Political System*, 1984—are more complete and evenhanded. Further perspective on his great contribution to party development can be found in Robert V. Remini, *Martin Van Buren and the Making of the Democratic Party*, 1951, and Richard Hofstadter, *The Idea of a Party System*, 1969. Two volumes devoted primarily to the presidential years are James C. Curtis, *The Fox at Bay: Martin Van Buren and the Presidency, 1837-1841*, 1973, and Major L. Wilson, *The Presidency of Martin Van Buren*, 1984. All direct quotations in the present article are drawn from the last-named work. The interested reader will also want to consult Martin Van Buren, *Inquiry into the Origin and Course of Political Parties in the United States*, 1867, and *The Autobiography of Martin Van Buren*, 1920.

WILLIAM HENRY HARRISON

1841

William Henry Harrison was the oldest man to serve in the presidency before Ronald Reagan. Sixty-eight years old at the time of his inauguration, in 1841, Harrison served only one month before he died from pneumonia. His early death made Harrison's presidency the shortest in the history of the United States, and provided the final irony in a life full of color and controversy.

The son of a signer of the Declaration of Independence, Harrison was born in 1773 at his family's famous Berkeley Plantation in Virginia. He attended Hampden-Sydney College, and briefly undertook the study of medicine under the noted physician Benjamin Rush.

Indian Fighter, Legislator, Diplomat

In 1791, Harrison entered the army serving in the campaigns against the Indians in the Northwest Territory and eventually becoming a lieutenant and aide-de-camp to the commander, General Anthony Wayne. With the conclusion of peace, he remained on garrison duty in the vicinity of Cincinnati. Harrison resigned from the army in 1798 and accepted an appointment as secretary of the Northwest Territory, from which he was elected first delegate to Congress in 1799. With the division of the Northwest Territory into the territories of Ohio and Indiana, Harrison was appointed governor of the Indiana Territory.

Harrison was given a nearly impossible mission: to win the friendship and trust of the Indians and to protect them from the rapaciousness of white settlers, yet to acquire for the government as much land as he could secure from the Western tribes. Apparently, Harrison had a genuine concern for the plight of the Indians, ordering a campaign of inoculation to protect them from the scourge of smallpox and banning the sale of liquor to them. He actively pursued the acquisition of Indian lands, however, and in 1809, he negotiated a treaty with Indian leaders that transferred some 2.9 million acres in the vicinity of the White and Wabash rivers to the United States. This cession exacerbated the tensions between red and white men in the Northwest and triggered the activities on which Harrison's fame and later career were founded.

Given the uneasy relationship between the United States and Great Britain, many Americans assumed that the "Indian troubles" of the interior were encouraged and fomented by the British. In reality, the growing hostility of the Western tribes was largely an indigenous reaction to the constant encroachments on their lands by white settlers. The Indians' frustrations were finally focused through the leadership of two Shawnee half brothers, the chief Tecumseh and a one-eyed medicine man called The Prophet. Tecumseh developed the concept of a great Indian confederation, arguing that Indian lands were held in common by all the tribes and could not be bargained away without their unanimous consent. The Prophet promoted a puritanical religious philosophy, and as his following grew, religion and politics gradually merged.

Harrison developed a healthy respect for the brothers' abilities, and he hoped at first that they could be placated. Finally, however, in what must be considered an aggressive move, Harrison marched a force of about one thousand men north from his capital at Vincennes toward Indian lands in northwestern Indiana. On November 7, 1811, Harrison's encampment near an Indian settlement called Prophetstown, near the confluence of the Tippecanoe and Wabash rivers, suffered an early morning surprise attack. Tecumseh was in the South organizing the tribes of that area, so the Indians who attacked Harrison were led, or at least inspired, by The Prophet. Harrison's forces beat back the attackers and later burned the Indian settlement.

Almost immediately, controversy arose concerning the particulars of the Battle of Tippecanoe and Harrison's performance. Were his troops prepared for the Indian attack? Why had they camped in a vulnerable position? Had Harrison or his companion officers actually commanded the defenses? Were Harrison's men outnumbered? What, in fact, was the size of the attacking Indian force? In the face of such critical questions, Harrison, who was not a paragon of modesty, and his supporters immediately began to construct the legend of a "Washington of the West" who represented the bravery and ambitions of Western Americans.

During the War of 1812 with Great Britain, Harrison served in several military positions and eventually became supreme commander of the Army of the Northwest. He broke the power of the British and the Indians in the Northwest and in southern Canada, with the culminating victory in early October, 1813, at the Battle of the Thames. Again controversy followed Harrison's military performance, although his reputation among the general public was apparently enhanced. In May, 1814, he resigned from the army and took up residence on a farm at North Bend, Ohio, on the bank of the Ohio River near Cincinnati.

At North Bend Harrison engaged in farming and several unsuccessful commercial ventures, and the foundation for another aspect of his public

TECUMSEH

PHOTOGRAPH OF THE ORIGINAL WATER COLOR PORTRAIT OF TECUMSEH
BY MATHIAS NOHEIMER. THE ORIGINAL HANGS IN THE INDIAN ROOM OF
THE ROSS COUNTY HISTORICAL SOCIETY MUSEUM

(Courtesy of the Library of Congress, Washington, D.C.)

image was established. Harrison's home at North Bend was a commodious dwelling of sixteen rooms, but it was built around the nucleus of a log cabin and became one of the misrepresented symbols of "Old Tip's" 1840 presidential campaign. In 1816 Harrison was elected to the United States House of Representatives, serving until 1819 with no real distinction. In 1825, he was elected to the United States Senate by the Ohio legislature. He became chairman of the Military Affairs Committee but resigned in 1828 to accept an appointment as United States minister to Colombia. His career as a diplomat was not particularly successful, but when he was recalled after about a year by President Andrew Jackson it was largely for political reasons.

Following his return from Colombia, Harrison experienced a continuing series of financial and family misfortunes and supplemented his resources by serving as clerk of the Cincinnati Court of Common Pleas. He was observed at this time by a French traveler who described him as "a man of about medium height, stout and muscular, and of about the age of sixty years yet with the active step and lively air of youth." A visitor to the "log cabin," on the other hand, considered Harrison "a small and rather sallow-looking man, who does not exactly meet the associations that connect themselves with the name of general."

The Election of 1840: "Tippecanoe and Tyler Too"

During the height of "Jacksonian Democracy," many displayed a growing concern about the alleged pretensions of "King Andrew" Jackson, which contributed to the emergence of the Whig Party. Old National Republicans, former anti-Masons, and various others who reacted strongly against the president or his policies began to work together, and in 1836 the Whigs made their first run for the presidency against Jackson's chosen successor, Martin Van Buren. William Henry Harrison ran as the candidate of Western Whigs, showed promise as a vote getter, and thus became a leading contender for the nomination in 1840.

By now widely known as "Old Tippecanoe," Harrison the military hero presented an obvious opportunity for the Whigs to borrow the tactics of the Democrats who had exploited "Old Hickory," Andrew Jackson, to great success. Harrison's position on key issues of the day—banking policy, internal improvements, the tariff, abolition—was almost irrelevant, for the old general was to be nominated as a symbol of military glory and the development of the West. The Whigs wanted a candidate who would appeal to a broad range of voters and who was not too closely identified with the issues of the Jacksonian era. They did not offer a real platform, only a pledge to "correct the abuses" of the current administration. If the campaign were successful, the real decisions in a Harrison Administration would be made by Whig leaders in Congress.

Harrison's age and health became immediate issues in the campaign, and he traveled from Ohio to Virginia so that he could be seen and "counteract the opinion, which has been industriously circulated, that *I was an old broken-down feeble man*." One observer who met the candidate described him as "about 5 feet 9 inches in hight [*sic*], very slender and thin in flesh, with a noble and benignant expression—a penetrating eye, expansive forehead and Roman nose. He is not bald but gray, and walks about very quick, and seems to be as active as a man of 45." During a later trip that Harrison made through New Jersey, a newspaper reported that "his appearance is that of a hale, hearty Ohio Farmer, of about fifty years of age."

Souvenir from the First Modern Presidential Campaign

The tone and lasting fame of the campaign were established during the battle for the nomination when a partisan of one of his Whig rivals suggested that Harrison should be allowed to enjoy his log cabin and hard cider in peace. An opposition party paper then picked up the idea and said, "Give him a barrel of hard cider and a pension of two thousand a year... he will sit the remainder of his days in a log cabin... and study moral philosophy." Whig strategists knew a good thing when they read it, and they created a winning campaign around the portrayal of Harrison as a man of the people, a wise yet simple hero whose log cabin and hard cider were highly preferable to the haughty attitude and trickery of "Old Kinderhook" Martin Van Buren. In the process, the Whigs waged the first modern presidential campaign as they sold souvenirs, published and widely distributed campaign materials, flooded the country with speakers, and employed songs, slogans, and verses, the most famous being their cry of "Tippecanoe and Tyler too."

A One-Month Presidency and Its Lasting Consequences

Harrison's presidency was anticlimactic. He traveled to Washington before his inauguration and was well received both by his former opponent, President Van Buren, and by members of Congress. His inaugural address was widely praised, even though it lasted more than two hours, but it had unexpected results. The day was cold and rainy, and the new president caught a cold, which continued to nag him. Harrison was besieged by people who wanted favors and offices, and he attempted to escape from this pressure by immersing himself in minor details. He visited various government offices to see if they were operating efficiently, and he even concerned himself with the routine matters of running and purchasing supplies for the White House. The development of a legislative program was left to Whig leaders in Congress, and settlement of the Caroline affair, with Great Britain, growing out of American involvement in an abortive Canadian Rebellion in 1837, the only major problem of his brief tenure, was entrusted to the hands of Secretary of State Daniel Webster.

On a cold March morning, the president ventured out to purchase vegetables for the White House. He suffered a chill, which aggravated the cold he had contracted on inauguration day. The cold developed into pneumonia, and on April 4, 1841, Harrison died in the White House. His body was returned to North Bend for burial. Old Tippecanoe had virtually no direct impact on the office of the presidency itself, yet the method of his election and the circumstances of his death were of lasting importance. The 1840 campaign had established a new style of presidential campaigning, and Harrison's death forced the nation for the first time to experience the elevation of a vice president to the Oval Office, an event that established a landmark Constitutional precedent.

James E. Fickle

Bibliographical References

The major biographies of William Henry Harrison are Freeman Cleaves, *Old Tippecanoe: William Henry Harrison and His Times*, 1939, and Dorothy B. Goebel, *William Henry Harrison: A Political Biography*, 1926. Robert G. Gunderson, *The Log-Cabin Campaign*, 1957, is the major work describing the election of 1840. James A. Green, *William Henry Harrison, His Life and Times*, 1941, is a laudatory popular account.

John Tyler

JOHN TYLER

1841–1845

John Tyler is one of the least-known yet most controversial presidents in American history. The first vice president to succeed to the presidency upon the death of a chief executive, Tyler established the precedent that in such circumstances the new president holds the office both in fact and in name. Public and political opinion about Tyler was badly divided in his own time, and later historians have continued to debate his motives, ability, and performance. President Theodore Roosevelt said, "Tyler has been called a mediocre man, but this is unwarranted flattery. He was a politician of monumental littleness." He is often portrayed as a stubborn, vain, and inconsistent leader who was one of the worst presidents. Other writers portray him as a president with strong principles and great integrity who remained true to his beliefs despite tremendous political pressure. They say that even though Tyler was the first president threatened with impeachment and the only one to be formally expelled from his own political party, he deserves recognition as a competent and courageous chief executive.

A Singular Political Course

Tyler was born March 29, 1790, in tidewater Virginia near Richmond, the son of a distinguished Virginian who served as governor, speaker of the Virginia House of Delegates, and as a judge. His father was a strict constructionist Jeffersonian Republican. John absorbed and remained deeply imbued with this philosophy throughout his life. He was reared in an atmosphere of aristocratic privilege and refinement, becoming something of a stereotypical representative of the tidewater aristocracy in his beliefs and values.

Upon his graduation from William and Mary, where he had been an excellent student with a growing interest in political theory and practice, Tyler at the age of seventeen began to read law under his father. He was admitted to the Virginia bar in 1809. At the age of twenty-one he was elected to the Virginia House of Delegates. After brief military service in the War of 1812, he returned to politics and was elected to the United States House of Representatives in 1816. As a congressman, Tyler stood for strict interpretation of the Constitution and limitation of the powers of the federal government. He resisted national internal improvements because they might extend the power of the federal government, and he opposed the first Bank of the United States for the same reason, as well as on constitutional and other grounds. He did not favor the slave trade, but he voted against the Missouri Compromise, believing that time and the social climate would eventually doom the "peculiar institution." Defeated in an election for the United States Senate at the age of thirty-one, Tyler served briefly as chancellor of William and Mary, and then as governor of Virginia. He was finally elected to the Senate in 1827 and began to achieve a degree of national prominence.

Remaining true to his constitutional principles, Tyler found himself in an ambiguous political situation. As a Republican, he supported William H. Crawford for the presidency in 1824 and was elected to the Senate as an anti-Jacksonian. He was repelled both by Old Hickory's authoritarianism and by the rising influence of Jacksonian democracy. Tyler was very cordial and effective when dealing with members of his own class, but common folk and their heroes made him uncomfortable. "The barking of newspapers and the brawling of demagogues can never drive me from my course," said Tyler. "If I am to go into retirement, I will at least take care to do so with a pure and unsullied conscience." Nevertheless, in 1828 Tyler supported Jackson and agreed with his opposition to the rechartering of the Bank of the United States. Tyler's principles, however, led him to split with the Tennessean and the Democratic Party.

Although Tyler favored the positions the president took on certain key issues, he considered Jackson's methods unacceptable, particularly in the nullification crisis and in dealing with the bank. Nullification became an issue during Jackson's presidency because of the linkage of two developments affecting the South. First was the tariff. In 1828, Congress passed a high protective tariff, which Southern planters, dependent on an export economy, strongly opposed. They called it the "Tariff of Abominations," and Tyler was among the senators who spoke and voted against it. Second was the fact that with the increasing political integration of the Northwest and Northeast, Southerners were coming to constitute only a minority in national politics. Some Southerners were beginning to talk about separation from the Union in order to escape from the tyranny of the majority. Vice President John C. Calhoun of South Carolina understood Southern frustration, yet he wanted to preserve the Union, and therefore developed the theory of nullification as a permanent protection for minority sections within the Union.

Nullification and the tariff were linked when South Carolina threatened to declare the Tariff of Abominations null and void within its borders if it were not repealed by Congress. Despite passage of a new compromise tariff, South Carolina began the nullification process. President Jackson issued an extremely strong proclamation rejecting South Carolina's position, and Congress passed the Force Act, authorizing the president to use force to make sure that federal laws were obeyed. Even though South Carolina eventually backed down and the crisis passed, Tyler found himself in a troubling situation. He shared the general Southern opposition to high tariffs, but he did not agree with the theory of nullification. Still, he believed that Jackson's nullification proclamation was a violation of the Constitution, and he was the only senator to vote against the Force Act. Further, he was repelled by the vehemence of Jackson's reaction to South Carolina's challenge.

The bank question raised similar contradictions for Tyler. Like Jackson, he opposed the attempt to recharter the Bank of the United States, on constitutional as well as on other grounds. Yet, when Jackson attempted to destroy the bank before its charter expired by removing the federal government's deposits from its vaults, Tyler supported resolutions in the Senate condemning the president's action. When the Virginia legislature ordered him to vote for a motion to expunge the resolutions, Tyler resigned from the Senate and left the Democratic Party.

Tyler was now in strange political territory. He had left Andrew Jackson's party and had begun drifting along with other Southern expatriates into the ranks of the emerging Whig Party, which was coalescing in opposition to the executive tyranny of "King Andrew." Yet Tyler had not departed from his constitutional or political principles, and these were not consistent with those of many Whig leaders. The Whig Party was a loose coalition of diverse groups, however, and seemed at first to accommodate considerable philosophical latitude. Defeated in a Senate election in 1839, Tyler was nominated for the vice presidency on the Harrison ticket the following year, in an obvious effort by the Whigs to attract Southern states' rights advocates.

Succession to the Presidency: A Historic Precedent

The Virginia politician whose name became part of the most famous campaign slogan in American political history—Tippecanoe and Tyler too—had matured into a dignified and appealing figure. Although remaining distant from the masses, Tyler was a polished and effective orator. He was patient, considerate, good-humored, and friendly. Even his political enemies found it difficult to dislike him. Tyler was scrupulously honest and had no major vices. He drank, but always in moderation, and he used profanity, but only of the mildest sort. Physically striking, he was six feet tall and slender. He was very fair, with a high forehead and aquiline nose, brilliant eyes, and a ready smile. Observers said he reminded them of a Roman statesman or of Cicero. Some said he was vain, but he did have some justification for vanity.

The Harrison and Tyler ticket won the election easily, but within a month of his inauguration "Old Tippecanoe" was dead. Supposedly, his dying words, intended for the vice president, were "Sir—I wish you to understand the true principles of Government. I wish them carried out. I ask nothing more."

Were William Henry Harrison's principles shared by Tyler? Despite the Virginian's long political career and philosophical and constitutional consistency, contemporary observers professed not to know. Tyler had scarcely known Harrison and had not particularly liked what he knew of him. Tyler was a close friend of Henry Clay, and many, probably including Clay, believed that he would support the programs, including plans for a new central bank, that the Kentuckian planned to introduce in Congress. Tyler's oratory in the campaign had been sufficiently vague to offer some justification for such a belief. Yet within a short period of time Clay would be a political enemy, attacking Tyler as a traitor to the Whig Party.

The first question was fundamental. What was Tyler's status upon Harrison's death? The Constitution is vague, saying that "in case of the removal of the President from office, or of his death, resignation, or inability to discharge the powers and duties of the said office, the same shall devolve on the Vice President. . . ." Does this mean the office itself, or simply the duties of the office? No precedents existed, and in this important crisis Tyler, the strict constructionist, interpreted the Constitution very broadly and claimed all the rights and privileges of the presidency. Although there was some criticism of his interpretation, it has been accepted and followed since that time.

Tyler kept the Harrison cabinet members, reinforcing the Whig perception that little would change. Almost immediately, Henry Clay submitted a legislative program calling for a new Bank of the United States and a higher tariff. Clay quickly discovered that he had badly misread the situation. When Congress enacted legislation creating the new bank and a higher tariff, the president vetoed both, in language reminiscent of Andrew Jackson. Some charged that this was treachery; others held that Tyler was jealous of Clay's assumption of leadership. In fact, Tyler was simply being consistent with the strict constructionist, Southern agrarian views that he had held all along. He stood firm despite recriminations from Clay, tremendous pressure from majoritarian Whigs, and outcries from the public, including a rock-throwing mob that attacked the White House.

Conflicts with Congress: A President Without a Party

Tyler argued that the proposed bank violated constitutional principles and also posed the threat of an economic monopoly. He suggested a modified "exchequer system" as a compromise, but the Whigs in Congress forged ahead with another attempt to create a bank, thinly disguised as a "fiscal corporation." Tyler vetoed that too, and the situation rapidly deteriorated into open warfare between the Whig president and his colleagues in Congress. After Tyler, using the veto as actively as Andrew Jackson, struck down Clay's distribution program and other legislation, the Kentuckian resigned from the Senate in frustration. There were public demonstrations against the president, he was burned in effigy, and the entire cabinet, with the exception of Secretary of State Daniel Webster, who was involved in sensitive negotiations with Great Britain, resigned. They were replaced by men like Tyler himself, former Democrats who shared his views. In January, 1843, the Whigs brought impeachment charges against the man they now called "His Accidency." They failed, but proceeded formally to expel Tyler from the Whig Party, which was in shambles.

The president, now a man without a party, continued to perform the duties of his office, loyal to his principles and in apparent good humor. He actually managed to achieve some successes and even considered an attempt to retain the presidency in the 1844 campaign as an independent candidate. In 1841, he approved the Preemption Act, which made land more accessible to settlers rather than to speculators and stimulated the development of the Northwestern states of Iowa, Illinois, Wisconsin, and Minnesota. He helped to end the Seminole War in 1842. The same year, the dispute with Great Britain over the boundary between the United States and Canada in the Northeast was resolved through the Webster-Ashburton Treaty, and in 1844 the United States signed a treaty with China opening the Orient to American commerce for the first time. Although Tyler did not occupy the limelight in these diplomatic matters, he wielded considerable influence behind the scenes.

(Courtesy of the Library of Congress, Washington, D.C.)

Map of Texas and the Country Adjacent, 1844

The president built his hopes for election in 1844 on the Texas annexation question. Originally a province of Mexico largely populated by slaveholding American settlers, Texas successfully rebelled in 1836 and hoped for annexation to the United States. The issue was troublesome because of the growing sectional controversy over slavery, and so for several years Texas remained an independent republic. Tyler genuinely believed that the annexation of Texas would be good for the United States, and he was hopeful that advocacy of such an action would generate support for his candidacy in the Southern slave states. He correctly anticipated the developing expansionist impulse in the country, but his personal ambitions were ill founded. When significant support failed to materialize, Tyler withdrew and endorsed Democrat James K. Polk, who ran on an expansionist platform and won. Following the election, Congress passed and Tyler signed a joint resolution of annexation for Texas. Two days later, during his last full day in office, the Virginian signed a bill admitting Florida to the Union.

Tyler then retired to his plantation home on Virginia's James River. He was coolly received by his neighbors, many of whom were Whigs, but his graciousness, character, and obvious goodwill gradually won them over. The former president became an honored citizen, and as the passions of sectional turmoil built in the 1850's, he was an influential sectional leader. Loyal to the Union, he attempted to promote compromise but finally voted in favor of secession as a delegate to the Virginia secession convention. He served in the provisional Congress of the Confederacy and was elected to the Confederate House of Representatives, but he died on January 18, 1862, before taking his seat. He was buried in Richmond.

Tyler's Achievements: A Reassessment

The first vice president to inherit the presidency upon the death of a president, the first chief executive to face impeachment charges, and the only one to be officially expelled from his party, John Tyler has been remembered primarily as a historical footnote. He deserves better. Although one can disagree with his reasoning on the issues, it is difficult to conclude that he acted out of malice or political expediency. Tyler remained true to his constitutional and political principles, displaying a consistency and courage rare in political leaders. He achieved some positive accomplishments despite the turmoil of his presidency, and he significantly shaped the theory of vice presidential succession under the United States Constitution.

James E. Fickle

Bibliographical References

The standard biography of John Tyler is Oliver Perry Chitwood's dated

John Tyler, Champion of the Old South, 1939. Robert Seager II, *And Tyler Too*, 1963, is a more recent joint biography of Tyler and his second wife, Julia Gardiner Tyler. Tyler's presidency is the focus of Robert J. Morgan, *A Whig Embattled*, 1954, and of Oscar Doane Lambert, *Presidential Politics in the United States, 1841–1844*, 1936. Tyler's role in the 1840 presidential campaign is discussed in Robert G. Gunderson, *The Log-Cabin Campaign*, 1957. Daniel Walker Howe analyzes the anti-Jackson movement in *The Political Culture of the American Whigs*, 1979.

JAMES K. POLK

1845–1849

James Knox Polk (1795-1849), eleventh president of the United States, was elected in November, 1844, and held office for one term, from March 4, 1845, to March 3, 1849, at age forty-nine the youngest president until the twentieth century. He declined to be considered for reelection. Although he was not widely known at the time of his election, he had served fourteen years in the House of Representatives (four of them as speaker) and one term as governor of his home state of Tennessee. As a protégé of Andrew Jackson (he was often called Young Hickory), Polk had represented the interests of the Jackson Administration in the lower house of Congress and was recognized as the floor leader in securing Jacksonian legislation. His presidency was the strongest and most vigorous of those between Jackson and Abraham Lincoln. Besides being a loyal Jacksonian Democrat in matters of domestic policy, Polk shared the expansionist fervor of his generation and as president presided over the nation's most dramatic period of territorial expansion. In the brief space of three years, Texas was annexed, the Oregon country was acquired, and a half-million square miles of Mexican territory was ceded to the United States as a result of the Mexican War. As America's first wartime president since James Madison, Polk did much to define the role of the president as commander in chief. The Mexican War dominated his administration and has influenced his reputation ever since. In spite of the controversy that has often been aroused over Polk's involvement in the war, he has fared well in presidential evaluations, as historians consistently place him among the top ten or twelve presidents of the United States.

Early Life

James K. Polk was born on November 2, 1795, in Mecklenburg County, North Carolina. His family, of sturdy Scotch-Irish stock and staunchly Presbyterian, had been in America since the seventeenth century, settling first in Maryland, moving to Pennsylvania, and from there sweeping southwestward with the great migration of Scotch-Irish to up-country North Carolina. Fiercely independent, the Polks resented British rule and were among the earliest to support separation from the mother country. Many of them served in the revolutionary army. By the late eighteenth century, the family was among the most prominent in the region.

James K. Polk was the eldest of the ten children of Samuel and Jane Knox Polk. His father was a well-to-do farmer and, like the rest of the family, strongly Jeffersonian in politics. His mother, said to be descended from the Scottish religious leader John Knox, was a tenacious Presbyterian whose life revolved around the Bible and the teachings of the church. Nurtured on tales of America's War of Independence, Polk derived from his parents a strong patriotism, a keen interest in politics, and deep religious convictions.

Like so many North Carolinians following the Revolution, members of Polk's family invested heavily in land in the state's western district, later the state of Tennessee. In 1806, when Polk was eleven years old, his parents moved to a farm in the Duck River Valley, near Columbia in Maury County, Tennessee. His father expanded his interests from farming to mercantile activity and continued to engage in land speculation during the economic boom that followed the War of 1812.

Because of his frail health, Polk began his formal education later than most youths of his generation. After preparation in Presbyterian academies in Tennessee, he entered the University of North Carolina in Chapel Hill in 1815 as a sophomore, where he studied the classics and mathematics, two subjects he believed would best discipline his mind. He was graduated first in his class in 1818. The following year, he took up the study of law in the office of Felix Grundy, a successful Nashville lawyer and former congressman, and in 1820 was admitted to the bar. Polk established his practice in his hometown of Columbia and prospered almost immediately, thanks to the business his family placed in his charge.

It was not the law, however, but politics that stirred Polk's interest. The times were filled with opportunity for an aspiring politician. The panic of 1819 awakened the American people, jolting them out of their indifference and ushering in a period of change and uncertainty that would lead to new political alignments. In Tennessee, as elsewhere, the economic distress aroused demands that the government be more responsive to the needs of the people. A "new politics" (however vaguely defined) was called for. Symbolizing the rising dissatisfaction with the existing system was Andrew Jackson, the hero of New Orleans.

In 1819, Polk assumed his first political post, that of clerk of the state senate, and four years later he was elected to the lower house of the Tennessee legislature. His academic background, readiness in debate, and persistent application quickly marked him as a promising young leader in Tennessee politics. He supported legislation that would relieve the banking crisis in the state and bring order to the state's tangled land problems, and in 1823 he voted for Jackson for United States senator. At the same time, he married Sarah Childress, daughter of a well-to-do farmer and Murfreesboro businessman, a well-educated, refined, and cultured woman who would be an important asset to his career. She would become one of the most respected first ladies to occupy the White House.

Polk's success as a legislator led him to seek election to Congress. The presidential election of 1824 promised to be one of the most important in years. Jackson had been nominated by the Tennessee legislature two years before, and his election to the Senate further boosted his candidacy. Although his triumph seemed sure, the results of the contest indicated otherwise. Jackson received more electoral and popular votes than any other candidate, but none of the four contenders (Jackson, William H. Crawford, John Quincy Adams, and Henry Clay) received the required majority. The election was placed before the House of Representatives, where in February, 1825, Adams was elected. The cry of "bargain and corruption" was immediately raised by the outraged Jacksonians. Polk shared the belief that Jackson had not only lost because of a nefarious plot involving Adams and Clay but also that his defeat had robbed the people of their choice. The outcome of the election gave new meaning to Polk's campaign for Congress; in August, 1825, he was easily elected from his four-county district in south central Tennessee.

Jacksonian Congressman

Although Polk proved extraordinarily successful in his appeals for the votes of his constituents—he served in the House of Representatives for seven successive terms, fourteen years—he lacked the charismatic quality that brought so many Americans to the side of Jackson. Of somewhat less than middle height, unprepossessing in demeanor, he often gave the appearance of dullness. He had but few intimate friends. Formal and stiff in his bearing, he was always concerned to maintain his dignity. When he presided over the House of Representatives as speaker during the last four years of his service, it was said that he appeared "in the chair as if he were at a dinner party." Thoughtful and reserved, his speaking style reflected his personality. His political statements lacked the ornamental flourishes common to early nineteenth-century political rhetoric; instead, they were plain, sincere, and convincing, demonstrating a command of facts and principles and exhibiting a practical common sense.

John Quincy Adams once characterized Polk's speaking ability as having "no wit, no literature, no point of argument, no gracefulness of delivery, no elegance of language, no philosophy, no pathos, no felicitous impromptus; nothing that can constitute an orator, but confidence, fluency, and labor." Adams spoke as an opponent; others were more charitable.

The charge that Polk had no philosophy was unfair. The aftermath of the panic and the outcome of the presidential election brought his views into sharper focus. The Jeffersonian convictions he had absorbed from his family and the intellectual discipline he had derived from the Presbyterian influence formed the basis on which he built his political outlook. His exposure to moral philosophy at Chapel Hill gave him a well-defined sense of republican virtue and of the obligations that rested on citizens of a republic. The troubled atmosphere of the 1820's, however, revealed the need for something more. Polk found the missing ingredient in the new democratic currents of his time.

Polk prized individual freedom, the rights of the states against the centralizing tendencies of the national government, and a strict interpretation of the Constitution. The sovereignty of the people, he believed, was unquestioned and absolute. In one of his first pronouncements as a congressman, Polk declared his faith in the popular will. "That this is a Government based upon the will of the People," he stated, "that all power emanates from them; and that a majority should rule; are, as I conceive, vital principles in this Government, never to be sacrificed or abandoned, under any circumstances." He would return America's republican government to its beginnings: "I would bring the Government back to what it was intended to be—a plain economical Government."

Polk entered Congress in December, 1825, determined to vindicate Jackson from his defeat by the Adams-Clay combination. One of his first actions was to support the effort to amend the Constitution to prevent future presidential contests from being decided in the House of Representatives. He proposed that the selection of presidential electors be made uniform throughout the country and argued that election by districts was the fairest, most democratic mode. He agreed with some that the electoral college should be abandoned altogether in favor of a direct vote for president but realized the futility of proposing such a radical change.

Although the movement to amend the Constitution did not succeed, it enabled Polk to express his views on the nature of the presidential office. The president, he believed, was the chief executive of all the people, the only federal officer to be elected by all the people, and the only elected official whose constituency was the entire nation. More than any other officer, the president best reflected the popular will; therefore, he was responsible only to the people.

Polk's course in the House of Representatives established him as a loyal, orthodox Jacksonian. When Jackson defeated Adams in 1828, Polk felt that the people had been vindicated. The election was fought, he wrote, "between the virtue and rights of the people on the one hand and the power and patronage of their rules on the other."

Before long, Polk was recognized as the voice of the Jackson Administration in the House of Representatives. He remained in close correspondence with the president, and Jackson frequently sent him directives and thinly veiled suggestions as to the course the House should pursue. Polk proved a trustworthy lieutenant. He waged continual war on Henry Clay's American System ("falsely called," said Polk) and warned against the "splendid Government, differing . . . only in name from a consolidated empire" that Clay's program would create. He fought efforts to fund internal improvement projects with federal money, and when the celebrated bill providing for a road from Maysville to Lexington, Kentucky, came before the House, he was assigned the task of leading the administration forces against it. The bill passed but was struck down in the first of Jackson's important vetoes. On the question of the protective tariff, Polk supported the reduction of duties without ever totally rejecting the principle of protection. When the nullification crisis pitted South Carolina against Jackson and the federal government, Polk was quick to side with the president. He assisted in drafting a compromise tariff that he hoped would placate South Carolina, but when his effort was superseded by Henry Clay's compromise bill, he gave the Kentuckian his full support. Polk was consistent in his stand on behalf of the Union, even though some have found in his support of Jackson's position a contradiction of his Old Republican views.

Polk's appointment to the House Ways and Means Committee and his subsequent designation as its chairman placed him in an advantageous position to defend Jackson's assault against the Second United States Bank. In early 1833, Polk took exception to the committee's report declaring the bank's soundness and prepared a minority report in which he detailed the weakness and irresponsibility of the institution. A year later, as chairman of the committee, he issued a report sanctioning Jackson's removal of deposits from the bank; its adoption by the House of Representatives was a deathblow to the probank forces. In one of his most powerful speeches as a congressman, Polk inveighed against the "despotism of money" and warned that, if not checked, the power of money would soon "control your election of President, of your Senators, and of your Representatives." To Polk, the forces of money and privilege constituted the gravest threat to America's republican system of government.

Polk's election as speaker of the House of Representatives during his last two terms in Congress, from 1835 to 1839, was a tribute to his leadership, his party loyalty, and his administrative ability. As speaker, Polk demonstrated the same relentless devotion to the responsibilities of the post that he exhibited in other offices he had held. During Martin Van Buren's troubled administration, he tried desperately (and not always with success) to hold the Jacksonian coalition together. He wielded a tight and virtually absolute control over the deliberations of the House, for which he was frequently criticized by his opponents. When he left the speakership, he boasted, without exaggeration, that he had decided more difficult and complex questions of parliamentary law and order than had been decided by all of his predecessors.

Polk preferred to remain in the House of Representatives and could easily have been reelected in 1839. Instead, he was persuaded to run for governor of Tennessee, a move his associates believed would redeem the state from Whig control, weaken the opposition, and influence the 1840 presidential election. Polk was elected, but his term of office (two years) was anticlimactic and uneventful. It was not a good time for Democrats, as much of the public's attention was focused on the effects of the panic of 1837. The party's position in the state was not strengthened. Polk was defeated for reelection in 1841, and two years later he was defeated again. The magic of the Jacksonian appeal was gone, the voters had turned away from the party of their hero, and Polk suddenly seemed an anachronism. At the age of forty-eight, after almost twenty years of public activity and service to his state and nation, his political career appeared to be over.

"Who Is James K. Polk?"

Nine months after his second defeat for the governorship of Tennessee, in an incredible turnaround of his political fortunes, Polk was nominated for president of the United States by the Democratic Party. "Who is James K. Polk?" asked startled Whigs. Historians, taking their cue, have explained the unexpectedness of Polk's nomination by insisting that he was the nation's first "dark horse" candidate. In fact, Polk was not unknown (the Whigs knew very well who he was), nor was he so dark a horse.

When the delegates gathered at the Democratic National Convention in Baltimore in May, 1844, the name of James K. Polk was hardly mentioned. To be sure, Polk's ambitions for a place in the nation's executive branch had been aroused, but it was for the vice presidency, not the presidency. Four years before, as the parties maneuvered for the 1840 election, his name was paired with that of Van Buren. The Tennessee legislature nominated a Van Buren-Polk ticket, friends worked for his nomination among party leaders in Washington, and Andrew Jackson gave it his endorsement. Polk's place on the ticket, it was thought, would offset Van Buren's lack of popularity among Southerners. Polk, however, was not nominated, giving way to Kentucky's Richard Mentor Johnson, and Van Buren lost the election. Both men set their sights on 1844.

Martin Van Buren was the leading contender for the nomination in 1844, long before the convention met. His nomination seemed a foregone conclusion. His delegate strength mounted as state conventions pledged their support (although often without enthusiasm). The presidential race, as everyone seemed to expect, would be run between Van Buren and Henry Clay. Whigs were confident that they would be able to repeat their triumph of four years before.

As Van Buren's candidacy became more and more certain, Polk revived his quest for the vice presidential nomination. Someone acceptable to both the West and the South, he thought, would be sought, and who better to fill the need than himself? Once again, the aid of his friends, including the aged and ailing Andrew Jackson, was enlisted. Polk's record in the House of Representatives as a steadfast and "unterrified" defender of Jacksonian democracy was publicized. His supporters doubled their efforts to advance Van Buren's candidacy for the presidential nomination under the assumption that Polk would get the second position. By the spring of 1844, it appeared that the efforts on Polk's behalf would fall short, as they had four years before, and that Richard M. Johnson would likely be the candidate a second time.

Then on April 27, a bombshell was tossed into the campaign. On that day, Washington newspapers carried letters from both Henry Clay and Van Buren announcing their opposition to the immediate annexation of Texas to the United States, on the ground that such a move would constitute aggression against Mexico. Van Buren's statement threw his party into confusion, desertions from his ranks began, and his opponents were handed an issue with which to defeat his nomination. The hopes of Van Buren's rivals were raised, and some sent out feelers to Polk seeking the latter's endorsement in return for the vice presidency. To Polk and his supporters, however, Van Buren's downfall suggested a different strategy.

From one of his closest friends, Polk received the suggestion that "if Van Buren is to be thrown over... we must have an entirely new man." There was no doubt who that new man should be. Jackson, both disappointed and angered at Van Buren's statement, insisted that the presidential candidate "should be an annexation man and reside in the Southwest" and suggested that Polk would be the "most available." Of one thing Polk was sure: If Van Buren's name were withdrawn, the balance of power in the convention would be held by his supporters; they would be able to control the nominations. "I have never aspired so high," Polk assured his friends, but while he reiterated his ambition for "the 2nd office," he made it clear that they could use his name in any way they thought fit.

Polk's credentials as a Jacksonian were impeccable, as his record in the House of Representatives attested. That he also shared Jackson's strong desire to see Texas annexed to the United States was without question. Ever since Texas' break with Mexico during the last year of his presidency, Jackson had favored annexation, although he declined to make any move in that direction because of the dangers it might create for the Union. By the early 1840's, however, the question could no longer be repressed. "It is the greatest question of the *Age*," declared one political leader, as Americans in the West and South gathered in rallies and demonstrations to demand government action. With an eye on the 1844 election, President John Tyler promoted annexation, and Democratic leaders carried the demand into Congress. Even before Van Buren's fateful statement, Texas annexationists in the West had been looking for another candidate.

Jackson joined the cry with a letter to one of Polk's close friends in which he urged immediate annexation. Although the letter was not made public until a year later, his position was well-known to Polk. A few days before Van Buren's letter was published, Polk made his views known in response to an inquiry from a committee of Ohio Democrats. Like Jackson, he strongly favored the immediate annexation of Texas, arguing that Texas had been a part of the United States before John Quincy Adams had given it up to Spain in the Adams-Onís Treaty of 1819. He feared, as did many Western Democrats, the rise of British influence in Texas and placed his argument in the broader context of hemispheric security. Unlike Jackson, Polk linked his demand for Texas with the demand that the authority and laws of the United States be also extended to the Oregon country.

(Courtesy of the Library of Congress, Washington, D.C.)

Political Cartoon Favoring Annexation of Texas, 1844

Democratic delegates gathered in Baltimore amid fears that the party would be seriously divided over the Texas issue and Van Buren's candidacy. Although commanding the support of a majority of the delegates, Van Buren faced a growing opposition from the West and South, and when his opponents succeeded in reaffirming the rule requiring a two-thirds majority for the nomination, his chances diminished rapidly. After several inconclusive ballots, on the convention's third day, Polk's name was formally presented to the body as a candidate for the presidential nomination, and before the day ended, he had received the necessary two-thirds vote.

Polk's nomination was a compromise between the opposing camps. It was acceptable to the Van Buren forces (one of Van Buren's most trusted lieutenants declared Polk to be his second choice), in part because his nomination denied the prize as well to Van Buren's rivals. The steadfastness with which Polk himself stuck to his support of Van Buren (hoping to get the vice presidential nomination) was impressive. It was New England, notably Massachusetts delegate George Bancroft, which first put his name before the convention. Polk's nomination, however, upset many rank-and-file Van Buren supporters; because it was unexpected, stories of intrigue and chicanery were circulated. Charges that his nomination had been hatched in the Hermitage were made, and the Whigs were quick to exploit them. With Polk's nomination, however, the Democratic Party acquired a candidate whose orthodoxy was above reproach—"a pure, whole-hogged democrat," as one delegate put it. Polk was also an unequivocal proponent of Texas annexation, and in 1844, that is what counted most.

The remainder of the convention was anticlimactic. For vice president, the delegates' first choice was New York's Silas Wright, but Wright refused the nomination. The weary delegates then turned to George M. Dallas of Pennsylvania. With the nominations completed, the platform was adopted almost as an afterthought. To a traditional statement of Jacksonian principles—strict construction, states' rights, opposition to a national bank, a high tariff, and federally funded internal improvements—the convention added one new plank. The title of the United States to "the whole of the Territory of Oregon" was "clear and unquestionable"; "the reoccupation of Oregon and the reannexation of Texas, at the earliest practicable period, are great American measures, which this convention recommends to the cordial support of the democracy of the Union."

The Whigs, who had already nominated Henry Clay, were startled at the turn taken by the Democrats, unbelieving and joyous that their opponents had made such a "ridiculous" nomination. Clay, in a fit of arrogant self-confidence, regretted that a person "more worthy of a contest" had not been chosen.

Clay need not have worried, for the campaign of 1844 was a hard-fought and bitter contest. The parties were evenly matched, a sign that the party system had reached a stage of maturity. Clay was moved to acts of desperation, which in the end cost him dearly. At the last minute, he experienced a sudden change of heart on the Texas question and joined the annexationists, and his efforts to dissociate himself from Northern abolitionists drove their support away, especially in New York. There, the Liberty Party candidate, James G. Birney, took enough voters away from the Whig column to give the state to Polk; it was Polk's victory in New York, in turn, that gave the Democrats their electoral majority.

Polk won the presidency with 170 electoral votes to Clay's 105. His popular vote exceeded that of Clay by only 38,000 out of a total of almost 2,700,000 votes cast. Polk's nomination and election, following so quickly after his failures to win the governorship of Tennessee, has been judged well-nigh miraculous. Although many unique circumstances involving issues, partisanship, and power contributed to his success, Charles Sellers, Polk's biographer, gives the larger share of credit to "the behavior of a remarkably audacious, self-controlled, and prescient politician" who shaped his course "with impressive skill and coolness."

A Continental Vision

Polk's inaugural address was in sharp contrast to the gloomy, rainy weather in Washington on March 4, 1845. It was a message of hope and confidence for a youthful nation from a president who was younger than any of his predecessors. A paean to America's republican system, it exhibited the ardor that many people felt toward the nation's future. The United States, "this Heaven-favored land," he declared, enjoyed the "most admirable and wisest system of well-regulated self-government among men ever devised by human minds." It was the "noblest structure of human wisdom," wherein burned the fire of liberty, warming and animating "the hearts of happy millions" and inviting "all the nations of the earth to imitate our example." Under the benign influence of their government, the American people were "free to improve their condition by the legitimate exercise of all their mental and physical powers."

The sheet anchor of American republicanism was the Union; to protect and preserve the Union was the sacred duty of every American. Warning against the forces of sectionalism that would disturb and destroy the Union, Polk struck out at those "misguided persons" whose object was the "destruction of domestic institutions existing in other sections." a reference to the abolitionists. The consequences of their agitation could only be the dissolution of the Union and the "destruction of our happy form of government." Preserved and protected, the Union was the guarantee that the "blessings of civil and religious liberty" would be transmitted to "distant generations." "Who shall assign limits to the achievements of free minds and free hands under the protection of this glorious Union?" he asked.

In a confession of his Jacksonian faith, Polk called for a strict adherence to the Constitution and a scrupulous respect for the rights of the states, each sovereign "within the sphere of its reserved powers." The government must be returned to the "plain and frugal" system intended by its founders. There was no need for national banks "or other extraneous institutions"; in levying tariff duties, revenue must be the object and protection only incidental.

More than a third of his address was devoted to the new spirit of continental expansion. He rejected the pessimistic view of some Americans that the nation's system of government could not be successfully applied to a large extent of territory. On the contrary, Polk insisted, the "federative system" was well adapted to territorial expansion, and as the nation's boundaries were enlarged, it acquired "additional strength and security." The annexation of Texas, "once a part of our country" that was "unwisely ceded away," was of first importance, and Polk lauded Congress for taking the initial steps to effect the reunion of Texas with the United States. To the settlement of the Oregon question, he stated, he was no less dedicated. America's title to the region was "clear and unquestionable." Thousands of Americans, moreover, were establishing their homes in this far-flung corner, and the extension of the jurisdiction and benefits of the country's republican institutions to the area was an inescapable duty.

Whereas the inaugural address provided the general direction of the course that President Polk had charted for himself, a statement made to the historian George Bancroft supplied the specifics. He intended, he told Bancroft at the time of his inauguration, to accomplish four great measures during his administration. Two of them related to his vision of continental expansion: the settlement of the Oregon boundary question with Great Britain and the acquisition of California. (It is interesting to note that aside from a general concern over the fate of California and the impulsive capture and brief occupation of Monterey by American naval forces in 1842, California had not been seriously mentioned as a target for American expansion.) The third was the reduction of the tariff to a revenue level, and the last was the establishment of the independent treasury system, the Democrats' alternative to a third national bank. The independent Treasury had been created by Congress in the waning days of the Van Buren Administration, only to be repealed by the Whigs in 1841.

It was a large order for the new president, the more so since he had pledged to serve only a single term. Following his nomination, Polk made the promise in order to secure the support of Van Buren's leading rivals, men such as Lewis Cass, James Buchanan, and John C. Calhoun, whose hopes would be dashed if they had to wait eight more years to pursue their presidential ambitions. Concerned lest he appear to be favoring one or another for the succession, Polk refused to select any presidential aspirant for his cabinet. His appointees were to be men devoted to him and not to their own, or someone else's, advancement. He later regretted that he had taken at face value the disclaimer of James Buchanan, whom he appointed secretary of state. Polk would thread his way carefully through the cliques and factions of the party, determined to maintain his independence. "I intend to be myself President of the U.S.," he wrote a friend.

Missing from Polk's list of intended achievements was the annexation of Texas, for by the time he was inaugurated, the annexation had already been set in motion. As president-elect, Polk played an important part in the movement. His election in November, 1844, was viewed as a mandate for annexation, and steps were immediately taken in the short session of Congress that followed. Polk himself favored a settlement of the issue before he should be inaugurated. The only question to be resolved was which plan to effect annexation would be adopted—a House resolution to annex simply by a joint resolution of Congress or a Senate bill that called for the appointment of commissioners to negotiate an agreement with Texas. Although he favored the former, Polk sought to avoid an impasse by proposing a compromise, whereby the two modes would be combined as alternatives, with the president empowered to choose between them. the assumption was that the decision would be made by the new president, Polk, rather than by John Tyler, the outgoing president. The measure passed Congress in the last days of the session and was signed by Tyler on March 1. To Congress' surprise, however, it was Tyler who acted quickly to exercise the option; he dispatched a messenger to Texas with the offer of annexation.

It remained only for Polk to complete the process following his inauguration. He could have reversed Tyler's decision (and some senators expected him to do so), but Polk let it stand. In the face of mounting public excitement for annexation in both the United States and Texas, the Texas government assented, but only after the American emissaries (and Polk) agreed to recognize Texas' claim to the Rio Grande boundary and to provide military protection to Texas as soon as annexation had been accepted. On July 4, a Texas convention voted to accept annexation and proceeded to draw up a state constitution; later in December, Congress admitted Texas to the Union as a state. Polk's role in the annexation of Texas has been closely scrutinized by historians, and some have argued that his insistence on the Rio Grande boundary and his dispatch of troops into Texas were part of a deliberate scheme to provoke Mexico to war and thus open the way for the acquisition of California. Certainly, relations between the United States and Mexico, which had been deteriorating for years, worsened, as the Mexican government charged the United States with an act of aggression against Mexico and recalled its minister from Washington.

With the Texas issue moving toward a resolution, Polk turned his attention to the Oregon boundary question. Although the Democratic platform and Polk's inaugural statements brought the question to a head, the dispute with Great Britain had been of long duration. Unable to settle their conflicting claims to the region, the two countries had negotiated a joint occupation agreement in 1818, at the time the boundary between the United States and British North America east of the Rocky Mountains was drawn along the forty-ninth parallel. The agreement, originally to run for ten years, was renewed for an indefinite period in 1827, with the proviso that either country might terminate the agreement by giving the other country one year's notice. Repeated efforts were made to resolve the dispute, the United States offering to extend the forty-ninth parallel to the Pacific and the British insisting on the Columbia River as the boundary. Neither side was willing to give in to the other.

British fur-trading interests were active in the Oregon country during the early years of the century, but no attempts to settle it permanently were undertaken. Little was done by the United States to challenge the British presence, even though sentiment favored the ultimate extension of American sovereignty to the region. The situation changed in the 1830's when American missionaries arrived in Oregon; their reports were widely publicized and did much to arouse public feeling in support of an American occupation of the far Northwest. Indeed, the missionary efforts were responsible for the first movement of permanent settlers to Oregon's western valleys. The distress experienced by Western farmers in the aftermath of the panic of 1837 turned further attention to Oregon's rich soil and salubrious climate. Before long, an "Oregon Fever" raged, especially in the Mississippi Valley; people gathered in meetings and demonstrations to sing the praises of the new land and to voice their demands that the United States act quickly to extend its laws and institutions to Oregon's growing population.

(Courtesy of the Library of Congress, Washington, D.C.)

Handcart Immigration on the Oregon Trail

Each year, large numbers of families gathered in their wagons in Independence, Missouri (the jumping-off point), and prepared to make the long trek over the Oregon Trail to the Pacific Northwest. As the population of Oregon grew, the settlers became increasingly impatient with the apparent reluctance of the United States government to recognize their needs. Beginning in 1841, they took steps to establish a provisional government of their own that would at least provide a semblance of law and order, but their uppermost desire was to be reunited with their country. The expansionist fervor of Western Democrats, fueled by the movement of Americans to Oregon, found expression in the repudiation of Martin Van Buren's candidacy and in the election of Polk to the presidency.

Following the 1844 election, the Oregon question became a heated national issue, as its supporters moved to the more radical demand that all of Oregon be acquired, meaning all that territory from the forty-second parallel north to fifty-four degrees forty minutes. "Fifty-four Forty or Fight" became a new rallying cry. Polk seemed to endorse this new extreme in his inaugural address, although privately he still believed that the extension of the forty-ninth parallel, America's traditional position, was the most feasible solution. The British government became alarmed at the bellicose tone of the American demands and feared that war might break out between the two countries.

Polk had no more intention than the British of fighting a war over the Oregon country, but he was not above using the more radical demands to strengthen his efforts to settle the boundary dispute. As in the case of the Texas issue, the Tyler Administration had taken steps to settle the question, and Polk's first actions were based on those of his predecessor. In July, he offered once again to draw the line along the forty-ninth parallel, without at the same time surrendering the American claim to the whole of Oregon. The offer was categorically rejected by the British minister in Washington without transmitting it to his government in London. Polk was both shocked and furious. He had made the offer, he said, out of deference to his predecessors; the offer was withdrawn, and the claim to all of Oregon was reasserted. The ball was now in the British court.

Polk was playing a dangerous game. Amid fears that his unyielding attitude would involve the United States in a war with Great Britain, Polk refused to back down. "The only way to treat John Bull," he confided to his diary, "was to look him straight in the eye." At the same time, the issue assumed an added urgency. Relations with Mexico were approaching a crisis, and Polk's attention was divided between the two situations. As with his Texas policy, there were hints that California was in his mind. The settlement of the Oregon question might deter Great Britain from acquiring California (perceived as a real threat in 1845), leaving the way open for an American acquisition through negotiations with Mexico.

Polk's course was bold and daring; at the same time, he was convinced that it was a peaceful one. In his first message to Congress, in December, 1845, he asked Congress to provide the one year's notice that the United States was terminating the joint occupation agreement with Great Britain. Furthermore, he asked that jurisdiction be extended over the Americans living in Oregon and that steps be taken to provide military protection to emigrants along the route to Oregon. Finally, he restated the Monroe Doctrine against any further colonization of North America by a European power, a reference to the British designs on California. Congress responded but not until the spring of 1846, when the one year's notice resolution was finally approved.

As Polk had expected, the passage of the resolution spurred the British government to make a new offer to the United States. It was tantamount to a surrender to the traditional American position. An extension of the boundary along the forty-ninth parallel was proposed, with the provision that British settlers south of that line could retain title to their lands and that the great fur-trading organization, the Hudson's Bay Company, would be allowed the free navigation of the Columbia River. The latter stipulation was not crucial, for by 1846 the company had moved its operations to Vancouver Island in anticipation of the boundary settlement. Polk stood firm but offered to seek the advice of the Senate. When the Senate advised the president by an overwhelming vote to accept the terms, Polk relented, and on June 15, 1846, a treaty was signed by the two powers that brought an end to the boundary dispute.

The settlement of the Oregon boundary has often been seen as a compromise between the United States and Great Britain. Insofar as the United States receded from its extreme demand for all of Oregon, it perhaps was. In the perspective of the long history of negotiations, however, the treaty was clearly a diplomatic victory for the United States—and that is how Polk viewed it. He had secured all that he initially sought; his firm stance had paid off. Western expansionist Democrats saw the result as neither a victory nor a compromise; to them, it was an abject surrender of an unquestioned American claim. Some of them never forgave Polk.

Within fifteen months of his inauguration, Polk had presided over the addition of two immense regions to the United States, Texas and Oregon, not only fulfilling the pledge in the Democratic platform on which he was elected but also bringing his dream of continental expansion closer to reality. There still remained the acquisition of California. That too had been set in motion; one month before the Oregon treaty was signed, Polk announced to Congress that war between the United States and Mexico had begun.

Relations with Mexico

In both Texas and Oregon, Polk carried to fruition problems that he had inherited from a previous administration to the ultimate advantage of the United States. The same was true with the deteriorated state of American-Mexican relations. Ever since Mexico had won its independence from Spain in the early 1820's, relations between the two countries had been on a downward slide. The initial enthusiasm expressed by Americans over the organization of a sister republic waned as Mexico became a country wracked by revolution and plagued by instability. The perception of Mexican irresponsibility (an attitude fomented among Europeans perhaps to a greater extent than among Americans) and of Mexico's inability to provide a sound and efficient republican system grew, and it was easy for critics to explain the situation in racial terms.

Two issues brought relations between the two countries to a crisis in the Polk Administration: the claims issue and the issue of Texas annexation. With independence from Spain, Mexico freed itself from the restrictive policies of Spanish mercantilism and opened its borders to foreign commercial activity. The frequency of revolution, exacerbated by an inability by foreigners to appreciate cultural differences, often resulted in the loss of property (and sometimes lives) by foreign nationals. Claims for compensation were lodged against the Mexican government; when it became obvious that Mexico was unable to pay, the claimants appealed to their governments—principally Great Britain, France, and the United States—for support. That the claims were often exaggerated did not lessen the determination of the governments to intervene on behalf of their aggrieved citizens.

The British and French solution was to exact payment by force. The French landed soldiers at Vera Cruz and fought a brief engagement (known as the Pastry War) with Mexican troops; Great Britain followed with a blockade of the Mexican coastline. Both Great Britain and France, with Spanish support, concluded that only the establishment of a monarchy in Mexico, headed by a European prince, could stabilize Mexico. The prospect horrified Americans.

Although Jackson had once threatened war against Mexico over the claims issue, the course of the United States had been a peaceful one. The issue was submitted to arbitration, the size of the claim was scaled down by two-thirds, and Mexico agreed to make payments to the United States. After only a few installments, Mexico defaulted. The claims issue continued to fester. By 1845, when Polk was inaugurated, it had become a major source of contention between the two countries. Fears, fed by rumors, that California would be either ceded to or seized by the British in payment for the Mexican debt became magnified. To many Americans, California seemed suitable payment for Mexico's unpaid debt to the United States, especially since large numbers of emigrants were now crossing the plains and mountains to settle in California's interior valleys.

It was the annexation of Texas, however, that had a more immediate impact on American relations with Mexico. Ever since Texas had won its independence in 1836, Mexico had nurtured plans for regaining the region. When Texas gave up its independence to accept integration into the American Union, such plans suffered a major setback. The issue became involved in Mexico's domestic politics, and no Mexican leader could ignore the rising anti-American sentiment in the country. Although the hard-line government of Santa Anna had been ousted by a coup in 1844 and replaced with the more liberal administration of José Joaquín Herrera, Mexico could ill afford to recognize the loss of Texas. On the contrary, the passage of the annexation resolution early in March, 1845, was viewed as equivalent to "a declaration of war against the Mexican Republic" and "sufficient for the immediate proclamation of war" on Mexico's part. The Mexican minister to Washington was recalled, and diplomatic relations between the two nations were broken off.

The volatility of the claims and Texas issues had never been so great as when Polk assumed office. His initial actions regarding Texas, the recognition of the Rio Grande boundary and the promise of military protection to the Texans, only aggravated the situation. United States Army troops, commanded by Zachary Taylor, entered Texas and took up positions at Corpus Christi, on the south bank of the Nueces River. Mexico responded by ordering an increase in the size of the Mexican army and threatened war against the United States as soon as the annexation process should be completed.

In the face of the heightened tension, Polk sent a personal representative, William S. Parrott (probably a poor choice inasmuch as Parrott was one of the largest claimants against the Mexican government), to probe the possibility of reopening diplomatic relations. When Parrott reported that the Herrera government would receive a qualified commissioner to negotiate the differences between the two countries, Polk moved to the next step. He chose John Slidell, congressman from Louisiana, to go to Mexico with instructions to secure Mexican recognition of the Rio Grande boundary in exchange for the cancellation of the claims and to offer to purchase California and New Mexico for an undetermined sum of money. The threat of British seizure of California seemed real: Parrott had emphasized it in his report from Mexico City, and Polk was determined to frustrate it.

Slidell went to Mexico, however, not only as a commissioner to negotiate a settlement of the disputes but also as a fully accredited minister, an effort on Polk's part to reopen diplomatic relations but one that would place Herrera in jeopardy if accepted. Slidell's arrival in Mexico was greeted by an outburst of anti-American activity as reports spread that Slidell intended to secure for the United States not only Texas but also the northern Mexican borderlands. Under the circumstances, the Herrera government could not receive Slidell; the rebuff, however, did not save it. A revolution forced Herrera out of office, and his place was taken by General Mariano Paredes, a monarchist who almost immediately contacted European powers with the intention of establishing a monarchy in Mexico as the only way the country could be saved from the United States.

Texas was admitted to the Union as a state in December, 1845, and shortly afterward, Taylor's army was ordered to new positions along the Rio Grande; by the end of March, 1846, he had arrived opposite the Mexican town of Matamoros. In the meantime, Slidell applied for recognition to Paredes, but with no different result. If Slidell should be rejected a second time, Secretary of State Buchanan had written, "the cup of forbearance will then have been exhausted." Nothing remained, he stated, "but to take the redress of the injuries to our citizens and the insults to our Government into our hands."

In rejecting Slidell, the Paredes government reiterated the position that the annexation of Texas was a cause for war between the two countries. Paredes followed with an order to mobilize Mexico's armed forces and to reinforce Mexican troops on the south bank of the Rio Grande. Taylor had been told to regard any Mexican attempt to cross the Rio Grande as an act of war, whereas the Mexican commander viewed Taylor's refusal to pull back as an act of war. Paredes further emphasized the Mexican position by declaring a "defensive war" against the United States in April. There matters between the two countries stood in the spring of 1846. Sentiment for war was on the increase in both countries. With European encouragement, Mexico was led to believe that a conflict with the United States would result in easy victory, and Americans, gripped by an expansionist fervor, resentful of supposed insults to their sovereignty and threats against their republican system, were equally persuaded that a war against Mexico would be quick and smooth.

With the arrival of news in Washington that Slidell's mission had failed, Polk was prepared to adopt "strong measures towards Mexico" but delayed until the Oregon question, then reaching its climax, should be settled. When Slidell returned to the capital and reported to the president, Polk agreed that action against Mexico must be taken. After securing cabinet approval, he decided to recommend a declaration of war to Congress. That night, he received a dispatch from General Taylor. Mexican forces had crossed the Rio Grande and had engaged American troops, resulting in some loss of life. To Polk, there no longer was any question as to what policy should be followed.

On May 11, 1846, Polk sent his war message to Congress. "The grievous wrongs perpetrated by Mexico upon our citizens," he declared, "remain unredressed, and solemn treaties pledging [Mexico's] public faith for this redress have been disregarded." The United States, he continued, in what some regarded as an exaggeration, had "tried every effort at reconciliation" but to no avail. "The cup of forbearance had been exhausted even before the recent information from the frontier of the Del Norte [Rio Grande]. But now, after reiterated menaces, Mexico has passed the boundary of the United States, has invaded our territory and shed American blood upon the American soil... As war exists, and, notwithstanding all our efforts to avoid it, exists by the act of Mexico herself, we are called upon by every consideration of duty and patriotism to vindicate with decision the honor, the rights, and the interests of our country."

Two days later, Congress, by a decisive vote, recognized a state of war between the United States and Mexico, empowered the president to use the army and navy against Mexico, appropriated $10 million for military purposes, and authorized the enlistment of fifty thousand volunteer troops. A short time later, Polk told his cabinet that "in making peace with our adversary, we shall acquire California, New Mexico, and other further territory, as an indemnity for this war, if we can."

The War with Mexico

The war with Mexico was a short war, as wars go, yet it was an extremely important conflict for the United States. Stung by the taunts of European powers that republics were ill equipped to fight wars and, because they eschewed professional standing armies, helpless to defend themselves, Americans saw in the war an opportunity to strengthen republicanism, both at home and abroad. Those who were uncomfortable with a conflict between two republics were also aware that Mexico's republican institutions had never been allowed to work, that repeated revolution and turmoil had destroyed their effectiveness, and that, in fact, the nation, through much of its life, had been ruled as a military dictatorship. Thus the war for many assumed an idealistic character.

At the same time, it was clear that the United States would benefit greatly by a victory over Mexico. Polk's continental vision would become a reality and his dream of adding California to the nation would be fulfilled. The war was a natural outgrowth of the expansionist feeling of the 1840's, a feeling that Polk shared. Although he denied that it was being fought for conquest, the circumstances of its origin suggested otherwise. As a result, Polk's role has been a controversial one in American historiography, as some historians have insisted that he deliberately provoked an unjust war in order to satisfy his lust for more territory.

Following the call for volunteers, a wave of war excitement passed over the country. Men flocked to the colors, many more than could be handled, and the quotas assigned some of the states were oversubscribed. The war, fought in a distant exotic land, held a romantic appeal for those who volunteered, an appeal that soon faded as the fighting began. The response to the volunteer calls, however, confirmed the belief that the republic could rely on its citizen-soldiers during times of crisis.

The problems faced by the Polk Administration in fighting the war were enormous; that they were met and for the most part solved was a tribute to the president's administrative ability. For the first time, the country was compelled to raise large numbers of troops in a short time, to train, equip, and move them quickly to distant points. Knowledge of Mexico was sketchy and the means for gathering intelligence either nonexistent or crude. War material had to be produced on an unprecedented scale, and quartermaster stores (everything necessary to support an army in the field) had to be provided without delay. Ships were built, purchased, or chartered to carry the men to the battle areas. The need to coordinate naval and land operations and to direct the movement of troops in enemy territory placed a premium on military skill and ingenuity.

(Courtesy of the Library of Congress, Washington, D.C.)

Landing of the Troops at Vera Cruz
Lithograph by Wagner and McGulgan

Military operations were mounted in three areas. General Zachary Taylor crossed the Rio Grande and moved into northern Mexico, fighting a desperate and costly battle for Monterrey in September, 1846, and achieving one of the greatest victories of the war at the Battle of Buena Vista in February, 1847. A second army, commanded by General Stephen Watts Kearny, moved west from Missouri over the Santa Fe Trail, occupying New Mexico and, in conjunction with naval forces, taking possession of California. A third front was opened in the spring of 1847 when General Winfield Scott, in the greatest amphibious operation to that time, landed twelve thousand soldiers at Vera Cruz. Marching inland along the route of Hernán Cortés' sixteenth-century invasion, Scott's army fought several sharp engagements, including a series of battles in the vicinity of Mexico City, before occupying the Mexican capital in September, 1847. With the occupation of Mexico City, the fighting came to an end, except for sporadic guerrilla activity along the lines of supply.

In his administration of the war, Polk contributed significantly to a definition of the president's role as commander in chief, and his exercise of military power became a model for future presidents. He assumed full responsibility for the conduct of the war, taking the initiative in securing war legislation and finance, deciding on military strategy, appointing generals and drafting their instructions, directing the supply efforts, and coordinating the work of the various bureaus and cabinet departments. He insisted on being informed of every decision that was made by his cabinet officers. Polk was, as one author has written, "the center on which all else depended."

There were problems, however, on which Polk faltered. He was bothered by the fact that the two senior officers in the army, Winfield Scott and Zachary Taylor, were both Whigs. He had no choice but to rely on them, in spite of the uncomfortable prospect that their exploits would advance their prestige and lead to presidential ambitions. To allay his doubts, he made a clumsy effort to persuade Congress to revive the rank of lieutenant general so that he might appoint a Democrat to this high-ranking post. Congress refused. His dislike for Scott was deep seated, culminating in Polk's unfair treatment of the general at the end of the war when Scott was relieved of his command and recalled to face a military inquiry. At the same time, Polk made some disastrous appointments of civilians to military commands, the most notorious being that of his former law partner, Gideon Pillow. On balance, however, Polk's conduct of the war was good. There were limits to even his endurance, and the long hours he devoted to his task and his intense application of energy eventually undermined his health.

When Polk delivered his war message to Congress, he anticipated a short conflict. Indeed, he expected Mexico to sue for peace in the very first weeks and months of the war, but the Mexican government, in spite of an unbroken series of military defeats, refused to give up. Almost as soon as the war began, Polk was seeking ways to end it. He made overtures to the Paredes government in the summer of 1846, but without success. At the same time, he entered into discussions with Santa Anna, exiled in Havana, offering to help restore the former Mexican leader to power in return for a peaceful settlement of the conflict. Santa Anna gave his assurances, and Polk foolishly believed him. Following his return to Mexico, Santa Anna assumed personal command of the army, increased its size, and took the field against the Americans.

With the failure of his peace efforts, Polk decided to open an offensive against Mexico City from Vera Cruz and reluctantly placed Scott in charge. Confident that this operation would bring the war to an end, he appointed Nicholas Trist, chief clerk of the State Department, to accompany Scott and granted him authority to suspend hostilities and enter into peace negotiations whenever Mexico might appear receptive. His instructions called for the cession of Upper and Lower California and New Mexico, the cancellation of the claims, and the payment of $15 million to Mexico.

Trist's task was not an easy one. He became involved in bitter personal quarrels with Scott, who resented the encroachment on his own authority, although relations between the two men later improved. Mexico was still unwilling to end the war, and Trist's efforts to lure Mexican representatives to the peace table, including an abortive plan to bribe Santa Anna, proved futile. It was not until the end of the summer, with Scott's army in the environs of Mexico City, that Santa Anna finally appointed commissioners to deal with Trist. Still, there was no meeting of the minds. Polk's impatience mounted. Extreme expansionists in the United States were demanding all of Mexico, and Polk himself apparently concluded that more territory should be taken from Mexico. Finally, in October, 1847, frustrated and at the end of his patience, Polk recalled Trist.

Trist, however, was determined to conclude a peace treaty with Mexico. He disregarded Polk's order and remained in touch with his Mexican counterparts, confident that no one else Polk might send could do better than he. The discussions continued, Polk became exasperated at Trist's arrogance, and Scott began making preparations to resume military operations. British diplomats urged the Mexican government to make peace; the country was rapidly falling into disarray. Santa Anna finally relented at the end of January, 1848.

The Treaty of Guadalupe Hidalgo, named after the town in which the document was signed, followed Trist's original instructions (except for the cession of Lower California). Mexico agreed to recognize the Rio Grande as the boundary of Texas and to cede New Mexico and Upper California to the United States; the United States assumed all the claims against Mexico and agreed to pay Mexico $15 million. Although Trist negotiated and signed the settlement without diplomatic authority, Polk accepted it and in late February transmitted the treaty to the Senate for ratification. By the end of May, the treaty was ratified by Mexico. Dispatched by special messenger to Washington, the document was delivered to Polk on July 4, when he proclaimed an end to the war amid the festivities celebrating America's independence.

When Polk submitted his fourth and last annual message to Congress in December, 1848, he pointed proudly to the fulfillment of America's expansionist destiny. The acquisition of California and New Mexico, the settlement of the Oregon boundary, and the annexation of Texas, he declared, "are the results which . . . will add more to the strength and wealth of the nation than any which have preceded them since the adoption of the Constitution." Within less than four years, almost 1,200,000 square miles of territory had been added to the United States, an area half as large as the nation before the acquisition. The geographic configuration of the country had undergone a profound change, for "the Mississippi, so lately the frontier of our country, is now only its center."

The war with Mexico, he continued, belied the assertions of Europeans that the United States was a weak and ineffective power. The United States had demonstrated "the capacity of republican governments to prosecute successfully a just and necessary foreign war with all the vigor usually attributed to more arbitrary forms of government." There could no longer be any doubt that a "popular representative government" was equal to any emergency likely to arise. The war had increased American prestige abroad, and even at that moment, Polk declared, European countries were struggling to erect republican governments on the American model.

"Peace, plenty, and contentment reign throughout our borders, and our beloved country presents a sublime moral spectacle to the world. . . . We are the most favored people on the face of the earth."

Slavery

With the advantage of hindsight, one can now wonder at Polk's optimistic faith in the future of his country, for although the Mexican War resulted in the addition of vast new regions to the republic, it also raised an issue that would rock the nation to its foundations.

It was inevitable that the question of territorial expansion would become involved with that of slavery. The first warning had in fact been sounded in 1819 when Missouri applied for admission to the Union as a slave state. The Missouri Compromise of 1820 resolved the issue, but few Americans believed it to be finally settled. The emergence of a militant abolition movement in sections of the North was a clear indication that the problem would only become more acute. Northern antislavery and abolitionist elements, a small but growing minority, strenuously opposed the annexation of Texas on the ground that it would strengthen the institution of slavery. Later, they took a strong stand against the Mexican War, in the mistaken belief that the war was a grand plot of the slave power to extend the institution to new areas, and they vented their spleen against Polk as one of the leading conspirators. Although their cries were drowned out in the enthusiasm that followed the opening of the war, they constituted a formidable political force.

It was not an abolitionist, however, but a disgruntled Pennsylvania Democratic congressman who first interjected the slavery issue into the deliberations on the war. David Wilmot, who believed that the Western territories should be reserved for free white settlers but who also had clashed with President Polk over the latter's tariff and internal improvements policies, introduced a resolution in August, 1846, that would bar slavery forever from all territory taken from Mexico. The so-called Wilmot Proviso, attached to an appropriation bill, became a rallying point for antislavery people and a focus for opposition to the war itself.

Although Polk was a slaveholder with plantations in Tennessee and Mississippi, he had never actively defended the institution. As a member of Congress, he had deplored the persistent agitation of the issue and believed that it only hampered the deliberation of more important questions. He had supported the gag rule, by which antislavery petitions were automatically tabled without being read, and as speaker of the House of Representatives he had enforced it. At the same time, he viewed slavery as an evil that affected not only the South but the entire nation as well, insisting that slaves were a species of property with a difference, inasmuch as they were also rational human beings. Although abolitionists believed otherwise, Polk had never linked his continental vision with a desire to extend slavery throughout the West.

Polk was shocked and dismayed by Wilmot's move, calling the resolution a "mischievous & foolish amendment." He feared that it would only entangle and frustrate his efforts to make peace with Mexico. "What connection slavery has with making peace with Mexico," he confided, "it is difficult to conceive." Still, the issue would not go away. Although it was never adopted by both houses of Congress, the Wilmot Proviso was raised in the following years, gathering momentum and strengthening the antislavery forces that were opposed to the war. Discussions in Congress became more heated, and Polk worried lest they sidetrack needed war legislation and jeopardize the acquisition of California and New Mexico. The question, he argued, was an abstract one, for not only had Mexico abolished slavery in the territory in question, but also slavery could never exist there. He blamed the "ultra" Northerners and the "ultra" Southerners for placing the Union in danger by their demands. "There is no patriotism on either side," he wrote, "it is a most wicked agitation that can end in no good and must produce infinite mischief."

With the end of the war and the ratification of the Treaty of Guadalupe Hidalgo, the discussion shifted to the question of providing territorial governments for the new lands. In August, 1848, Congress, after much debate, finally agreed on a bill organizing a territorial government for Oregon, with slavery prohibited in keeping with the wishes of the population, and Polk signed it into law, pointing out that the territory lay wholly north of the Missouri Compromise line.

Governments for California and New Mexico were not so easily established. Polk would have been happy to see the Missouri Compromise line extended to the Pacific, but Northern antislavery elements had already defeated that proposal. He was strongly opposed to the Wilmot Proviso's prohibition of slavery in the area because he believed that it would divide the nation, not because he was anxious to see slavery spread. At the same time, he tried to point out that the slavery question involved much more than a matter of property rights to the people in the South. The question "ascends far higher, and involves the domestic peace and security of every family." By the time Congress was able to agree on the organization of governments for California and New Mexico, Polk had not only left office but had also died.

Young Hickory

Although Polk's Administration was dominated by territorial expansion and the war with Mexico, other matters on his agenda also demanded his attention. As a lifelong disciple of Andrew Jackson, he was determined to reinstate the Jacksonian program that had suffered erosion under the Whigs following the election of 1840. The modification of the tariff and the establishment of the independent treasury system, both mentioned to Bancroft, formed the core of his domestic program. Equally important was his determination to enforce Jacksonian scruples against the passage of internal improvements legislation by Congress. His program constituted a full-scale attack on Henry Clay's American System.

He succeeded in all three areas. Following the guidelines Polk set forth in his first message to Congress in December, 1845, new tariff legislation was introduced that would reduce the rates established by the Whigs in 1842 and place them on an *ad valorem* basis. In keeping with Jacksonian orthodoxy, the tariff was designed for revenue only, with protection merely incidental. Polk kept a close eye on the bill's progress, exerted pressure on wavering congressmen, and held numerous conferences with Democratic leaders. In August, 1846, the bill passed and was signed. Almost simultaneously, legislation restoring the independent treasury system, or constitutional Treasury, as Polk called it, became law. The system, Polk hoped, would end all connection between the government and banks, whether state or national. Henceforth, the government would be the custodian of its own funds, depositing revenues in treasury vaults and disbursing them as the government's business might require. Polk placed great emphasis on these achievements, commenting that "the public good, as well as my own power and the glory of my administration" depended upon their success.

The question of internal improvements had long been a source of contention between the parties. For the Whigs, it served as an important element in their platform, alongside the protective tariff and the United States Bank. Although Andrew Jackson had not always been consistent in the matter, he made opposition to internal improvements projects that were essentially local in nature a primary characteristic of Democratic Party ideology. Polk shared Jackson's conviction that internal improvements bills were violations of constitutional authority.

In 1846, the same year in which the tariff and independent treasury bills passed Congress, a comprehensive river and harbors bill, to which scores of internal improvement projects had been added, was enacted. Polk promptly vetoed it in one of the most important actions of his administration. The legislation, he insisted, was not authorized by the Constitution. "The whole frame of the Federal Constitution," he wrote, "proves that the Government which it creates was intended to be one of limited and specified powers." An interpretation of the Constitution as broad as that argued by the bill's supporters, he warned, would head "imperceptibly to a consolidation of power in a Government intended by the framers to be thus limited in its authority."

Polk's veto aroused a fierce opposition among many Democrats, especially in the Western sections of the country where internal improvements were deemed essential to economic development, but Polk was unmoved by their protests. The principle behind the question of internal improvements struck at his concept of limited national government and strong states' rights. "I am thoroughly convinced," he wrote, "that I am right on this subject."

Polk stood by his pledge to serve only one term as president and, in spite of the appeals of many of his friends, refused to allow his name to be presented to the Democratic convention in 1848. He also declined to express a preference for his party's nominee. The conflict over the extension of slavery to the Mexican cession continued to worry him, and as it became clear that the party was seriously divided on the question, concern gave way to depression. All that he had worked to achieve seemed threatened by an issue that he had not foreseen. The pressures of the presidential office began to take their toll on his health. When Zachary Taylor won election as president, Polk confided his deep regret to his diary. Taylor, he feared, had no opinions of his own; he would be wholly controlled by the leaders of the Whig Party. "The country," he was sure, "will be the loser by his election." On March 5, 1849, Taylor assumed the reins of government (March 4 had fallen on a Sunday), and that evening Polk and his wife began their journey home.

Polk returned to Tennessee physically exhausted and in ill health. On June 15, 1849, barely three months after he left office, he died unexpectedly. He was fifty-four years old.

Although lacking in charisma and judged by many of his contemporaries to be dull and colorless, Polk brought to the presidency a dynamic quality that few occupants of the office have had. He devoted his full energy to his duties, working tirelessly to achieve his goals. He put in long hours; twelve-hour days were not uncommon. "I am the hardest working man in this country," he once remarked. Polk seldom left the national capital and during his four years as president took only one brief vacation. "No President," he insisted, "who performs his duty faithfully and conscientiously can have any leisure." He maintained a constant surveillance over the departments of the government and kept in constant touch with the leadership in Congress. Polk was his own man, made his own decisions, and seldom allowed them to be changed. Even Jackson found that he could not influence Polk.

Polk left behind a monument to his energy and his dogged determination. Seldom has a president carried out such an ambitious and far-reaching program as did Polk in the brief space of four years. To George Bancroft, one of Polk's devoted supporters and friends, he was "one of the very foremost of our public men and one of the very best and most honest and most successful Presidents the country ever had." To another, a political leader who had tangled with Polk on more than one occasion, he was "the partisan of a principle—of a system of measures and policy which he believed to be essential to the purity and perpetuity of our republican institutions . . . [who] consecrated his life to the cause, and staked his fortunes on the result."

Robert W. Johannsen

Bibliographical References

Indispensable to a study of Polk's presidency is the diary he maintained during his administration, *The Diary of James K. Polk During His Presidency, 1845 to 1849*, 4 vols., 1910. Charles G. Sellers, Jr., has written two volumes of a projected three-volume definitive biography: *James K. Polk: Jacksonian, 1795-1843*, 1957, and *James K. Polk: Continentalist, 1843-1846*, 1966. An early biography is by Eugene I. McCormac, *James K. Polk: A Political Biography*, 1922. A study of Polk's conduct of the presidency is Charles A. McCoy, *Polk and the Presidency*, 1960.

ZACHARY TAYLOR

1849–1850

Zachary Taylor entered the White House as a former professional soldier who had never voted in an election nor run for public office before the presidential election of 1848. Although he died before completing even half of his term, he exhibited strong leadership during a dangerous period of domestic crisis.

A Military Heritage

Born at Montebello, Orange County, Virginia, on November 24, 1784, Taylor could claim descent from distinguished forebears. One ancestor arrived in North America on the *Mayflower*, and James Madison was the Taylors' second cousin. The family also counted Robert E. Lee as a distant relative. One of seven children born to Revolutionary War veteran Lieutenant Colonel Richard Taylor and his wife, Sarah Dabney Strother Taylor, young Zachary was still an infant when the family moved to Jefferson County, Kentucky. He grew up on a farm near Louisville with the benefit of little formal schooling.

In 1808, Taylor was commissioned a lieutenant of infantry and won promotion to captain two years later in the minuscule regular army of the United States. During the War of 1812 he repeatedly distinguished himself in action. In September, 1812, his determined defense of Fort Harrison in the Indiana Territory won for him a brevet promotion to major. In 1814, he led troops against a superior force of British and Indians at Credit Island on the Mississippi, attacking aggressively before being forced to withdraw in the face of overwhelming enemy strength. It was the first and last time that Taylor retreated during his military career.

In 1832, Colonel Taylor again served in combat during the brief and tragic Black Hawk War, which he regarded as a needless waste of lives and resources in a dubious cause. The conquered Chief Black Hawk later recalled Taylor's kind treatment of his people with great gratitude. From 1837 through 1840, he battled the Seminole Indians in Florida Territory. An ill-managed conflict fought under appalling conditions, the war brought Taylor brevet promotion to brigadier general as the result of his victory over the Seminoles at Lake Okeechobee in 1837. He finished his tour of duty in

Florida as commander of all the troops in the territory, having won a reputation for resourcefulness and dogged determination.

In 1810, Taylor married Margaret Mackall Smith, the daughter of a prominent Maryland family. She bore him five daughters and one son between 1811 and 1826, before becoming an invalid. In 1835 one of his daughters, Sara Knox Taylor, married Mississippian Jefferson Davis against her father's wishes. Three months later she died of malaria and Taylor remained embittered against Davis for more than a decade. Taylor's son, Richard, grew up to become one of the most prominent generals in the Confederate army. A second daughter, Mary Elizabeth, served as official hostess of the White House during Taylor's presidency. Despite his frequent absences on campaign or frontier service, Taylor remained a devoted husband to his ailing wife and an affectionate father to his children.

The Mexican War

In 1845, the sixty-year-old Taylor was well known in the army but still little known in the nation as a whole despite his victories in two wars. He was placed in command of the American troops stationed at Corpus Christi, Texas, that year and instructed to guard against Mexican incursions into the newly annexed state. Early in 1846, his "Army of Observation" marched south to the disputed territory between the Rio Grande and Nueces rivers and encamped on the eastern bank of the Rio Grande across from Matamoras, Mexico. Fighting erupted in April, 1846, when Mexican troops ambushed an American patrol on the north bank of the Rio Grande. On May 8 and 9, Taylor met and defeated a Mexican army in pitched battles at Palo Alto and Resaca de la Palma. The enemy fled across the Rio Grande, leaving Taylor a new national hero in the United States while giving open justification to President Polk's call for a declaration of war against Mexico.

An aggressive commander, Taylor chose to maintain the momentum of his success by pursuing the beaten Mexicans across the Rio Grande and driving south against the city of Monterrey, a key city in the northern portion of the country. It fell to his troops after fierce fighting raged through the suburbs and streets from September 21 to 23. The defeated defenders were allowed to withdraw their forces under a truce granted by Taylor. This act of chivalry angered President Polk, who desired the swiftest possible conclusion to the war while fearing Taylor's potential rise as a political rival to candidates of his own Democratic Party.

Polk's concerns led him to choose General Winfield Scott rather than Taylor to lead the main American offensive aimed at the conquest of Mexico City. A large portion of Taylor's command was taken from him and assigned to reinforce Scott's expeditionary force as it prepared to drive inland to the west after making an amphibious landing at Vera Cruz on the Gulf coast. Taylor was left to secure control of northern Mexico with a badly depleted army.

From February 21 to 23, 1847, General Antonio Lopez de Santa Anna learned of the enemy forces' division and decided to strike north to destroy Taylor before turning to face Scott's thrust from the coast. Santa Anna attacked Taylor at Buena Vista, a stretch of rugged, hilly terrain south of Saltillo. Although some of the American volunteers panicked under fire, Taylor masterfully held his line together and bloodily repulsed the enemy assaults with musketry and skillfully handled artillery. The five thousand Americans inflicted heavy casualties on the twenty thousand Mexicans and forced Santa Anna to withdraw in frustration. Buena Vista was the most spectacular victory of Taylor's military career, and it had more to do with his subsequent election to the presidency than any single factor.

(Courtesy of the Library of Congress, Washington, D.C.)

Scott successfully captured Mexico City at the climax of his offensive, and a peace treaty was signed at Guadalupe Hidalgo early in 1848. The United States had won vast new southwestern territories extending from the Rio Grande to the Pacific, and Taylor returned home a hero despite Polk's attempts to belittle his fame.

Taylor as President: Free States and Threats of Secession
The Whig Party had last won the White House in 1840 with William

Henry Harrison, a part-time soldier with enduring political aspirations. In June, 1848, the Whigs eagerly nominated Zachary Taylor, an even more glamorous military figure, as their presidential candidate. "Old Rough and Ready," as his soldiers called him, was the perfect candidate for the times. His earthy, unassuming personality and reputation for courage and decisiveness were complemented by an obscure record on the prevailing political issues. His ancestry and ownership of slaves and a cotton plantation made him attractive to Southern voters, while his lack of prior political involvement meant that he had said or done nothing to offend groups in other parts of the country.

The Democrats countered with Lewis Cass of Michigan, a colorless party figure. Cass joined Taylor in conducting a campaign that was purposely vague on the pressing issues of the day: slavery and the future of the new western territories. Even before the war had ended, debate had raged in Congress over whether slavery should be permitted in the new territories won from Mexico. Many Northern abolitionists demanded a permanent prohibition against slavery in the new lands, whereas moderates favored the concept of popular or "squatter" sovereignty, which would allow the residents of those territories to make independent decisions on the issue. Neither Taylor nor Cass openly committed himself to either side of the debate, a prudent attempt to win votes by not antagonizing any group in the electorate.

The campaign was complicated by the appearance of the Free-Soil Party. Its candidate, Martin Van Buren, continually agitated against the expansion of slavery westward and attempted to goad his opponents into confronting the issue in a decisive manner. Taylor won a narrow victory, with 1,360,967 popular votes to 1,222,342 for Cass and only 291,253 for Van Buren. In the electoral college Taylor received 163 votes to 127 for Cass and none for Van Buren. It is probable, however, that Van Buren deflected enough Democratic votes from Cass in New York to throw the contest to Taylor.

Taylor was the first man to enter the White House with no previous political experience or training. He was also the first professional soldier to hold the office. Although a Southerner and a slaveholder on his Louisiana plantation, he had acquired a national outlook from his military service and was no friend to sectional extremists of any stripe.

Congress had failed to provide any form of civil government for the new territories before Taylor's election, and he disliked the prospect of administration by military governors. The new president wanted both California and New Mexico brought promptly into the Union. Once they had achieved statehood they could dispose of the slavery issue as their citizens desired.

California, where the Gold Rush had resulted in a rapid rise in population and demands for statehood, quickly adopted a constitution that prohibited slavery. When Congress convened in December, 1849, Taylor urged

California's admission while calling for popular sovereignty in New Mexico—that is, allowing the people, acting through their legislature, to decide whether the territory should permit slavery. His recommendations were ignored by the bitterly divided Congress. Southern legislators feared that the admission of California would weaken their position in the Senate, and numerous other sectional issues began to be joined with that of what to do about slavery in California and New Mexico.

Determined abolitionists wanted slavery barred from the District of Columbia. Southerners countered that only the state of Maryland could authorize such a measure, for it had donated the land from which the district was organized. Even if Maryland consented to the prohibition, the South could not countenance an act that would place a national stigma on its "peculiar institution."

Southerners were also nettled by Northern sympathy and aid extended to runaway bondsmen. Northern state laws—personal liberty laws—that barred courts and law enforcement agencies from assisting Southerners in finding and returning runaways led them to agitate for a strictly enforced national law which would require Northern assistance in such efforts. This proposal, seen as an attempt to force complicity in slavery, deeply angered abolitionists.

Another sensitive issue arose over Texas' claim to the eastern part of New Mexico Territory. Texans fought what they considered an attempt to annex a portion of their domain to another state and asked the national government to assume their share of the debt which they had incurred in fighting the Mexican War. Anti-slavery Northerners opposed their claims in an effort to reduce the size of at least one slave state.

The South as a whole was angered and alarmed by the possibility of a new bloc of free states entering the Union. In 1849, the number of free and slave states was equally balanced at fifteen. Only in the Senate did the South retain numerical equality in representation. Moreover, Southerners resented the affront to their honor implied by the enactment of any national law prohibiting slavery in the territories. Many talked of secession, and members of Congress appeared armed in its chambers and corridors. President Taylor faced a major crisis of the Union as 1850 began.

Taylor chose nation over section in his response to the crisis. Supported by most of his fellow-Whigs on the issues, he took a firm stand in dealing with the volatile mixture of Democrats and Free-Soilers in Congress. Speaking for the South, John C. Calhoun demanded full rights for the slaveholders in the West and protection for their property in the East. Abolitionists, such as William H. Seward and Salmon P. Chase, decried any compromise with slavery, talked of a higher law than the Constitution—the law of God, which slavery contravened—and demanded that slavery be prohibited in all the territories. Henry Clay, meanwhile, joined by Daniel

Webster and Stephen A. Douglas, led moderate Northerners in seeking a compromise.

Clay's compromise proposals met with continued Southern opposition, but President Taylor persisted in his insistence that California be admitted to the Union before other issues were considered. He made it clear that Southern recourse to secession would be met with force, and that he was willing personally to lead troops against his native section if it should become necessary to preserve the Union. The stalemate in Congress persisted, but Taylor's blunt response had effectively called the South's bluff on the threat to secede.

As Congress remained deadlocked, Taylor was suddenly stricken with a violent stomach disorder following an attack of heat prostration. He died on July 9, 1850, and was succeeded by Vice President Millard Fillmore. Taylor's death may have sobered the sectional and antislavery zealots in the government, for an amended version of Clay's original "omnibus bill" was eventually agreed upon by Congress and enacted by mid-September. Passed as five separate measures, the Compromise of 1850 provided for: the admission of California as a free state; the creation of New Mexico Territory without reference to slavery and the payment of $10 million to Texas for relinquishing to New Mexico its claim to the disputed area east of the Rio Grande; the formation of the Territory of Utah without reference to slavery; a strong fugitive slave act; and the abolition of the slave trade in the District of Columbia. With the achievement of this compromise the survival of the Union was assured for another troubled decade.

In contrast to strife and turmoil on the domestic scene, foreign affairs during Taylor's brief administration were calm and uneventful. The only happening of significance was the signing of the Clayton-Bulwer Treaty with Great Britain. By its terms the two nations agreed to join in promoting a canal across Central America which neither nation should ever fortify or put under its exclusive control. Furthermore, neither party was ever to occupy or claim sovereignty over any part of Central America.

Taylor's Legacy

Zachary Taylor was an able and dedicated soldier. His intelligence, ingenuity, and aggressiveness served the United States well from the War of 1812 through the Mexican conflict. Although he cannot be rated as one of the truly great captains cast in the mold of Robert E. Lee, Ulysses Grant, or Dwight D. Eisenhower, his skillful handling of a greatly outnumbered American force at Buena Vista averted what could have been a costly defeat and a serious setback to the achievement of national aims in the Mexican War. At a time when many Americans suspected the officer corps of harboring aristocratic pretensions, Taylor's simple dignity and lack of pomp won the popular confidence in both his person and his profession.

As president Taylor left no great body of legislation behind him. He coined no ringing slogans and led the nation on no great crusades. His major contribution as president was his firm and resolute adherence to the old Union. A slaveholder himself, he had no desire to interfere with the practice where it already existed, but he was determined that it be permitted neither to expand nor to imperil the Union. A Southerner, but also a son of the Western frontier and a staunch nationalist, he displayed great moral courage in defending the Constitution against domestic as well as foreign enemies.

Wayne R. Austerman

Bibliographical References
A recent biography of Taylor is Brainerd Dyer, *Zachary Taylor*, 1946. Also useful is Holman Hamilton's study, *Zachary Taylor*, 1941. The military phase of Taylor's life is ably dealt with in such works as K. Jack Bauer, *The Mexican War, 1846-1848*, Robert S. Henry, *The Story of the Mexican War*, 1950, and Otis A. Singletary, *The Mexican War*, 1960. Taylor's own correspondence during the 1846-1848 period is preserved in *Letters of Zachary Taylor, from the Battlefields of the Mexican War*, 1908. The Taylor presidency and related matters have inspired an extensive literature. Milo M. Quaife edited *The Diary of James K. Polk During his Presidency*, 1910. This four-volume work contains useful insights on Taylor's Mexican War role and his subsequent rise to political prominence. Holman Hamilton's valuable *Prologue to Conflict*, 1964, deals with the events surrounding the Compromise of 1850 and Taylor's impact on the sectional crisis.

MILLARD FILLMORE

1850–1853

Millard Fillmore has been characterized as a "handsome, dignified man of no great abilities." Although perhaps harsh, this comment underscores the truth that Fillmore was a man of unrealized expectations. He became president by a tragic fluke of fate, and although possessing some genuine administrative ability, he never displayed the leadership qualities of his predecessor, Zachary Taylor.

An Education in Practical Politics

Fillmore was one of the few prominent nineteenth-century American politicians who could truthfully boast of having been born in a log cabin. The second of six children born to a poverty-stricken family in Cayuga County, New York, Fillmore entered the world on the bitter winter day of January 7, 1800. His father apprenticed him in boyhood to a cloth-dressing and carding business in the hope that he would learn a useful trade.

Young Fillmore felt the stirrings of higher ambition and purchased a release from his apprenticeship to pursue an education. While still working at the textile mill, he had already enrolled as a part-time student at an academy in Mount Hope, New York. In 1819, his father obtained for him a clerkship in the office of Judge Walter Wood in Montville, New York. Fillmore clerked for Wood's firm and for another firm in Buffalo, New York, for several years. He also supplemented his meager income by teaching school. In 1823, he was admitted to the state bar and began his own practice in East Aurora, New York. As his business prospered, he hired a student clerk, Nathan K. Hall, who would subsequently become his law partner, political associate, and presidential cabinet member. In 1826, Fillmore married Abigail Powers, the daughter of a Moravia, New York, clergyman and sister of a local judge. She bore him a daughter in 1828 and another in 1832. The marriage endured until her death in 1853. Fillmore remained a widower until 1858, when he married a wealthy widow from Albany, Caroline Carmichael McIntosh. Her income allowed the Fillmores to live fashionably in a handsome mansion on Niagara Square in Buffalo.

In 1826, Fillmore joined the Anti-Masonic Party. This, the first organized third party in American history, originated in the 1820's in western New

York in opposition to the Society of Freemasons and other secret, exclusive, and presumably undemocratic organizations. Fillmore soon became closely linked to the movement's leaders, William H. Seward, Thurlow Weed, and Francis Granger. Marked as a rising figure in local politics, Fillmore rode the Anti-Masonic fervor to win three terms in the state assembly. An amiable legislator, he gained some distinction by sponsoring a bill to abolish imprisonment for debt.

In 1830, Fillmore moved to Buffalo and became a prominent member of the Unitarian church while continuing to enjoy a thriving legal partnership with Hall. A popular figure in Erie County, he won a seat in Congress in 1832, still upholding the Anti-Masonic banner. By 1834, he was following Weed's leadership as a newly converted Whig but declined the party's congressional nomination for fear of alienating his Anti-Masonic supporters at home. He astutely strengthened his political base by securing the editorship of the *Buffalo Commercial Advertiser* for a close associate.

Reelected to Congress in 1836 as a Whig, he enjoyed three consecutive terms before declining to run again in 1842. Fillmore was a convinced protectionist and used his position as chairman of the Ways and Means Committee to secure passage of the 1842 tariff bill through the House of Representatives.

Spurred by his increasing ambition, Fillmore began to chafe at Weed's continued dominance of the New York Whigs. He supported Granger, Weed's rival, for the state governorship in 1838, only to see him lose the nomination to Seward, a Weed ally. Fillmore subsequently declined Seward's offer of a post with the state but secured for Granger the office of postmaster general in the Harrison Administration.

Although Fillmore was a liberal Whig and leader of the party's antislavery faction, he opposed interference with the institution where it already existed, even as he staunchly opposed its expansion elsewhere. Like many New Yorkers, Fillmore was preoccupied by the perceived threat of massive foreign immigration, and he led the nativist opposition against fellow Whigs such as Seward and Weed, who saw the influx of foreigners as a way to forge new alliances and win added support for the party.

The Taylor-Fillmore Ticket

Accepting the gubernatorial nomination in 1844, Fillmore lost to his Democratic opponent. He blamed his defeat on "abolitionists and foreign Catholics" and accused Seward and Weed of having placed him in a doomed contest. Serving as state comptroller in 1847, Fillmore sponsored internal reforms in the office and designed a currency system that later served as a model for the National Banking Act of 1863. The following year he returned to the national stage as Zachary Taylor's vice presidential running mate. It was a purely pragmatic move by the Whigs, for Taylor's nomination had antagonized Henry Clay's supporters and antislavery partisans. Fillmore was viewed as a healing agent and assured winner for the ticket in New York State.

The 1848 election gave the Whigs a slim victory in a climate of rising sectional tension as debate flared over the westward expansion of slavery. Fillmore mistakenly believed that the Whigs' victory had ended "all ideas of disunion." The Taylor-Fillmore Administration was instead witness to the greatest domestic political crisis the nation had faced since that over the admission of Missouri to the Union as a slave state in 1820. In addition, Fillmore's experience with the traditional frustrations associated with the vice presidency was made even more bitter by internal bickering within the Whig Party. A patronage struggle between Fillmore and Seward ended with Taylor supporting Seward's rival and awarding him control of all patronage appointments in the state of New York. It was typical of Fillmore that he should be personally involved in such minor matters as the nation began to divide ever more deeply along sectional lines.

The long-simmering dispute over slavery threatened to boil over in the wake of the Mexican War. The Wilmot Proviso of 1846 had never become law, but its proposed ban on the importation of slaves into the territories won from Mexico was still a popular rallying point for antislavery Northerners in Congress. Southern demands for a stringent fugitive slave law, Northern attacks on the existence of slavery in the District of Columbia, and a Texas claim on portions of New Mexico created a sharply divided body when Congress convened in December, 1849.

The House of Representatives numbered 112 Democrats, 105 Whigs, 12 Free-Soilers, and 1 Native American. Sectional rivalry prevented any party from forming a stable majority, and a deadlock resulted whenever an attempt was made to determine the status of the new territories or their eventual acceptance into the Union as slave or free states. Frustrated Southerners spoke openly of convening a secession convention the following June.

The nation's political leadership offered a variety of proposals to defuse the crisis. President Taylor pressed for the immediate admission of California as a free state, while warning that any attempt at secession would be suppressed with the full force of the government. John C. Calhoun led the South in demanding equal rights for slaveholders in the West and blanket protection for the institution where it already existed. Henry Clay of Kentucky joined Daniel Webster of Massachusetts and Stephen A. Douglas of Illinois in sponsoring a compromise settlement. Fillmore joined Taylor in opposing any extension of slavery and hoped to avoid an open breach in the Union. He was disturbed by Seward's adamant refusal to support any compromise with slaveholders.

In May, 1850, Clay's "omnibus bill" presented the compromise package to a restive Congress. Clay proposed that California be admitted as a free state, that in the rest of the Mexican cession territorial governments be formed without restrictions on slavery, that Texas yield her land claims in New Mexico in exchange for compensation, that the slave trade, but not slavery itself, be abolished in the District of Columbia, and that a strict fugitive slave law be passed.

Earlier versions of this compromise had sparked violent debates in Congress, and sectional suspicions still made agreement over Clay's simplified version difficult.

Inheriting the Presidency: The Compromise of 1850

President Taylor's death in July, 1850, thrust the burden of leadership upon Fillmore, and although he lacked the blunt forcefulness of his predecessor, the unqualified support he and his cabinet gave to Clay's efforts proved decisive. Fillmore's choice of John J. Crittenden as attorney general and Webster as secretary of state, both moderates, was open indication of his desire for a compromise. His August message to Congress called for indemnification of Texas in exchange for that state surrendering its claim to New Mexico territory. Understanding the importance of give and take, however, Fillmore also sought to placate the South by including an affirmation of states' rights in his first annual message. Such gestures helped to win passage and acceptance for the Compromise of 1850 while soothing the inflamed feelings of the South.

The Compromise of 1850 can rightfully be called the apogee of Fillmore's presidency and public career. In other matters, his administration emphasized national economic development by fostering internal improvements and the growth of overseas trade. Commodore Matthew C. Perry used diplomacy and the implicit threat of his warships to secure open commerce with Japan, which enhanced American interest in Asia and the Pacific. The patronage issue remained a domestic irritant, causing further conflict with Seward and his allies in the party as Postmaster General Hall used his influence to weaken their hold on the system in New York State so that more conservative Whigs could gain posts.

A Career in Decline

In 1852, Fillmore enjoyed strong support from Southern and Northern conservative Whigs for the presidential nomination, but Webster's bid also gained conservative and moderate strength, dividing the party. General Winfield Scott claimed the nomination as the antislavery faction's candidate. Denied renomination by his own party, a disappointed Fillmore went home to Buffalo in 1853 after the inauguration of his successor, Franklin Pierce, and became the chief spokesman for the rapidly growing nativist Know-Nothing Party. The rise of the avowedly sectionalist Republican Party concerned him, but his 1856 candidacy for the Know-Nothings saw him finish far behind James Buchanan of the Democrats, the victor, and John C. Fremont of the Republicans.

Realizing that his national political career was over, Fillmore watched the nation drift toward disunion with mounting alarm. He deplored Abraham Lincoln's election in 1860 and saw little hope of averting a violent Southern response. Although Fillmore remained loyal to the national government during the Civil War, he blamed the Republicans for what he considered a needless tragedy. In 1864, he supported Democrat George B. McClellan against Lincoln. After the war, when the Radical Republicans attacked Andrew Johnson, he sympathized with the embattled president.

Domestic and local affairs also occupied much of Fillmore's attention after leaving the White House. He was the first chancellor of the University of Buffalo, serving from 1846 until his death. He also helped to establish Buffalo General Hospital and was a patron and first president of the Buffalo Historical Society. His wife became a chronic invalid during the 1860's, which made further demands on Fillmore's time, but their marriage remained stable and happy. Fillmore remained the well-spoken and kindly retired politico until he suffered a paralytic stroke in February, 1874. A second stroke followed, and Fillmore died on March 8, 1874.

Millard Fillmore was a skilled and insightful practical politician. He understood the psychology of his own New York electorate and grasped how issues and personalities could be molded to reach effective compromises in the flow of politics. Well read and surprisingly devoid of the overweening egotism that afflicted many of his fellow politicians, Fillmore was essentially a good man of limited perceptions and talents. He was generous and public spirited among his native New Yorkers, but he feared the influx of foreigners and joined in the persecution of the Masons. Animated by both moral and pragmatic sentiments in his opposition to slavery, he sought accommodation and not confrontation in dealing with Southern threats of secession over the issue. Sadly shortsighted on the major issues of his day, Fillmore was at least skilled and fortunate enough to delay the Union's dissolution by a decade while avoiding a genuine confrontation with the ills that beset it. Unlike Zachary Taylor, he habitually chose the path of least resistance.

Wayne R. Austerman

Bibliographical References

Fillmore's papers reside in the Buffalo Historical Society. They have also been edited for publication by Frank H. Severance in the *Buffalo Historical Society Publications*, vols. 10 and 11, 1907. Among the notable biographies are William E. Griffis, *Millard Fillmore*, 1915, and Robert J. Rayback,

Millard Fillmore, Biography of a President, 1959. Edward Everett Hale, *William H. Seward*, 1910, is a useful study of Fillmore's chief rival. Ulrich B. Phillips' study, *The Southern Whigs, 1834-1854*, 1910, provides insights on the rise and fall of Fillmore's party. Ray Allen Billington, *The Protestant Crusade, 1800-1860*, 1938, treats Fillmore's involvement with the Know-Nothings in an evenhanded manner. Holman Hamilton, *Prologue to Conflict*, 1964, is an invaluable aid to understanding the skein of issues, men, and events surrounding the Compromise of 1850. Useful general studies of the period can be found in Avery O. Craven, *The Growth of Southern Nationalism, 1848-1861*, 1953, and Allan Nevins, *Ordeal of the Union: Fruits of Manifest Destiny*, vol. 1, 1947.

FRANKLIN PIERCE

1853–1857

Franklin Pierce was probably the most obscure man ever elected president. Although he had served in both the House and the Senate, he had been out of national politics for a decade when he was nominated in 1852 and was barely known outside his native state of New Hampshire. Indicative of his lack of national stature, the president-elect stopped in New York City on his way to Washington for the inauguration and strolled down a crowded Broadway without once being recognized.

Pierce's unexpected nomination grew out of the deep divisions within the Democratic Party. Factionalism, personal rivalries, and divisions over a number of issues including the expansion of slavery and the Compromise of 1850 increasingly plagued the party. As a result the 1852 Democratic convention deadlocked, with none of the leading contenders able to secure the necessary two-thirds vote for nomination. In this situation a number of dark horse possibilities were brought forward, and on the forty-ninth ballot the delegates in a stampede named the little-known Concord lawyer. Lacking any knowledge of Pierce or his principles, most delegates blindly accepted assurances that he was sound on the Compromise of 1850 and would be evenhanded in distributing patronage.

Born in 1804, the Democratic nominee was the son of General Benjamin Pierce, a prominent New Hampshire politician. In 1824 he was graduated from Bowdoin College, where he formed a lifelong friendship with Nathaniel Hawthorne. Five years later, aided by his name (which the family pronounced "purse"), Pierce entered the state legislature. He subsequently served three terms in the national House of Representatives, where he was a strong supporter of Andrew Jackson, and was elected senator in 1836. The youngest member of the Senate, he was a dogged party man, hardworking but unimaginative. Pierce resigned in 1842 before the end of his term. His decision to leave national politics stemmed in part from his wife's dislike of political life and his inability to resist the temptations of Washington society. Genial and well-liked, Pierce was fond of liquor, for which he had a low tolerance and which earned for him a certain notoriety. He became a temperance advocate in the 1840's and struggled the rest of his life with varying success to forgo stimulants. Indeed, his wife, remembering his earlier behavior, collapsed when news arrived of his nomination for president.

Following his retirement from the Senate, Pierce resumed his career as a lawyer, but he reentered public life during the Mexican War as a brigadier general in the army. His military career was also undistinguished, its most notable aspect being his fainting after his horse fell during the Battle of Contreras. On his return home, he resumed his place as a leader of the state Democratic Party but did not hold public office again until his election as president.

An Ill-Starred Administration

Pierce scored a clear victory in the 1852 election. Carrying every state but four, he won a majority of the popular votes, which was increasingly an unusual feat. Pierce's triumph was soon scarred by tragedy, however, as his only surviving child, Benjamin, was gruesomely killed in January, 1853, in a train wreck before his horrified parents' eyes. Plagued for years by religious self-doubt, Pierce was haunted by guilt over his son's death, which he feared was punishment for his own religious shortcomings. A pall of tragedy hung over the entire gloomy Pierce presidency, with Mrs. Pierce in mourning and social life held to a cheerless minimum. The accident undermined Pierce's none-too-large self-confidence at the crucial beginning of his ill-starred term in the White House.

When he assumed office, Pierce was forty-eight, the youngest chief executive the country had ever elected. His program to reunite the Democratic Party was twofold. First, he planned to use the federal patronage to heal the rifts in the party. He announced that the past would be forgotten and all factions recognized in appointments. In particular, the president intended to welcome back into the party's good graces the Van Burenite barnburners, who had bolted in 1848 and helped defeat Lewis Cass, the party's presidential candidate, and the radical states' rights men in the South, who had advocated secession following passage of the Compromise of 1850.

His second policy was territorial expansion, which he believed was generally popular and would especially appeal to Democrats. Ignoring the deep divisions that the territorial question had recently produced, Pierce confidently announced in his inaugural address, "My administration will not be controlled by any timid forebodings of evil from expansion." His major goal was to acquire Cuba, long an object of desire for American expansionists and proslavery men. He also hoped to gain more territory southward, especially from Mexico. That slavery would be suitable in most if not all of this territory seemed to Pierce, who had long denounced abolitionists and believed the slavery issue had no place in national politics, an unimportant consideration.

Physically unimposing, Pierce was only five feet nine inches tall and of wiry build, but he was a genuinely handsome man, with pale coloring, thin features, and a full head of hair. Graceful and well-mannered, he exuded a boyish charm mingled with a good dose of vanity. For all his personal attractiveness, however, his flawed character was inadequate to meet the challenge before him. Known as Frank to his intimates, he was a weak and indecisive person, without intellectual depth and excessively optimistic, who when challenged took refuge in stubborn inflexibility. The new president knew few Democratic power brokers when he took office, and the party's real leaders, especially in the Senate, were unwilling to defer to one they considered a nonentity. Social and affable, Pierce desperately wanted to be liked, and rather than confront those he disagreed with, he preferred to seem to endorse whatever policy was recommended to him regardless of whether he agreed with it. Men who left believing that Pierce concurred with them only to see him ultimately adopt a different course naturally accused him of disingenuousness and came to distrust him thoroughly.

Pierce's inexperience and ineptitude came to the fore immediately. He wanted an old friend, John A. Dix of New York, a barnburner who had reluctantly bolted the Democratic Party in 1848, to head his cabinet as secretary of state, and he offered Dix the post. When Southerners and anti-Van Burenites objected, rather than insisting on his right to name his cabinet and on the necessity for all party members to accept his policy of reconciliation, Pierce backed down and withdrew the tendered appointment. Keen-sighted politicians saw that Pierce lacked the inner strength to command acceptance of his policies and could be intimidated.

As finally constituted, Pierce's cabinet was not without talent. Its leading members were Secretary of State William L. Marcy, Secretary of War James K. Polk, a leading advocate of accepting the barnburners back into the regular party organization, Secretary of War Jefferson Davis, who represented the anti-Compromise Southern wing of the party, and Attorney General Caleb Cushing, a man of distinguished intellectual ability but without any firm political principles. Pierce intended that Marcy, the most politically experienced and capable of the group, be the premier, but the New Yorker was quickly shunted aside in the administration's councils by Davis and Cushing. This development was one pregnant with potential disaster, especially under a weak and vacillating leader such as Pierce. Davis and Cushing were efficient subordinates, but they were too extreme to be given any important say in policy. More and more, they directed the administration along a pro-Southern, proslavery course that badly weakened the party in the North. Pierce's diplomatic appointments were equally unfortunate; they included a gang of romantic adventurers, bumptious representatives of the proexpansion Young America movement, whose antics brought ridicule on the administration, involved the country in a series of unnecessary imbroglios, and helped undermine the president's foreign policy. Compounding Pierce's problems was his failure to put the administration organ, the *Washington Union*, in loyal hands. Of its two editors, A. O. P. Nicholson, a Cass man, feuded with several members of the cabinet, whereas the talented John W. Forney was personally loyal to James Buchanan and deserted Pierce in 1856.

Repeal of the Missouri Compromise: The Kansas Crises

Problems were not long in developing. The administration's patronage policies satisfied no one. Not enough jobs existed to buy off every faction, and in any event men resented recognition of their rivals. Such problems plagued the party in virtually every state, although the situation in New York was the most intractable and ominous for the party's future. There dissident Democrats refused to accede to the administration's appointment of former Free Soilers and ran a separate state ticket in 1853, thereby handing control of the nation's leading state back to the Whigs.

Such was the condition of the Democracy, with its ranks in complete disarray and the party seemingly rudderless, when Congress assembled in December, 1853. Some men, such as Stephen A. Douglas of Illinois, believed that without vigorous new leadership the party would soon fall apart, whereas a number of powerful Southern senators saw in the existing political chaos a chance to impose new policies and erect a new test of party orthodoxy for Pierce's despised Free Soil nominees, who had to be confirmed in the upcoming session. The Missouri Compromise of 1820 had forever prohibited slavery in the remaining portion of the Louisiana Purchase, but Southerners now demanded that the principle of popular sovereignty—that the residents of the territory (at some unspecified time) decide whether they wanted slavery—be applied to this region. To be confirmed, Pierce's barnburner nominees would be required to endorse this policy, a bitter pill since they had earlier favored the Wilmot Proviso, which sought to bar slavery from all the territory acquired from Mexico.

Under pressure Douglas, who was preparing a bill to organize the Kansas and Nebraska territories, agreed to repeal the time-honored Missouri Compromise, but the Illinois senator wanted the administration's endorsement before proceeding with such a controversial move. In a rare Sunday interview at the White House on January 22, 1854, Douglas and a group of Southern leaders induced Pierce to accept the proposed repeal of the 1820 compromise as the unspoken price to get his appointments through the Senate. Knowing the president's unreliability, Douglas insisted that Pierce put his support in writing. In taking this step, Pierce ignored Marcy's advice and was influenced instead by Davis and Cushing, the latter of whom convinced him that the Missouri Compromise was unconstitutional anyway; he was also eager to repel the damaging accusation that his administration was Free Soil in its sympathies. Pierce's acceptance of the repeal of the Missouri

Compromise was the most fateful day of his presidency. Not only did it make a mockery of the 1852 platform's pledge not to reopen the sectional controversy but it also precipitated a series of problems that ultimately drove Pierce from office.

Once committed, Pierce threw the power of the administration behind the Kansas-Nebraska bill. No record remains of the specific means used to secure support for the bill, but aided by these efforts the bill finally passed the House in early May by a vote of 113–100, with Northern Democrats evenly divided. Hailing it as the first great measure of his administration, Pierce signed the bill on May 30. Compounding this error, the *Union* officially announced in another serious blunder that support of the law was a test of party regularity. A number of Northern Democrats refused to support the law and bolted in the fall elections; before long many of these dissidents would join the new Republican Party, which the Kansas-Nebraska Act spawned. The Nebraska issue contributed to the Democratic Party's crushing defeat in the 1854 elections; the party lost sixty-six Northern seats and control of the House of Representatives, dooming Pierce's legislative program.

Trouble soon erupted in the Territory of Kansas. Southerners believed that an unspoken agreement existed that Kansas would be a slave state and Nebraska free, and Pierce certainly acted as if this were the case. Northerners opposed to the repeal of the Missouri Compromise, however, had no intention of conceding Kansas to slavery. Almost immediately a race developed between pro- and antislavery elements to settle the region, and elections in the territory were marred by massive illegal voting by Missourians. When Pierce upheld the fraudulently elected proslavery territorial legislature, which expelled the legally elected free state members, enacted a thoroughly unfair election law, and passed a harsh legal code to protect slavery and silence critics, free state men organized their own "state" government, defied the territorial authorities, and petitioned Congress for admission as a free state. With two governments in existence, fighting soon erupted and flared off and on for the next two years.

What would have been a disorganized situation anyway was made worse by Pierce's unfortunate territorial appointments, headed by the volatile Samuel Lecompte, an aggressively proslavery Southerner, as chief justice, and Andrew Reeder, a local Democratic politician from Pennsylvania of no significance and without administrative experience, as governor. Tactless and erratic, Reeder was soon at odds with the legislature, and in response to heavy Southern pressure Pierce finally replaced him with former Governor Wilson Shannon of Ohio, an even worse choice. Shannon was incompetent and a tool of the proslavery interests in the territory. In 1856, with the territory ablaze, he resigned and fled in panic. That more capable governors could have completely forestalled the violence in the territory is perhaps doubtful, but poor leadership unquestionably made the situation worse.

Pierce's one-sided response to the Kansas crisis greatly contributed to the welling anger in the North as well. In his discussions of territorial affairs, Pierce took the Southern side and blamed all the troubles on Northern efforts to colonize the territory and on the illegal free state movement. These criticisms were not completely misdirected, but to overlook or excuse the illegal voting by Missourians, the unconstitutional laws passed by the territorial legislature, and the acts of violence by Southerners destroyed whatever influence Pierce might have exercised. Events reached a climax in May, 1856, with the caning of Senator Charles Sumner by the fiery-tempered Preston Brooks, a member of Congress from South Carolina, for a speech Sumner delivered on affairs in Kansas and the raid on Lawrence, Kansas, headquarters of the free state movement, by a proslavery band. These two events dealt the final blow to Pierce's fading chances for renomination.

Democratic leaders recognized that Kansas could not continue to bleed until the 1856 presidential election. They exerted pressure to force the administration to retreat from its plan to try free state leaders for treason. More important, Pierce finally selected in John W. Geary a man capable of handling the duties of territorial governor. Energetically governing in an evenhanded manner, Geary brought some semblance of law and order to the territory for the first time. By then, however, Pierce's political career had been irreparably destroyed. More than anything else, bleeding Kansas sank Pierce and almost sent the Democratic Party with him.

In domestic matter Pierce adhered to the limited government philosophy of the Democratic Party. He vetoed several internal improvement bills, as well as a proposal to dedicate part of the proceeds from public land sales to care for the insane. Pierce's unwillingness to use government power to encourage economic development alienated many business interests, especially in the North. The president and his advisers displayed a positive genius for needlessly making enemies and letting chances to gain friends slip through their fingers.

The Decline of Manifest Destiny

Pierce's foreign policy was equally controversial. Cuba remained the main object of desire. Initially, the administration quietly encouraged the schemes of the proslavery filibusterer John Quitman of Mississippi, who endlessly planned to invade the island, but suddenly in 1854 Pierce shifted to a policy of acquiring Cuba through diplomacy. His program ran athwart his foreign appointments. Prodded by Pierce, three American ministers, led by the theatrical Pierre Soulé, in 1854 drafted the Ostend Manifesto, which urged that the United States offer up to $120 million for Cuba and if Spain refused to sell, seize the island by force. The memo was intended to be secret, but its contents soon became public, and in the ensuing outcry the administration felt compelled to repudiate it. A public relations disaster, the manifesto discredited the doctrine of Manifest Destiny in the eyes of many Americans by linking it to naked aggression, and it exposed the administration as a group of bumbling incompetents. At the same time it reinforced the idea of an aggressive slave power bent on using any means to strengthen slavery and expand the institution's domain. The renewal of sectional agitation rendered any effort to obtain Cuba futile for the remainder of the decade.

More successful were his efforts to secure additional territory from Mexico. Pierce's negotiator, James A. Gadsden, a South Carolina railroad promoter, was unable to gain Lower California or a port on the Gulf of California as Pierce desired, but he did obtain territory south of the Gila River, which afforded the best route for a Pacific railroad from New Orleans. Critics charged that the administration bought the land to facilitate selection of a southern rather than a central or northern route, but as with other programs the growing sectional conflict blocked all efforts to construct a transcontinental railroad. The Senate ratified the Gadsden Treaty only after reducing the amount of territory annexed.

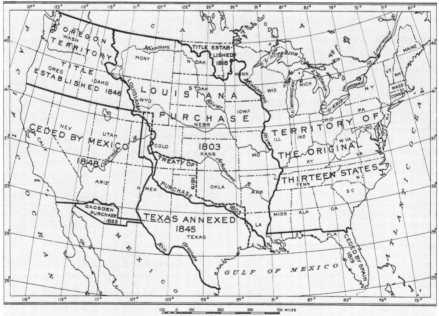

(Courtesy of the Library of Congress, Washington, D.C.)

Boundaries of the United States Showing
Acquisitions of Territory from 1803 to 1853

It is clear in retrospect that these efforts marked the decline of Manifest Destiny until after the Civil War. A growing number of Northerners opposed expansion, since it would inevitably be to the south and thus would strengthen slavery. Although the seeming endorsement of the use of force alienated a minority of antebellum Americans, it was the fear of slavery expansion rekindled by the Kansas-Nebraska Act that doomed the administration's program of territorial acquisition. Pierce's failure to recognize this consequence when confronted with the demand for the repeal of the Missouri Compromise is testimony to his lack of political acumen.

The High Cost of Pierce's Presidency

Pierce actively sought renomination in 1856, but party leaders realized that a new choice was necessary for the party to beat back the challenge of the suddenly powerful Republican Party. At the Cincinnati convention, Pierce had some support among Southern delegations, but his strength soon melted away, and in the end the party nominated James Buchanan. So unpopular had Pierce become in the North that had he been renominated, he almost certainly would have been defeated. Few presidents have squandered so much goodwill at the beginning of their term in such a short time. Pierce remains the only elected president not to be renominated by his party.

Pierce did not play an active role in politics after he left the White House. When war broke out in 1861, he tepidly backed the Union cause, but he became a strident critic of the Emancipation Proclamation and the Lincoln Administration's regulation of civil liberties. He died in 1869, largely a forgotten man without influence.

Although Pierce's impact on the office of president was negligible, his role in American history was crucial. Taking office at a time when the slavery issue was declining in force, he recklessly reopened the sectional conflict, and his ill-advised policies made the crisis steadily worse. By such actions he significantly contributed to the events that led to civil war. Pierce should be ranked a failure as president.

William E. Gienapp

Bibliographical References

Pierce apparently destroyed most of his personal papers relating to his presidency, and hence its history must be written from widely scattered sources. In general, historians have been too charitable in evaluating his performance. The only modern full-length biography is Roy F. Nichols, *Franklin Pierce: Young Hickory of the Granite Hills*, 2d rev. ed., 1969, a work based on a wide knowledge of the sources. Nichols displays a sure grasp of the intricacies of Democratic politics, but he is overly generous in his judgments and does not create a vivid portrait of Pierce's character and personality. The most important reminiscence is by Pierce's private secretary, Sidney Webster, *Franklin Pierce and His Administration*, 1892. Three members of the Pierce cabinet have modern biographies: Claude Feuss, *The Life of Caleb Cushing*, 2 vols., 1923; Ivor D. Spencer, *The Victor and the Spoils: A Life of William L. Marcy*, 1959, a good study; and Clement Eaton, *Jefferson Davis*, 1977. The best discussion of the origins of the repeal of the Missouri Compromise is Roy F. Nichols, "The Kansas-Nebraska Act: A Century of Historiography," *Mississippi Valley Historical Review* 53 (September, 1956): 187–212. Histories of the coming of the Civil War perforce devote considerable attention to Pierce's term in office. Of particular importance are Allan Nevins, *Ordeal of the Union*, 2 vols., 1947, the second volume of which covers Pierce's administration, and David M. Potter, *The Impending Crisis, 1848–1861*, completed and edited by Don E. Fehrenbacher, 1976. These works will guide the interested reader to many specialized studies of American history during this period.

James Buchanan

JAMES BUCHANAN

1857–1861

Few men have entered the presidency with as much political experience as James Buchanan. A veteran of more than forty years of public service, the Pennsylvania leader had served in the state legislature, in both houses of Congress, as secretary of state in the Polk Administration, and most recently as minister to Great Britain under Franklin Pierce. With legislative, administrative, and diplomatic experience, Buchanan seemed eminently qualified to be president.

He had been born in 1791 of Scotch-Irish ancestry, the son of a Pennsylvania farmer and merchant. Hardworking and ambitious, he compiled an excellent record at Dickinson College and then trained for a career in the law. He was a successful lawyer, and through diligence, thrift, and shrewd investments amassed a fortune of some $300,000 during his lifetime. In 1819 his life was forever altered, however, when his fiancée, who had broken off their engagement after a quarrel, suddenly died. In reaction, Buchanan vowed that he would never marry; he is the only bachelor president in American history.

Buchanan commenced his political career as a Federalist, but he eventually became a loyal follower of Andrew Jackson and steadily rose in the ranks of the Democratic Party. A loyal party man, he shrank from controversy and built up a large personal following through a voluminous correspondence. After several unsuccessful attempts to gain the party's presidential nomination, he finally secured the prize in 1856, in large measure because he had the good fortune to be out of the country in 1854 and 1855 and was not identified with either the repeal of the Missouri Compromise or the troubles in Kansas. Party managers turned to Buchanan, who seemed a safe, experienced, conservative choice.

Buchanan and the Forces of Sectionalism: A Failure of Understanding

To Buchanan the main issue of the 1856 contest was the Union. The Democratic standard bearer viewed the Republican Party as a fanatical organization and predicted that if the party carried the election, disunion "will be immediate and inevitable." Aided by the division of the opposition, Buchanan was elected despite winning only a plurality (45 percent) of the popular vote, but the Union had had a narrow escape. In its first national campaign, the sectional Republican party had come very close to electing a president, and in the aftermath of his victory Buchanan indicated that his major goal as president would be to defuse the territorial crisis and "destroy" the Republican party, which was the main threat to the Union.

Tall and heavyset, with a large head, snow white hair, and a ruddy complexion, the fifteenth president was a gentleman of the old school. He dressed impeccably but in an old-fashioned style, cultivated courtly manners, and had a well-developed taste for fine liquor and cigars. Because of a vision defect, he tilted his head forward and sideways in conversation, which reinforced the impression of great courteousness. He was rather fussy and vain—Washington dubbed him "Miss Nancy"—and was extremely sensitive to criticism or personal slights. Lonely and never completely adjusted emotionally, he was stiff and formal and allowed little familiarity; he had few close friends and rarely revealed his feelings on controversial matters to anyone. He had a peculiar relationship with Senator William R. King of Alabama, with whom he lived for many years when in Washington, that led one Tennessee congressman to refer to them as "Buchanan and *his wife*." Ill at ease with confrontation, he was timid and indecisive and often relied on stronger men, yet in spite of his conciliatory nature he could be petty and vindictive when attacked. Like many insecure men, Buchanan was unable to admit that he had been wrong, and once he made up his mind he tenaciously held to his position.

Buchanan's greatest handicap was not his irresolute character but his lack of understanding of the conflict between the North and the South. Although he termed slavery a wrong in his memoirs, he felt no great moral indignation over the institution, harbored a deep hatred of abolitionists, and had long contended that Northern agitation of the slavery question was solely responsible for the sectional crisis. Few Northern politicians were so pro-Southern in their policies and feelings, and for many years his closest friends had been Southerners. Willing to see slavery expand, he had wanted to annex more territory from Mexico in 1848 while secretary of state, and he had signed the infamous Ostend Manifesto in 1854, which advocated that the United States acquire Cuba by force if necessary. He had not witnessed at firsthand the Northern protest over the Kansas-Nebraska Act and had no appreciation of how much Northern public opinion had changed in a few years. Devoid of any real comprehension of the Republican Party or the reasons for its success, he was intellectually and emotionally unsuited to deal with the forces of sectionalism in American politics.

Less than two months shy of his sixty-sixth birthday when he took the presidential oath, Buchanan, who was uncomfortable around men of intellectual distinction, surrounded himself with an undistinguished cabinet. The only member of national stature was Secretary of State Lewis Cass, who was indolent and no longer mentally alert; Buchanan intended to direct foreign policy himself. A few of the other members had some experience in national politics, but they were all men of limited vision and talent. The strongest personalities in the cabinet were Howell Cobb of Georgia (Treasury), Jacob Thompson of Mississippi (Interior), and Jeremiah S. Black, an old political associate from Pennsylvania who was attorney general. Cobb and Thompson were strongly proslavery, and Black, although no advocate of the institution, usually sided with them on narrowly legalistic grounds. Together they dominated the cabinet and with it the president, who normally followed the collective will of his advisers, although the idea that they constituted a "directory" and ran the government virtually without consulting him is exaggerated. The president's closest adviser outside the cabinet was Senator John Slidell of Louisiana, who despite his New York origins was an ardent Southerner, ready with Cobb and Thompson to push extreme measures to protect the South. None was a very astute judge of Northern public opinion or of the political consequences of their policies, and unfortunately Buchanan lacked the ability to compensate for their shortcomings.

The Dred Scott Decision

Most presidents have had a period of time to get their administration organized before dealing with major problems. Buchanan enjoyed no such luxury. His term began in controversy. Two days after his inauguration the Supreme Court handed down its decision in the famous Dred Scott case. The Court majority (five Southerners joined by one Northerner) ruled that blacks could not be citizens of the United States, that Congress had no power to prohibit slavery from the territories, and that the Missouri Compromise of 1820, which had banned slavery from most of the Louisiana Purchase territory and which had been repealed by the Kansas-Nebraska Act, was unconstitutional. Republicans were incensed, for not only did the Court ignore countless past precedents in propounding this ruling but the opinion also negated the party's platform.

Buchanan, in fact, had played an important and highly improper role in the decision. Secretly informed of the Court's deliberations, he urged a Northern justice who was undecided to support the majority point of view. Then, knowing that the decision would be favorable to slavery, he announced in his inaugural address with seeming innocence that the Court was about to rule on the question of slavery in the territories and lectured that all good Americans would cheerfully acquiesce in the decision "whatever it may be." In the ensuing outcry, Republicans bitterly denounced the Court and its decision, and, although not informed of his intervention in its deliberations, accused Buchanan of conspiring to extend slavery. Contrary to Buchanan's naïve expectations, the decision did nothing to quiet agitation over slavery or heal sectional animosities. That he thought the decision would have such an effect revealed how little he understood the nature and causes of the sectional conflict.

A second event in 1857 that weakened the administration was the onset in August of a depression. The economic downturn severely reduced government revenues and produced a growing clamor in the North to raise the tariff duties, both as a means to stimulate American manufacturing and to increase government revenues to meet expenditures. Pennsylvania, long a center of protariff sentiment because of its coal and iron industry, was especially prominent in demanding greater protection. Democratic leaders recognized that loss of the state, which Buchanan had carried in 1856, would be a devastating blow. In a rare display of political acumen, Buchanan favored revising tariff duties upward to what they had been under the 1846 Walker tariff, both to increase government revenue and to cool discontent in his home state. His Southern advisers, however, headed by Cobb in the Treasury, were inflexibly opposed to any increase. In their messages to Congress in December 1857, Buchanan and his secretary assumed opposite positions on the question, prompting Cobb's famous remark, often cited as evidence of Buchanan's weakness, that "Old Buck is opposing the Administration." Unwilling to impose his views on his subordinates, the president failed to muster the resources of his administration behind revision of the tariff, and all efforts at tariff reform failed during his term. Failure to increase the tariff alienated certain groups, especially in the business community, that up to this time had largely opposed the Republican Party.

The Kansas Controversy: A Disastrous Decision

The greatest problem that bedeviled Buchanan in his first year in office, however, was the continuing turmoil in Kansas. Buchanan was determined to bring Kansas into the Union and end the bitter controversy over the status of slavery in that territory. To accomplish this task he selected Robert J. Walker, his colleague in the Polk cabinet and one of the most talented politicians of his generation, to be territorial governor. Knowing Buchanan's tendency to waffle on disputed questions, Walker got the president to pledge in advance support for the policy of submitting the state constitution, which a convention was about to draft, to a fair vote of the territory's residents.

Once he took up his new post, the diminutive governor soon found himself enmeshed in a host of difficulties. Meeting in Lecompton, the constitutional convention, which had a proslavery majority because the free state men refused to vote despite Walker's pleas, drafted a constitution that protected slavery. Then, contrary to Walker's announced policy, the delegates submitted only the slavery clause rather than the entire constitution for popular ratification. Residents could vote for the constitution with more slavery or for the constitution with only the slaves already in the territory, but they could not vote against the entire constitution nor could they vote to abolish slavery. Denouncing the convention's action, Walker hurried to Washington and warned Buchanan that the Lecompton constitution was a fraud and represented the wishes of only a small minority of the residents of Kansas.

Buchanan was now caught in a dilemma. Reaffirming his earlier pledge to Walker, he had written the governor in July that he was willing to stand or fall "on the question of submitting the constitution to the bona fide residents of Kansas." Now he confronted a growing demand from the South and from his Southern advisers that Walker be removed. Their anger increased when the governor threw out obviously fraudulent returns in the legislative election, thereby handing control of the legislature to free state men for the first time in the territory's existence. Through a series of procedures that were outwardly legal, Southern Democrats had the opportunity to make Kansas a slave state, and they desperately grabbed at this chance. Walker, however, gained a powerful ally in Senator Stephen A. Douglas, who insisted that the Lecompton constitution made a mockery of popular sovereignty and demanded a full and fair vote on the constitution. In a stormy interview, Douglas warned Buchanan that endorsement of the Lecompton constitution would destroy the Democratic party in the North. Nursing a cordial hatred for the aggressive Illinois senator and badly overestimating his power to enforce party discipline, Buchanan affirmed his support for the constitution and warned Douglas, who considered the president a political pygmy, that he would be crushed if he opposed it.

Buchanan, the Democratic Party, and the nation now stood at the crossroads on the road to civil war. The president was about to make the most disastrous decision of his presidency. Warned by his governor that a large majority of the residents of the territory opposed the Lecompton constitution and wanted Kansas to be a free state and warned by the most popular Northern Democratic leader that the party could not carry the burden of the fraudulent Lecompton constitution in the free states, Buchanan nevertheless plunged ahead, swayed by his Southern sympathies and his obtuse advisers. Abandoned by the president, a disgusted Walker soon resigned. The referendum called by the constitutional convention produced a large majority in favor of the Lecompton constitution and slavery, but a separate vote a few weeks later scheduled by the antislavery legislature demonstrated quite clearly that a majority of the people of Kansas opposed the constitution. Nevertheless, in a special message in February, Buchanan urged Congress to admit Kansas under the Lecompton constitution.

The stage was now set for a titanic struggle in Congress in which Douglas openly opposed the administration. In this fight, Buchanan showed none of his customary indecisiveness. He bent every power to force the Lecompton constitution "naked through the House," as he phrased it, discharging opponents of Lecompton from federal offices, extending patronage to wavering congressmen, and even offering outright cash to secure the necessary votes. Northern representatives were more sensitive to public opinion, and in the end enough Northern Democrats defected to defeat Lecompton in the House by a tally of 120–112. At this point, the administration agreed to a face-saving compromise, which provided for the residents of the territory to vote on whether they would accept admission under the Lecompton constitution with a reduced land grant. On August 2, 1858, with the free state men participating, the voters of Kansas rejected the land grant and with it the Lecompton constitution by a vote of 11,812 to 1,926. The struggle over Kansas was at an end. Slavery was doomed there, and it was only a matter of time until the territory would have sufficient population to enter the Union as a free state (as it did in January, 1861).

Buchanan insisted that the immediate admission of Kansas under the Lecompton constitution would end the territorial controversy and destroy the appeal of the Republican Party. In reality, Buchanan's ill-advised policy had precisely the opposite effect. It strengthened the Northern belief in the slave power and linked the president directly to an alleged conspiracy to force slavery on the unwilling people of Kansas. It broadened the Republicans' appeal by allowing them to pose as the defenders of cherished democratic principles and procedures. Finally, it badly divided the Democratic Party, with Douglas the symbol of this division. The Democratic Party paid this heavy price needlessly, for even Buchanan realized that the South would not have seceded over this question.

The fall elections were a debacle for the administration and the Democratic Party. Republicans scored gains in a number of key Northern states, and Northern congressmen who had supported the Lecompton constitution went down to defeat in droves, while those who had stood with Douglas generally won reelection. The new House had an anti-Democratic majority. More ominous was the loss of Pennsylvania, which foreshadowed an impending Republican victory in 1860 unless there was a radical change in policy. To all of this Buchanan remained oblivious. His advisers dismissed the losses as the result of temporary causes rather than the administration's pro-Southern policies, and the president, unwilling to confront the harsh political truth, eagerly embraced this explanation.

Desperately needing to shore up the Democratic Party's support in the North, Buchanan instead alienated additional Northern groups by adhering to his outmoded Jacksonian economic principles. As he grew older, Buchanan became increasingly inflexible on economic matters, and during his presidency he consistently opposed using the federal government to promote economic growth. Southerners blocked all attempts to revise the tariff, and Buchanan vetoed several internal improvement bills that got through Congress, which angered popular opinion, especially in the Northwest. He also vetoed a homestead bill designed to appease Western sentiment. Another bill, which donated public land to states to found agricultural colleges, met a similar fate. These vetoes enabled Republicans to picture him as a tool of Southern interest, who used their stranglehold over the federal government to block Northern progress and development, and his actions further damaged the democratic cause in the free states.

More successful was his handling of the growing difficulties with the Mormons in the Utah territory. When not entirely accurate reports reached Washington that the Mormons under the leadership of Brigham Young were defying federal authority, Buchanan moved with uncharacteristic firmness. He dispatched twenty-five hundred troops to subdue the rebellious saints, but before they arrived in Utah his emissary negotiated a peaceful settlement under which the Mormons would not be interfered with in their religion but in temporal matters the federal government would be supreme. The so-called Mormon War thus came to an end without bloodshed and with federal authority intact.

In foreign affairs Buchanan's primary goals were to expand the national domain and check foreign influence in the New World. He did get the British to abandon some of their territorial aspirations in Central America, and he managed to secure commercial treaties with both China and Japan. His efforts to acquire additional territory, however, were doomed to failure. He was rebuffed by Congress when he requested the power to establish protectorates over the northern provinces of Mexico and when he sought authority to invade Mexico to gain redress for wrongs committed against American citizens. In addition, in 1860 the Senate rejected a treaty the administration negotiated with Mexico that would have given the United States the right of unilateral military intervention. Republican senators believed that the treaty's real purpose was to seize additional territory from Mexico and expand slavery. Buchanan also continued to push for the acquisition of Cuba, and in 1859 he backed a bill to appropriate $30 million for negotiations with Spain. Although it could have passed the Senate if brought to a vote, the bill stood no chance in the House, and its introduction was simply a futile gesture. Thus Buchanan's diplomatic record, while not a total failure, fell far short of the goals he had set when entering office.

Administrative Corruption: Damaging Revelations

More damaging to Buchanan's reputation were the revelations of a House committee chaired by John Covode of Pennsylvania, which was appointed to investigate charges of administrative corruption. Covode and his colleagues ferreted out massive amounts of evidence of wrongdoing. Indeed, when the investigation was completed, it was clear the Buchanan had presided over the most corrupt administration in American history up to that point. Testimony revealed that patronage and even money had been offered to editors and congressmen for their support, that campaign contributors had been rewarded with lucrative federal contracts, and that the huge profits from the public printing had been partially diverted to Democratic candidates. Evidence also came to light that completely discredited Secretary of War John Floyd, who had used his office to reward his friends and was criminally lax in his management of accounts. This was not all. It would later be discovered that Floyd had endorsed bills for army supplies before Congress appropriated the money and that he had continued this illegal practice even after Buchanan ordered him to stop. Moreover, some of these notes had been exchanged for $870,000 worth of bonds stolen from the Interior Department by one of the secretary's kinsmen. Although Floyd's malfeasance brought him into complete disgrace, he defiantly refused to resign when Buchanan through an intermediary asked him to do so, and the president meekly backed down. Buchanan had not profited personally from these activities, but the evidence fully documented his weakness of character and lack of judgment.

Buchanan's performance put the Democratic Party badly on the defensive in 1860, and party unity was essential if the Republican challenge were to be turned back. Motivated by narrow personal considerations, Buchanan re-

(Courtesy of the Lilly Library, Indiana University, Bloomington, Indiana)
Dividing the National Map
A division of political parties as they enter the campaign of 1860. Lincoln and Douglas struggle for the West, Breckenridge captures the South, Bell tries to repair the damage.

fused to make any effort to heal the breach with Douglas. The senator's supporters were proscribed or removed from federal office and some of his most bitter enemies appointed in their stead. Buchanan also threw the power of the administration against Douglas' bid to win the 1860 Democratic presidential nomination. Pressure was applied to federal officeholders to get anti-Douglas men elected to the national convention, and some of the president's closest associates went to Charleston for the sole purpose of defeating the Illinois senator. In the end the Democratic Party split, with the Northern wing nominating Douglas and the Southern wing Buchanan's vice president, John C. Breckinridge of Kentucky. Buchanan, who had not sought renomination, endorsed Breckinridge and the Southern platform, which demanded a federal slave code for the territories. With the Democratic Party hopelessly divided, Abraham Lincoln was easily elected the nation's first Republican president in November.

The Secession Crisis

With four months remaining until the end of his term, Buchanan now confronted the most serious crisis of his life. Following Lincoln's election, as the states of the Deep South began making preparations to leave the Union, Buchanan's cabinet, which had been noted for its harmony, became a deeply divided and quarrelsome body. Its Northern members, led by Black, heatedly denounced secession, whereas Southern members defended it and denied that the federal government could coerce a state to remain in the Union. Some members, most notably Cobb and Thompson, were merely waiting for their states to act before leaving the administration. Still attached to these men by feelings of affection, Buchanan could not bring himself to dismiss them and reorganize his administration on a pro-Union basis. Instead, he presented to the world the folly of maintaining in office men who now openly advocated disunion. Buchanan rationalized that their dismissal would strengthen secession sentiment in the South, but more revealing was his refusal to break with his personal organ, the *Constitution*, edited by William E. Browne, who was an outspoken secessionist. Not until January, 1861, did Buchanan cut off the paper's official patronage. He even gave his blessing for Thompson, who was still in the cabinet, to go to North Carolina as the representative of the seceded state of Mississippi. Never was his weakness more forcefully demonstrated.

This division in his official family badly paralyzed Buchanan, under whom decisions had usually been a joint effort. Never the most decisive of men, he was now a lame duck, and the recent election had deprived him of most of his political influence. The president immediately grasped the seriousness of the situation. He recognized that the South's fundamental grievance was the continuing agitation over slavery, and the main problem was its accompanying threat of insurrection. He had, however, no constructive ideas on how to deal with this crisis. He considered issuing a proclamation announcing his intention to enforce the laws in the South, but backed off from this idea because of the split in his cabinet. In his annual message of December 3, 1860, he again entirely blamed the North for the crisis and recommended that Congress call a constitutional convention to deal with Southern complaints. Embracing the most extreme Southern demands, he urged passage of amendments to secure the return of fugitive slaves and to protect slavery in the states and territories. The recent election had thoroughly repudiated this last idea, and Congress ignored his suggestions.

On the constitutional question of secession, the president's message was hopelessly inadequate. Devoted to Andrew Jackson's concept of a perpetual Union, Buchanan argued that secession was unconstitutional, but he went on to declare that he had no power to prevent it. The federal government, he asserted, could not coerce a state, but he mitigated the force of this statement by reaffirming his sworn duty to enforce the laws. Buchanan's message produced a chorus of indignation in the North. His constitutional argument was specious, since the federal government did not have to coerce states at all but could direct its authority against individuals. Although Buchanan vainly hoped that Congress would devise some sectional settlement, the day of compromise had passed. Neither secessionists nor Republicans were interested in compromise, and although Buchanan might have been more vigorous in promoting a solution, in the end his efforts would not have made any difference. Buchanan's policy was simply to hang on until his term was over without legally recognizing secession or starting a civil war.

Of fundamental importance in Buchanan's eventual response to the secession crisis was the reorganization of his cabinet. In little more than one month, beginning in early December, the secessionists in the cabinet resigned and were replaced by staunch Union men. Black, who took over the State Department, now emerged as the guiding force of the administration; he gained powerful allies in Edwin M. Stanton, who assumed Black's old post as attorney general, and Postmaster General (and subsequently Secretary of War) Joseph Holt. Together these men stiffened Buchanan's resolve not to surrender federal property or to forswear the use of force.

The major point of conflict ultimately was Fort Sumter in the middle of Charleston Harbor with its small federal garrison under the command of Major Robert Anderson. Influenced by Black, Stanton, and Holt, Buchanan resisted intense Southern pressure to abandon the fort, and on December 31 he authorized sending a relief expedition. The relief ship was driven off by batteries on the South Carolina shore, but the president was now fully committed to the doctrine, which he outlined in his special message to Congress on January 8, that he had the right to use military force defensively to protect federal property and enforce the laws. South Carolina officials now undertook to starve out the garrison, and Buchanan decided not to send any further supplies or reinforcements until Anderson requested aid. The stalemate that had developed in Charleston continued for the remainder of Buchanan's term. Up until Buchanan's last day in office, Anderson reported that he did not need any supplies or reinforcements.

On March 4, a relieved Buchanan turned the reins of government over to Lincoln. He had managed to leave office without compromising his successor by legally recognizing disunion or precipitating a war. "If you are as happy in entering the White House as I shall feel on returning [home]," he confessed to Lincoln, "you are a happy man indeed."

The Judgment of History

Buchanan retired to his estate, Wheatland. He came under heavy attack by partisan journalists during the war, but he publicly supported the war effort and opposed the peace plank in the 1864 Democratic platform. He was largely out of the public limelight, however, and he spent his retirement writing his memoirs. Published in 1866, they presented a full-scale defense of his actions as president. Finally, on June 1, 1968, death came to the former president at the age of seventy-seven. The day before he died he told a friend, "I have always felt and still feel that I discharged every public duty imposed on me conscientiously. I have no regret for any public act of my life, and history will vindicate my memory."

Historians have not been as charitable as Buchanan prophesied. Few administrations present such an unbroken record of misjudgments, short-sightedness, sordid corruption, and blundering. Ill-equipped to handle the sectional conflict and blind to the realities of Northern public opinion, Buchanan pursued a course that drove the sections further apart, ruptured his own party, and made a Republican victory all but inevitable in 1860. His incredible belief that the Supreme Court's Dred Scott decision would solve the crisis, his endorsement of the fraudulent Lecompton constitution, his destructive vendetta against Douglas, his zeal to add slave territory to the United States, and his obstruction of much desired economic legislation all aided the Republican Party to varying degrees. Desirous of healing the sectional breach, Buchanan instead promoted policies that escalated the crisis to the point where no compromise was possible. His failure as president had unprecedented tragic consequences for the nation.

William E. Gienapp

Bibliographical References

The best biography of Buchanan is Philip S. Klein, *President James Buchanan*, 1962. Although cognizant of his subject's shortcomings, Klein presents the most convincing defense possible of Buchanan and his policies.

George T. Curtis, *Life of James Buchanan*, 2 vols., 1883, prints some important documents and correspondence but is tedious. A brief, balanced treatment of Buchanan's presidential years is Elbert B. Smith, *The Presidency of James Buchanan*, 1975. John B. Moore, *The Works of James Buchanan*, 12 vols., 1908–1911, is a valuable selection of Buchanan's writings. Essential for understanding Buchanan's point of view and his limited insight into the crisis he confronted are his memoirs, *Mr. Buchanan's Administration on the Eve of the Rebellion*, 1866. Buchanan's presidency understandably has attracted considerable attention from historians of the sectional conflict. Allan Nevins, *The Emergence of Lincoln*, 2 vols., 1950, contains a full treatment of these crucial four years. Nevins is hostile to Buchanan and views him as a prisoner of the cabinet Directory, which, he argues, set policy. More balanced is Roy F. Nichols' magisterial *The Disruption of American Democracy*, 1948, a thorough examination of the politics of the Buchanan Administration. Nichols provides the best analysis of the impact of the Lecompton issue on the Democratic Party. The last half of David M. Potter, *The Impending Crisis, 1848–1861*, 1976, edited and completed by Don E. Fehrenbacher, is a superb analysis of the political developments of this period. David E. Meerse, "Presidential Leadership, Suffrage Qualifications, and Kansas: 1857," *Civil War History* 24 (December, 1978): 293–313, challenges the view that Buchanan changed his mind on submitting the Lecompton constitution to the voters of Kansas. The best study of the Dred Scott decision is Don E. Fehrenbacher, *The Dred Scott Case*, 1978, an exhaustive analysis that takes a broad view of its subject. For the Covode investigation and the scandals of Buchanan's administration, see David E. Meerse, "Buchanan, Corruption, and the Election of 1860," *Civil War History* 12 (June, 1966): 116–31. Kenneth M. Stampp, *And the War Came: The North and the Secession Crisis, 1860–61*, 1950, presents an acute analysis of Northern public opinion in the secession crisis. Indispensable on this crisis is Horatio King, *Turning on the Light*, 1895, the recollections of Buchanan's assistant postmaster general.